# The Parables of Jesus
# in Matthew 13

# The Parables of Jesus in Matthew 13

## A STUDY IN
## REDACTION-CRITICISM

J. D. Kingsbury

LONDON

S·P·C·K

*First published in 1969*
*Reissued in paperback 1977*
*Third impression 1978*
*S.P.C.K.*
*Holy Trinity Church*
*Marylebone Road*
*London NW1 4DU*

*Printed in Great Britain by*
*Whitstable Litho Ltd, Whitstable, Kent*

ISBN 0 281 02974 1

TO
*Amelia, my mother*
*Barbara, my wife*
AND IN MEMORY OF
*Alice, my aunt*

# CONTENTS

# PREFACE

This book is the revised version of a doctoral dissertation I originally submitted to the Faculty of Theology of the University of Basel in the summer of 1966. The publication of the dissertation is the final requirement for obtaining the degree of Doctor of Theology (D.Theol.). In preparing the manuscript for printing, I was able to take note of the literature pertaining to the subject which appeared up to the end of 1967. Works published in the latter part of the year, however, could be drawn upon only to a limited extent.

It now gives me great pleasure to express my gratitude to those who in special measure have aided me in this project. Professor Ernst Käsemann awakened in me a particular interest in the Gospel according to St Matthew through his lectures delivered in 1959–60 when I was a student at the University of Tübingen. Professor Bo Reicke, my "doctor father" at the University of Basel, directed me to the parables and faithfully lent counsel and guidance throughout the years of labour. As co-supervisor of my work, Professor Oscar Cullmann gave generously of his time and proved repeatedly to be both friend and counsellor. During his sabbatical year in Europe, Professor Frederick Danker of Concordia Seminary (St Louis) read the first section of the manuscript and offered valuable suggestions of a scholarly and technical nature. After the manuscript had been completed, Professor Anton Vögtle of the University of Freiburg in Breisgau (West Germany) graciously did me the personal favour of reading it through and relating to me in conversation and by letter his impressions of it. As a fellow-student both at Tübingen and Basel, Joseph Burgess, now professor at Boston College, was at every stage of the work an invaluable source of help, especially in bibliographical matters. When the manuscript was being prepared for publication, the Reverend Michael Perry of the S.P.C.K. gave unstintingly of his assistance as editor. In preparing the indexes, Mr Stanley Olson, my student assistant, also rendered valuable service. Last, it should go without saying that throughout the entire doctoral programme it was my wife who aided me most in turning dream into reality.

There are also many others to whom I am deeply indebted. By reason of space, however, it must suffice that I extend in print my heartiest thanks to Dr Ruth Wick, Director of International Exchange at the U.S.A. National Committee of the Lutheran World Federation, and to the scholarship committees of Concordia Seminary (St Louis) and of the Lutheran Brotherhood, for financial assistance granted me during my student days in Europe.

*Luther Theological Seminary*                                   J. D. K.
*St. Paul*

# ABBREVIATIONS

| | |
|---|---|
| Arndt – Gingrich | *A Greek-English Lexicon of the New Testament and Other Early Christian Literature* (*see* Selected Bibliography under "Bauer") |
| *BHH* | *Biblisch-Historisches Handwörterbuch* (*see* Selected Bibliography under "Reicke") |
| *Bib* | *Biblica* |
| Billerbeck | *Kommentar zum Neuen Testament aus Talmud und Midrasch* (see Selected Bibliography) |
| *BJRL* | *Bulletin of the John Rylands Library* |
| *BZ* | *Biblische Zeitschrift* |
| *CBQ* | *The Catholic Biblical Quarterly* |
| *DB* | *A Dictionary of the Bible* (*see* Selected Bibliography under "Hastings") |
| *DCG* | *A Dictionary of Christ and the Gospels* (*see* Selected Bibliography under "Hastings") |
| *DTT* | *Dansk Teologisk Tidsskrift* |
| ET | English Translation |
| *EvTh* | *Evangelische Theologie* |
| *ExpT* | *The Expository Times* |
| *HThR* | *Harvard Theological Review* |
| *JBL* | *Journal of Biblical Literature* |
| *JThS* | *The Journal of Theological Studies* |
| *KRS* | *Kirchenblatt für die reformierte Schweiz* |
| LXX | Septuagint |
| NEB | New English Bible |
| *NovTest* | *Novum Testamentum* |
| *NTS* | *New Testament Studies* |
| *PJ* | *Palästinajahrbuch* |
| *RB* | *Revue Biblique* |
| RSV | Revised Standard Version |
| *SJTh* | *Scottish Journal of Theology* |
| *StEv* | *Studia Evangelica* (*see* Selected Bibliography under "Cross") |
| *StTh* | *Studia Theologica* |

| | |
|---|---|
| *ThW* | *Theologisches Wörterbuch zum Neuen Testament* (*see* Selected Bibliography under "Kittel") |
| *ThZ* | *Theologische Zeitschrift* |
| *ZNW* | *Zeitschrift für die neutestamentliche Wissenschaft und die Kunde der älteren Kirche* |
| *ZThK* | *Zeitschrift für Theologie und Kirche* |

# CHAPTER 1

# Modern Trends in Parable Interpretation

---

Widespread scholarly opinion holds that the Gospel according to St Matthew was written in the latter decades of the first century to meet the needs of a specific body of Christians living somewhere within the Syrio-Phoenician regions of the Roman empire. The object of this study is to examine the thirteenth chapter of the Gospel, the so-called "parable chapter", in terms of the first evangelist's own age: his thought, theology, and situation.

Recent treatment of Gospel parables reflects persistent disagreement among scholars on the nature and function of parabolic speech. Therefore some preliminary discussion of matters relating to these questions is essential to the later investigation. To facilitate this discussion, we shall review briefly some of the modern trends in parable interpretation.

## A. JÜLICHER

It is generally recognized by scholars that A. Jülicher inaugurated the modern era of parable interpretation when he formulated his comprehensive parable theory some eighty years ago in the first part of a two-volume work.[1] The aim of Jülicher's parable theory can be seen in the categories into which he divides the parabolic speech of Jesus. Recently, there has been a pronounced tendency in some quarters to dismiss such categories on the grounds that the Hebrew counterpart of παραβολή, *mashal*, has an extremely broad range of meanings.[2] But if the interpreter adopts this position he unnecessarily forfeits a valuable tool for analysing the various forms in which the parabolic speech of Jesus has been preserved.

According to Jülicher, the two basic units in parabolic speech are the "simile" (*Vergleichung*) and the "metaphor".[3] The metaphor is a word that must be replaced by a second word that is somehow similar to the first. This substitution of one word for another, alleges Jülicher, is essential if the metaphor is ever to be intelligible to the reader or hearer. Thus, it is only by replacing the word "lion" with the word "Achilles" that the reader can comprehend the real intention of the otherwise enigmatic statement "A lion rushed on".

In the case of the simile, Jülicher argues that this process of translation vanishes completely.[4] Here the word-picture (*Bild*) and its object (*Sache*) are placed side by side so that the reader is informed at once how the one member is meant to illustrate the other. Hence, "Achilles rushed on like a lion" is a simile.

Jülicher is rigorous in his contention that the nature of the metaphor is essentially different from that of the simile.[5] The two have but one thing in common, namely, the ὅμοιον, i.e. in both one thing is regarded somehow as being "like" another. Beyond this, Jülicher holds that the antithesis between the simile and metaphor is absolute, and he accentuates this viewpoint by characterizing them as follows: the metaphor is non-literal speech (*uneigentliche Rede*), i.e. it says one thing but means another; the simile is literal speech (*eigentliche Rede*), i.e. each word is to be taken at face value; the metaphor demands an interpretation and remains a mystery outside of its context; the simile admits of no interpretation because it is always self-explanatory; the metaphor is intended to be interesting and puzzling, and to lead the mind from a lower to a higher sphere by spurring it on to ask, "What is this?"; the simile is intended to teach, and consequently leaves no grounds for questions.

The next two categories Jülicher discusses are the "similitude" (*Gleichnis*) and the "allegory".[6] The allegory is a string of metaphors that are all taken from the same sphere and so arranged as to form a coherent narrative. The similitude is merely an expanded simile. Whereas the simile is a comparison between individual words, the similitude is a comparison between two thoughts or sentences each of which contains a relationship. Accordingly, it is a similitude when we read with the psalmist (42.1), "As a hart longs for flowing streams, so longs my soul for thee, O God", for here the relationship of the hart longing for streams is comparable to that of the soul longing for God.

Because Jülicher derives the remainder of his categories from the similitude, he describes its properties as painstakingly as those of the simile.[7] He designates the two relationships that make up the similitude as the picture (*Bild* = hart longing for water) and the object (*Sache* = soul longing for God). These two relationships are always linked by a comparative particle, usually ὡς, and the function of the particle is to challenge the hearer to locate within the similitude its *tertium comparationis*, the one point at which the two relationships coincide. But this very structure discloses the purpose of the similitude: it is contrived to compel the reader or hearer to form a judgement; its intention is to prove.

Closely related to the similitude is what Jülicher considers to be the most famous category of parabolic speech, the "fable" (*Fabel*).[8] To avoid confusing the fable with animal stories, Jülicher is prepared to call it "a parable [*Parabel*] in the narrow sense" of the term.[9] The fable possesses all of the attributes of the similitude. Its uniqueness lies in the fact that the picture-half no longer consists of a single sentence expressing familiar reality or a universally recognized truth, but has been elaborated to form an imaginary story narrated in past time.

The final category Jülicher treats is the "example-story" (*Beispielerzählung*).[10] It diverges from the fable and similitude only to the extent that its narrative is itself an illustration of the truth it is intended to demonstrate. The example-story is designed to encourage the reader to draw the point of comparison directly between himself and the characters with whom he is confronted. In this way, it serves as a mirror by which the reader is enabled to form a judgement on his own behaviour (cf. Lk 10.30–7; 12.16–20; 16.19–31; 18.9–14).

To sum up, Jülicher holds that, though the parabolic speech of Jesus may vary as to form, the fundamental unit is always the simile. As a result, there can be only one point of contact between the picture-half and the object-half in any of the several types of parabolic sayings or stories of Jesus. With regard to their nature, all of these parabolic units are characterized by literal speech and are self-explanatory. With regard to their function, their purpose is to prove: to compel the reader or hearer to form a judgement.


## P. FIEBIG

Jülicher's antipathy towards the allegorical method of interpretation as it had been practised by scholars throughout the centuries was the impulse that motivated him to draft his parable theory precisely as he did.[11] In Jülicher's eyes, the allegorical approach to parabolic speech was unscientific: it defied adequate controls and readily lent itself to the caprice of the individual exegete. To counter it, Jülicher propounded principles of parable exegesis the application of which made it impossible to treat the parabolic speech of Jesus allegorically in any sense of the term.

At this point, C. A. Bugge (1903)[12] and especially P. Fiebig (1904)[13] provided a necessary corrective to Jülicher's stringent theory.[14] The substance of Fiebig's argument is that Jülicher erred in deriving his exegetical postulates from Aristotle. Instead, Jülicher should have turned to the *meshalim* of the Rabbis, since the *meshalim* in form and nature are by far the closest analogies we have to the parabolic speech of Jesus. This means that Jülicher's rigid antithesis between the simile and the metaphor, the similitude and the allegory, is untenable, for the Rabbis composed at once pure parables, allegories, and mixed-forms, i.e. allegorical parables and parabolic allegories. To prove this, it is only necessary to examine the *meshalim* themselves.

In his books Fiebig gathered together and investigated a considerable number of Rabbinic *meshalim*, demonstrating the general truth of his assertions. For our purposes it will suffice if we reproduce and analyse merely three such *meshalim*.

The following is an example of a Rabbinic *mashal* that is a pure parable:

> A *mashal*.
> To what is the matter like?
> To one who received a large field in a province of the sea (i.e. in the far distance, in the remote West) as inheritance. And he sold it for a trifle. And the buyer went there and dug it up and found in it treasures of silver and treasures of gold and precious stones and pearls. Then the seller began to choke himself [for anger].
> This is what the Egyptians did; for they sent away and did not know what they sent away; for it is written, "And they said, 'What is this we have done, that we have let Israel go from serving us?'" (Exod. 14.5).[15]

According to Jülicher's categories, this *mashal* would classify as a fable, or parable in the strict sense of the term, for the following reasons: the story is the product of the imagination, it has to do with a single event narrated in past time, and its sole aim is to compare the Egyptians in their angry remorse over the loss they suffered at the exodus of the Israelites from Egypt to a man who sold a precious field for a trifle. As an illustration, the story achieves its purpose well. An examination of its individual features discloses that none possess a figurative quality. Moreover, if we are not pedantic in our demands, the story may also be said to conform to real life.

The following is an example of a Rabbinic *mashal* that is an allegory:

> A *mashal*.
> To what is the matter like?
> To a man who became angry with his son and drove him out of the house.

Then his [the father's] friend went in to request of him [the father] that he should lead him [the son] back into his house. Then he [the father] said to him: Do you want to ask for anything else from me besides what concerns my son? Already long ago I made up with my son.

Thus "the Place" [God] said to him [Moses]: "Why do you cry out to me?" (Exod. 14.15). Long ago I was again well disposed towards them.[16]

If one interprets the house as the "presence of God", this pericope is a pure allegory. Otherwise, it must be classified as a parabolic allegory: an allegory with, in this instance, a single parabolic trait. The statement appended to the narrative tells us that the man in the story is God, the son Israel, and the friend Moses. When the story is "translated" as follows, it shows how neatly the allegory has been composed:

A *mashal.*

To what is the matter like?

To God who became angry with Israel and drove Israel out of his presence. Then Moses went into God's presence in order to request of him that he should lead Israel back into his presence. Then God said to Moses: Do you want to ask for anything else from me besides what concerns Israel? Already long ago I made up with Israel.

The following is an example of a Rabbinic *mashal* that is a mixed-form:

A *mashal.*

[It is like] a king who had a beautiful park. In it were beautiful first-fruits. And he placed two attendants in it, the one was lame and the other blind. Then the lame man said to the blind man: I see beautiful first-fruits in the park; come, take me on your shoulders and we will get them and eat them. The lame man climbed on the shoulders of the blind man, and they got them [down] and ate them up. After a while, the owner of the park came. He said to them: Where are the beautiful first-fruits? Then the lame man said to him: Have I then legs to walk? The blind man said to him: Have I then eyes to see? What did he do [the owner of the park]? He made the lame man climb on the shoulders of the blind man, and then he convicted them both together [lit. as one, as a unit].

So also the Holy One, blessed be he, brings the soul and sends it into the body, and then he judges them both together [as a unit]; for it is said: "He calls to the heavens above and to the earth, that he may judge his people" (Ps 50.4). "He calls to the heavens above": that refers to the soul; "and to the earth, that he may judge his people": that refers to the body.[17]

The immediate context reveals that the question to which this *mashal* is addressed is God's judgement of the soul as well as the body at the time of man's death. Of particular interest to us is the fact that this pericope, in structure and content, is a mixed-form.

With respect to the content, the speech of the story is primarily literal, though it does contain allegorical traits: the king represents God, the blind man the body, and the lame man the soul.

That particularly the blind man and the lame man are indeed metaphors is indicated by the circumstance that the narrator introduces them, not so much to serve as integral parts of the story he relates, but for the sake of the reality that he intends they should signify. Two factors support this view. From a negative standpoint, neither the blind man nor the lame man is well suited for the role ascribed to him in the story. It is inconceivable that a king who possessed a beautiful garden would assign the task of caretaker to one man who could not see and to another who could not walk. But this incongruity is not disturbing when we realize that the narrator is not, in fact, concerned with true-to-life caretakers. His real interest in the two characters is simply to establish them as symbols that will point to another reality. Yet it is precisely this property that is indicative of a metaphor.

From a positive standpoint, if we place ourselves in the position of the Rabbi who told this *mashal*, the blind man and the lame man serve as quite adequate metaphors for the body and the soul. The Rabbi reasons that the lame man is compelled to ride on the shoulders of the blind man just as the soul is compelled to reside in the body; similarly, the blind man is dependent on the lame man for direction just as the body receives its direction from the soul. Hence, from both a negative and positive point of view, one must conclude that the blind man and the lame man are metaphors for the body and the soul.

Regarding the structure of the *mashal*, we note that there can be no question of substituting the "body" and the "soul" for the "blind man" and the "lame man" in the story itself without reducing it to sheer nonsense. This is clearly an attribute of a parable. Were this *mashal* an allegory, it should be possible to translate the various metaphors as they appear in the story and still obtain coherent statements, as we did in the case of the allegory quoted above. Furthermore, all of the parts of the story, even those retaining an independent significance, harmonize to illustrate a single major thought, which is also characteristic of the parable. In this instance, the thought may be expressed as follows: even as the blind man and the lame man consort together to eat the first-fruits of the garden and are convicted by the king, so man's body and soul consort together for sin and stand under God's judgement.

On the basis of this analysis, it is obvious that the *mashal* before us

is a "mixed-form", or, more specifically, an "allegorical parable". It
is allegorical in that it contains metaphors, each of which requires
"translation", and therefore confronts the reader with more than one
point of contact between the unit's picture-half and object-half. At
the same time, this *mashal* is fundamentally a parable, for it has only
one major thought (which constitutes the culmination of the story)
and each of the principal traits, including the metaphors, are subordinate to this thought and advance the story towards it.

In summary, the contributions of Fiebig to parable exegesis consist
in his demonstrating that the closest analogies to the Gospel parables
at our disposal are the Rabbinic *meshalim*, and that the simile and
metaphor, because they are more similar than dissimilar, can naturally
be combined in a unit to produce mixed-forms, i.e. allegorical parables
and parabolic allegories. While these insights certainly do not negate
the validity and usefulness of Jülicher's categories, they none the less
invest them with a degree of latitude Jülicher himself did not envisage.

## THE FORM-CRITICS

Form-criticism did not emerge as the product of the co-ordinated
efforts of a school or group of scholars. On the contrary, four men
working independently of one another are commonly acknowledged
to be the founders of form-criticism: K. L. Schmidt (1919),[18] M.
Dibelius (1919),[19] R. Bultmann (1921),[20] and M. Albertz (1921).[21] Of
these four, only Dibelius and Bultmann deal with the parables as a
special block of material. Even so they do not endeavour to interpret
the parables, but attempt variously to classify them according to form,
to record their structural and stylistic features, and to determine the
*Sitz im Leben* in the early Church they appear to have served.[22]

Particularly significant are Bultmann's observations concerning the
formal characteristics of the parabolic speech of Jesus. He examines the
introduction, the conclusion, and the body of the numerous parabolic
units, and makes the following comments:[23]

> 1. The introduction may take the form of a question, or a statement contain-
> ing a comparative particle ("as", "like") or a comparative formula ("the
> kingdom of heaven is like . . ."), or be formulated as an imperative.
>
> 2. The conclusion may assume an even greater variety of dress. It may, for
> example, be absent altogether. Or it may constitute a question directed to the
> hearers, or contain the application of the narrative, or appear as an aphoristic
> logion, or develop into a lengthy interpretation of the story.
>
> 3. An analysis of the body of parabolic units reveals that specific techniques

for storytelling are employed as follows: (*a*) Brevity characterizes each narrative, particularly in terms of detail. Only necessary persons appear. The law of "scenic duality" reigns, i.e. only two persons at any given time speak or act. Groups are treated as individuals. (*b*) The story develops in rectilinear fashion, i.e. the action unfolds in a series of single incidents so that the eye never rests on two events occurring simultaneously. (*c*) Little attention is given to traits of personality; individuals are characterized by their conduct and speech, or judged by another person. (*d*) Emotions, too, are described only to the extent that they are essential to the point of the story. (*e*) Secondary characters are mentioned only as necessity demands. (*f*) Unless it serves the point of the story, no effort is made to inform the hearer of the motivation that dictates the behaviour of a character. (*g*) If the conclusion is considered to be self-evident, it fails. (*h*) Speech is concrete, and events are depicted as sparsely as are the characters. (*i*) Direct discourse is richly applied, including also the monologue. (*j*) The law of repetition is prominent: words or phrases will recur; the same type of character (guest, slave, etc.) may appear repeatedly. Whatever is most important, however, comes last. (*k*) Each story challenges the hearer to make some type of judgement.

In brief, the significance of the form-critics for our study is the following: by systematically cataloguing the structural and stylistic traits of parables, and by calling attention to the fact that the *Sitz im Leben* served by any given parable, whether in the early or later stages of the Gospel tradition, will necessarily have influenced the form in which we find that parable, the form-critics have facilitated a more proper analysis and interpretation of parabolic speech.

## A. T. CADOUX, C. H. DODD, J. JEREMIAS

A. T. Cadoux (1931),[24] C. H. Dodd (1935),[25] and J. Jeremias (1947),[26] who initiated a third phase in the modern era of parable interpretation, advanced the work of both Jülicher and the form-critics. With Jülicher, they reject the allegorical method of interpretation[27] and hold that the exegete should attempt to recover the parables of Jesus, as far as possible, in their pristine forms, i.e. just as Jesus first narrated them.[28] With the form-critics, they recognize the importance of the period of the oral tradition and the fact that the Gospel parables underwent change during this period; as a result, they acknowledge the need to distinguish between tradition and redaction and the value of the form-critical method for performing this task.[29]

At the same time, the programmes of Cadoux, Dodd, and Jeremias are unique in their own right. All three scholars concentrate their attention exclusively on the time of Jesus, and they examine his parabolic speech with two objectives in mind: methodologically, their goal is to recover that particular sociological situation in the ministry of Jesus in which he narrated any specific parable; theologically, their goal is to interpret the parables of Jesus, understood eschatologically,[30] in the light of such situations, so that they might secure from the parables a more adequate understanding of the person and message of Jesus.[31]

With this succinct characterization of their aims, the work of Cadoux, Dodd, and Jeremias has the following importance for us: because they inaugurated a "back to Jesus" campaign in the area of parable-exegesis which persists to the present day, with the consequence that scholars have generally ignored the need to understand the parables from the standpoint of the evangelists, they have indirectly determined the direction our study will take; they have demonstrated the advantage, indeed, the necessity, of interpreting a parable against the background of the setting in which it was delivered (though in our case this setting is not the ministry of Jesus but the situation of Matthew and his Church); and they, particularly Jeremias, have further developed and redefined those principles that have proved to be an invaluable aid in differentiating between tradition and redaction in analysing parabolic forms.

More recently, other contributions have also been made to the field of parable interpretation. E. Fuchs, for one, has developed a hermeneutical approach to the parabolic speech of Jesus according to which he concentrates on the very language of such speech, analysing types of parabolic units in terms of the "language movement" (*Sprachbewegung*) inherent in them.[32] In addition, Fuchs attempts through his existentialist interpretation (*existentiale Interpretation*) of the parables of Jesus to make the latter fruitful in the quest for the historical Jesus by using them to gain insights into Jesus' own peculiar situation.[33]

Following in the wake of Fuchs are his two pupils, E. Linnemann[34] and E. Jüngel.[35] Linnemann's book is perhaps noteworthy for the stress it places on the role the hearer played in those situations in which Jesus narrated his parables. Jüngel, in reflecting on the nature of parabolic speech, appears to strike a new note when he asserts that it is inaccurate to say that a parable is made up of a picture-half and an object-half with a *tertium comparationis* as the point at which the halves coincide; the reason is that Jesus employed his parables to the end that God's Kingdom, or kingly rule, should confront his hearers precisely in the parable as parable.[36] Yet Jüngel's contention, even if it should apply to Jesus' use of parables, is largely without relevance as far as the evangelists are concerned. For the most part, the evangelists construed the parables of Jesus paraenetically, i.e. as teaching *about* God's Kingdom, or rule, and not as the vehicle by which the Kingdom *per se* first comes to men. Accordingly, the distinction between the picture-half and the object-half of a parable retains its validity for our purposes. And because these most recent developments in parable interpretation have to do exclusively with the theology and situation of Jesus, they will have only marginal influence on our examination of Matthew's parable chapter.

## REDACTION-CRITICISM

Since it is our objective to understand the parables of Matthew 13 from Matthew's own point of view, the method we shall adopt in analysing them is what has popularly come to be known as redaction-criticism (*Redaktionsgeschichte*). The reader can find a suitable discussion of it in the first two chapters of J. Rohde's volume entitled *Die redaktionsgeschichtliche Methode*.[37]

In harmony with the tenets of redaction-criticism, our study of chapter 13 is based on the premiss that, just as Jesus employed parables to meet the demands of his own situation, so Matthew employed parables that had come down to him to meet the demands of the situation of the Church to which he belonged. If this assumption is valid, it follows that Matthew has placed the parables of chapter 13 in the service of his own age and theology, and that these parables, when studied within the context of his Gospel, will likewise reflect this age and theology. Accordingly, Matthew's Gospel itself, not some preconceived theory regarding the nature and function of parables and not the whole of the Scriptures or the later dogmatics of the Church, becomes the norm for interpreting the parables in chapter 13. Once this is recognized, the question of the legitimacy of "allegorizing" these parables can be seen to be a matter of ascertaining the intention of Matthew himself.

We speak repeatedly of "Matthew". Yet we do not attach to the designation of the first evangelist as Matthew any particular theory regarding authorship. This problem lies beyond the scope of our investigation. For our purposes, it is sufficient that the name Matthew should denote the person who is responsible for drafting the first Gospel as it has been preserved and handed down to us.

Finally, in treating any part of Matthew's Gospel, there is one matter that cannot be overlooked, but about which scholars have not been able to achieve anything like a consensus of opinion. We refer to the relationship between Matthew's Church and the Judaism of the time. Since we do not confront this subject in a fully adequate manner in chapter 13, we shall summarily state our view on it here at the outset.

The picture the first Gospel gives us of Matthew's community is one of a Church that had already attained a high degree of autonomy and even looked upon itself as the "true Israel". This Church was universally oriented, and its members were of both Jewish and Gentile origin. At the same time, it appears that it was in close contact with contemporary Pharisaic Judaism. It was concerned with justifying its existence over against the latter through self-assertion and self-defence, and with engaging in concerted missionary activity among Jews as well as Gentiles.

In view of this, the relationship between Matthew's Church and Pharisaic Judaism is characterized in the first Gospel by a tension between the autonomy of the Church on the one hand and its involvement with the Jews on the other. Consequently, we cannot endorse the positions of those scholars who either argue that Matthew's Gospel deals exclusively with intra-Church affairs,[38] or who contend that Matthew's Church by the time of the evangelist was no longer embroiled with Judaism and knew it only as a historical factor that had left its imprint upon the traditions of the Church,[39] or who assert that the link between Matthew's Church and Pharisaic Judaism factually exhausted itself in the evangelist's apologetic outbursts against the Jews.[40] By the same token, we are sceptical of how far one can go in the other direction, that of firmly aligning Matthew's Church within the association of Jewish synagogues.[41] In the last analysis, the interpreter must be aware of the tension we have defined, but for the present we are inclined to believe that one cannot go much beyond it with any degree of real precision.[42]

# CHAPTER 2

# Matthew 13
# Structure and Context

⬥━━◆━━⬥

## THE STRUCTURE OF MATTHEW 13

Chapter 13 is divided into two main sections: vv. 1–35 and 36–52. A comparison of these sections reveals that they possess a remarkably similar structure: each has its respective setting (vv. 1–3a, 36a); in each there is an "excursus" (vv. 10–23, 36b–43); in the first section there are four parables (Sower, Tares, Mustard Seed, Leaven), in the second three (Hidden Treasure, Pearl, Net [but cf. Treasures New and Old]); and each section has an appropriate conclusion (vv. 34f, 51f).

How did the materials in chapter 13 come to have this arrangement? A number of scholars look to source-criticism for an answer to this question.[1] An examination of the text, however, will demonstrate that Matthew himself is the one who designed chapter 13.

### Verses 1–35

A survey of 13.1–35 shows that both at the outset, except for vv. 16f (a Q logion), and at the end, Matthew does indeed follow one of his sources, namely, Mark (cf. vv. 1–23 to Mk 4.1–20; v. 34 to Mk 4.33f). But throughout the intervening block of material (vv. 24–33), the disposition of the pericopes is solely the work of Matthew, as can be proved from an analysis of the framework material.

The framework material of 13.24–33 consists of a series of transitional statements (vv. 24a, 31a, 33a) that bind together the parables of the Tares, of the Mustard Seed, and of the Leaven. These transitional statements are the threefold repetition of a single formula: "Ἄλλην παραβολὴν παρέθηκεν αὐτοῖς λέγων ("Another parable he put before them, saying . . ."). The slight alteration of the formula in v. 33a is due to its assimilation to the context both backwards and forwards (cf. v. 33a with vv. 24a, 31a, 34).

Now the component words of this formula indicate that it originated with Matthew. Ἄλλος, for example, occupies a preferred position in Matthew's vocabulary. Of the twenty-nine times he employs it, in only nine instances does it have a parallel in Mark and only twice in Luke (Q). In addition, it is used four times by Matthew in connection with parable transitions (13.24, 31, 33; 21.33). Although three of the parables that then follow have synoptic counterparts, it is singularly in the Matthaean transitions that ἄλλος appears.

Παραβολή attests to Matthaean authorship because it signals the great "turning point" to which Matthew calls attention in 13.1–35. *P3 ff* That the pronoun αὐτοῖς is of Matthaean origin can be seen from the fact that Matthew has elevated it in 13.1–35 to the status of a *terminus technicus*: it is his formal designation for the Jewish crowds (cf. 13.3, 10, 13, 24, 31, 33, 34).[3] This is in stark contrast to Mark, who uses αὐτοῖς indiscriminately in his parable chapter to refer now to the crowds and now to the disciples.[4] And the participial use of λέγω to introduce direct speech is further proof that Matthew formulated this transition, for here we have a literary device that is thoroughly characteristic of his style.[5]

This brings us to παρατίθημι. In view of the preceding arguments, it makes little difference that this verb, because it occurs so seldom in the synoptic Gospels, admits of no statement as regards the plausibility of our thesis. On the whole, the evidence is conclusive that the transitional formula we find in vv. 24a, 31a, and 33a is the product of Matthew himself. As a result, it stands to reason that Matthew was the one who gave order to the pericopes comprising *Conclusion* vv. 24–33.

This position is corroborated from a negative standpoint by the difficulties attached to the view that Matthew took 13.24–33 from a source at his disposal. For such a view compels one to assume variously that this early source was equal to Matthew (M) at the point of the parable of the Tares, equal to a conflation of Mark and Q at the point of the parable of the Mustard Seed, and equal to Q at the point of the parable of the Leaven. In other words, this source would itself necessarily be a compilation of other sources of both early and late date. But even if we were to presuppose this, how would we then explain that the transitional statements throughout vv. 24–33 should be completely Matthaean in style and content? Hence, the most natural supposition is that it was Matthew who gathered the pericopes in question from Mark, Q, and traditions peculiar to himself, arranged *Conclusion* them as he saw fit, and provided them with a framework.

*Verses 36–52*

In the second section of chapter 13, the framework material again indicates that the arrangement of the pericopes was the personal achievement of Matthew. Verse 36a–c, "Then he dismissed the crowds and went into the house; and his disciples came to him and said, 'Explain to us the parable of the darnel of the field'," introduces the Interpretation of the Parable of the Tares. It is plainly a Matthaean literary construction, for v. 36a has direct reference to 13.1f,[6] and v. 36b is patterned after 13.10a[7] and v. 36c after 15.15b.

The Interpretation of the Parable of the Tares is followed by the three parables of the Hidden Treasure, of the Pearl, and of the Net, after which this second section concludes with the pericope known as Treasures New and Old. The link that binds the three parables together is the word πάλιν ("again", "furthermore", vv. 45, 47). To be sure, πάλιν occurs only sixteen (seventeen) times in Matthew's Gospel as opposed to twenty-eight times in that of Mark. Still, Matthew betrays no particular dependence upon Mark in his use of it. In only five instances do Matthew and Mark have it in common (at 19.24; 21.36; 26.42, 43, 72), and once the parallel is at best distant (19.24). For Matthew, πάλιν is a connective, the function of which is to string together scenes (4.8; 20.5; 21.36; 22.4; 26.42, 43, 44), sayings (4.7; 5.33; 18.19; 19.24; 26.72; 27.50), and parables (13.45, 47; 22.1). This explains why, stylistically, Matthew, in contrast for example to Mark, quite regularly (eleven times) places it at the very head of a sentence, which is true of 13.45, 47. Consequently, both linguistically and stylistically, we have good reason to believe that πάλιν in 13.45, 47 points to the editorial hand of Matthew.

Two other factors confirm our conclusion. The parable formula "The Kingdom of Heaven is like . . ." (plus dative) is a standard feature in all three of these parables. As we shall see,[8] this formula is distinctive of Matthew's milieu, and most likely of the evangelist himself. In addition, the parable of the Net (13.47–50) and the parable of the Tares (13.24–30), to anticipate later discussion, are not companion parables.[9] Were this the case, the fact that the two are not found in juxtaposition in chapter 13 could argue for the hypothesis that Matthew was following a source and simply arranged them according to his document, i.e. apart from each other. But since the Net and the Tares are not companion parables, the position they occupy in chapter 13 cannot be used as an argument in favour of a source hypothesis.

For all these reasons, the current disposition of the parables of the

Hidden Treasure, of the Pearl, and of the Net can be seen to be the handiwork of Matthew. But in this event, Treasures New and Old, the conclusion to Matthew's parable chapter, would of necessity also owe its position to him. Accordingly, the section 13.36–52, like 13.24–33, is throughout a Matthaean composition.

Analysing framework material is not always one of the most exciting tasks of exegesis. Yet the importance of establishing the fact that Matthew was the architect who designed the structure of chapter 13 can hardly be overestimated. Our understanding of the parable of the Tares in its relationship both to the Interpretation of the Parable of the Tares and to the parable of the Net, to cite merely two examples, will be greatly affected by this recognition.

## THE CONTEXT OF MATTHEW 13

The context of chapter 13 is clearly marked off by the presence of a formula that appears periodically in Matthew's Gospel to alert the reader to several of the book's larger divisions. This formula occurs both at 11.1 and 13.53, and reads as follows: "And it happened when Jesus had finished . . .". By relating chapter 13 to its immediate context we can gain an initial insight into the subject matter that is to command our attention.

The division 11.2—13.53 is itself made up of two major parts, the break coming at the end of chapter 12. The central theme of the first part has to do with the rejection of Jesus. It evolves in such a manner that the intensity of the opposition against him steadily mounts.

The opening section is a longer unit that treats of the *doubt* of John the Baptist about the Messiahship of Jesus (11.2–19). At the time of Matthew, this may have been an issue for the Christians of his Church because of contact with certain Essenic elements.

The next section contains Jesus' woes against the Galilean cities of Chorazin, Bethsaida, and Capernaum (11.20–4). The heart of the matter is that these cities have *not repented* in response to the mighty works of Jesus. Might we conjecture that this situation reflects unsuccessful missionary activity in the region of Galilee on the part of Matthew's Church?

After a brief but theologically important excursus (11.25–30), Matthew pits Jesus against the (scribes and) Pharisees, the leaders of the Jews, in a series of *Streitgespräche* (conflict-discourses, 12.1–45). From the side of the Pharisees, the culminating accusation is that *Jesus, far from discharging a ministry authorized by God, is in league with the prince of demons* (12.23f). In Matthew's day, such an attack would be expressive of the animosity that typified the relationship of the Church to Pharisaic Judaism.

In the final pericope of chapters 11–12, the theme of the Jews' rejection of Jesus is developed by reverse example, i.e. by focusing on the true relatives of Jesus (12.46–50). Matthew pictures Jesus surrounded by the crowds. What is noteworthy is that he reshapes his Marcan text so that Jesus points beyond the Jewish crowds and his family towards the "disciples"; it is the disciples, that is to say, the Church, who are the true relatives of Jesus, because they do the will of the heavenly Father. With this scene the stage is set for chapter 13, the second major part of the division 11.2—13.53.

Throughout the entire first half of chapter 13 Matthew makes Jesus address the crowds. Previously (chaps. 11–12), Jesus was depicted in conflict with only individual segments of the Jewish nation. Now, however, he faces in the crowds the whole of unbelieving Judaism. So it is that Jesus in 13.1–35 vigorously assails the crowds for being *blind, deaf, and without understanding* in regard to the things of salvation (cf. 13.10–13). This harsh judgement is of the utmost significance, for through it Matthew informs us that the nature of the first chief part of Jesus' parable speech is that of the apology. In association with chapters 11–12, this apology represents the reaction of Jesus to his rejection by the Jews on all sides.

Thus far, there has been no particular difficulty in tracing the logical development of Matthew's text. But the sudden shift at 13.36 from the Jews to the disciples as Jesus' partners in discussion strikes one as being incongruous with the prevailing line of thought. This shift, however, is only apparently disruptive; it would seem that Matthew reasons as follows. In chapters 11–12, Jesus is rejected by the Jews; the result, in 13.1–35, is that he turns upon the Jews and in effect decries them as being a people that does not know and do the will of God. Then, in 13.36–52, Jesus dismisses the Jewish crowds and devotes the remainder of his parable discourse to his disciples, whom, we recall, represent the Church. In his address to them, Jesus essentially takes up his former statement in which he had described them as those who do comply with the will of the heavenly Father (12.49f), and enlarges upon it, in this way giving the disciples instruction on precisely what the doing of the will of God implies. Accordingly, the section 13.36–52 ties in very neatly with chapters 11–12 and the apology 13.1–35, so that the division 11.2—13.53 forms a coherent whole.

# CHAPTER 3

# Matthew's Concept of "The Kingdom of Heaven"

---

"The Kingdom of Heaven" is perhaps the most important single concept in Matthew's entire Gospel. From an exegetical standpoint, scholars such as G. Dalman,[1] H. Windisch,[2] and, more recently, W. Trilling[3] and G. Strecker[4] have made important contributions towards a better understanding of its meaning.

## THE KINGDOM OF HEAVEN IN THE PRESENT AND FUTURE

As an idiom, the Kingdom of Heaven appears only in the first Gospel. Nevertheless, Dalman has shown that there is no difference in definition between it and its counterpart, "the Kingdom of God".[5] Both expressions denote God's dominion, or kingly rule (*Gottesherrschaft*).[6]

According to first-century Jewish thought, God's kingly rule was eternal; it encompassed the entire world and all of the nations and powers in it.[7] In the present age, however, God's sovereignty was fully recognized only in Israel.[8] Consequently, it was the hope of the Jews that God would intervene in history, openly manifest himself as the Ruler of all, and, in so doing, free his people from heathen bondage and subject all nations to his holy will.[9]

This strong accent on the future can also be found in Matthew's concept of the Kingdom of Heaven. There is no question but that Matthew, like the Jews, looks forward to a final event in which God will break into history and openly reveal himself as Ruler over all nations to the salvation or damnation of men. This future event is explicitly delineated by Matthew, who maintains that it will unfold in the following sequence: the Son of Man will come very suddenly, all the nations will be gathered before him, he will separate them into two groups, and he will speak judgement on them, thus determining who will "inherit the Kingdom" that has been prepared from the foundation of the world and who will "go away into eternal punishment" (25.31–46; 13.40–43; 16.27; 24.27, 29ff, 37ff, 44, 50).

Other statements in the first Gospel likewise reveal that Matthew envisages the Kingdom of Heaven as a future reality. This is the case, for example, where Matthew, in only partial reliance on Mark and Q, tells of "entering",[10] "going into" (21.31), or "inheriting" (25.34) the Kingdom of Heaven, as is evident from parallel idioms that speak of "entering life",[11] "entering the joy of your Lord",[12] or "inheriting eternal life" (19.29).[13] Of course the contrary is equally true: one can "not enter",[14] be shut out (25.10), or be "thrown out"[15] and therefore excluded from God's latter-day Kingdom. Finally, Matthew also refers to the consummated Kingdom of Heaven under the imagery of a meal (8.11; 26.29), a concept that connotes bliss for the elect.[16]

The Kingdom of Heaven is not solely a future reality for Matthew. It is a past and present reality as well. Matthew believes that the Kingdom manifested itself in the person (1.23; 11.6, 27) and words (cf. the great discourses) and deeds (12.28; 11.2–6; chaps. 8–9) of Jesus in fulfilment of Old Testament prophecy (cf. the formula quotations). Indeed, such was the presence of the Kingdom in Jesus that the enemies of the Kingdom could even oppose it with force (11.12). In addition, the Kingdom manifested itself in the words and deeds of the Apostles. The Twelve received from Jesus the same message to proclaim (10.7=4.17) and the same works to perform[17] as he himself.

This tradition of Jesus and the Apostles is the foundation upon which Matthew squarely establishes the Church to which he belongs. As a result, he considers the Kingdom of Heaven to be a present reality in his own day. He asserts that the Church is the new "nation" to whom God gives his Kingdom (21.43),[18] and that it is here that "sons of the Kingdom" can be found (13.38) who hear and understand the "Word of the Kingdom" (13.19, 23), who know the "secrets of the Kingdom" (13.11), and who produce the "fruits" of the Kingdom (13.23; 21.43).

As to the manner in which the Kingdom of Heaven exists in the Church, Matthew holds that it is present in the rule of Jesus, who is now the exalted Kyrios.[19] Whichever attitude men assume towards Jesus, whether they confess and follow him as Kyrios or reject him, is the attitude they assume towards the Kingdom.[20] For those who do acknowledge Jesus as Kyrios, it is his will that they should be gathered into the Church, or ἐκκλησία, of which he is the head (28.18ff; 16.18), since it is here that he resides (18.20; 28.20), and it is this body to which he has delivered his authoritative Word (28.20; 11.25ff; 13.11) and to which he has entrusted the task until the close of the age of making "disciples of all nations" (20.19f).

The importance of the latter injunction lies in the fact that the rule of the Kyrios, and therefore the Kingdom of Heaven, is constantly being challenged by the Evil One, or Satan, who also rules in this world, exercising dominion over those who have become his sons (13.38f; 12.26). Because of this, the posture of the Christian who lives under the imperative of the Kingdom and awaits the Parousia must be one of prayer (6.10), of humility (5.3; 18.1–4), of preparedness in view of the coming of his Lord (chaps. 24–5), of a willingness to serve (20.20–8), suffer (5.10), or make whatever sacrifices necessity demands (19.12), and, contrariwise, of avoidance of the world, i.e. wordliness, which, for example, finds expression in the temptations of riches (4.8; 13.22; 19.23f). In brief, the Christian in this present age is to seek first the Kingdom (6.33), and this means pursuing the greater righteousness as exemplified and enjoined by Jesus (5.19f; 6.33).

## THE GOSPEL OF THE KINGDOM[21]

Since the genitive in the formula "the Gospel of the Kingdom" is objective, the phrase is best translated as "the Gospel *about* the Kingdom". It is an idiom peculiar to Matthew; twice it occurs as a designation for the message of Jesus (4.23; 9.35) and once as a designation for the message of the Church: that which is to "be proclaimed throughout the whole world as a testimony to all nations" before the end comes (24.14; cf. 26.13). Although, for technical and theological reasons, New Testament scholars are careful to distinguish between the message of Jesus, the historical person, and that of the Church, Matthew consciously summarizes both with the same words, because in this way he desires to emphasize that there is continuity between the historical Jesus and the Church. But this reveals that the expression "the Gospel about the Kingdom" is a summary theological formula that was current in Matthew's Church and denoted the total message of this church as we know it from the whole of Matthew's Gospel.[22]

Several facets of this Gospel about the Kingdom come to light in the "parables of the Kingdom", the special block of material that is of particular interest to us. The important place that the parables of the Kingdom occupy in Matthew's book is illustrated by the fact that whereas Mark and Luke have only two such parables,[23] Matthew has no fewer than eleven: the Tares (13.24–30), the Mustard Seed (13.31f), the Leaven (13.33), the Hidden Treasure (13.44), the Pearl

(13.45f), the Net (13.47–50), Treasures New and Old (13.51f), the Unforgiving Servant (18.23–35), the Labourers in the Vineyard (20.1–16), the Great Supper (22.1–14), and the Ten Virgins (25.1–13). Since only one of these parables, apart from the Mustard Seed and the Leaven, has even a loose synoptic parallel (the Great Supper, 22.1–14=Lk 14.15–24), the circumstance that a large group of parables are introduced with the formula "The Kingdom of Heaven is like (may be compared to, shall be compared to) . . ." is thoroughly indicative of the milieu of the first Gospel.

The underlying bond that unifies all the parables of the Kingdom is their ultimate orientation towards the rule of God as, admittedly, a present reality, but a present reality that is still to be consummated at the Parousia of the Son of Man. Only in this way can one adequately explain how it is that Matthew can apply some of these parables principally to the present, some principally to the future, and some to the present as conditioned by the future. Indeed, if we look closely at these parables, we find that they develop all of the following aspects concerning the Matthaean concept of the Kingdom of Heaven: that judgement will take place at the final coming of the Kingdom so that Christians are not now to pre-empt that judgement (Tares); that the activity of God in the present age will issue in the future, fuller realization of his Kingdom (Mustard Seed and Leaven); that Christians who now live under God's kingly rule in awareness of the future Judgement are to commit themselves without reserve to the doing of God's will (Hidden Treasure and Pearl); that the Church, too, must submit to the Final Judgement (Net); that the Christian who has been instructed about the Kingdom is like a scribe, for he both knows and does God's will (Treasures New and Old); that only the Christian who practises forgiveness towards his brother in the present age will persevere in the coming Judgement (Unforgiving Servant); that the Kingdom of the End will usher in a new order of things where "the last will be first, and the first last" (Labourers in the Vineyard); that while many are called into the Kingdom in this age, only a few will finally enter it at the Latter Day (Great Supper); and that although the coming of the Son of Man and the final appearance of the Kingdom are not known, Christians must keep themselves in a state of readiness as they anticipate their Lord's return (Ten Virgins).

When we consider the message of these parables as regards the Kingdom of Heaven even in this preliminary fashion, several factors stand out which we want to note because of the importance they will assume for the remainder of our investigation. First of all, through their message the parables of the Kingdom substantiate the assertion that Matthew viewed the Kingdom of Heaven both as a present and as a future reality. Moreover, they confirm that Matthew's Church possessed a keen awareness of being God's eschatological community, a community of "candidates" who await the appearance of the Kingdom in its cosmic dimensions and in whose midst the Kingdom even now manifests itself, directing the life of the members. In other respects, these parables disclose the great extent to which Matthew follows Jewish apocalyptic in the sense that he employs imagery depicting the Last Judgement in order to motivate the congregation ethically towards the doing of God's will. Last, these parables reflect in general how fully Matthew has placed them in the service of his paraenesis.

In summary, "the Kingdom of Heaven" in the first Gospel refers to God's Kingdom, or kingly rule, as a present and future reality. From a historical point of view, Matthew holds that God has always been the Ruler of the world and, in a special sense, of Israel. In Jesus, however, God has manifested his rule eschatologically, and, through Jesus, also in the Twelve. What is more, God continues to exercise his rule in the Church: through Jesus, the Kyrios. Finally, at the Parousia of Jesus, the Son of Man, God will manifest his rule in all its fullness and glory before the whole human race. From a dogmatic point of view, the Kingdom of Heaven denotes for Matthew no less than God's total salvation[24] for mankind as revealed, again, in Jesus. As a result, the term Kingdom of Heaven in its several variations can denote the message Matthew's Church proclaims, the doctrine it teaches, the hope it cherishes, and the life it is to lead,[25] without, however, ever being identified with it, the ἐκκλησία, as such.

# CHAPTER 4

# Jesus' Parables to the
# Jewish Crowds beside the Sea
# (13.1–35)

## THE SETTING (13.1–3a)

*(1) On that day Jesus went out of the house and was sitting by the sea. (2) And large crowds gathered around him so that he got into a boat and sat down, and all the people were standing on the shore. (3) And he told them many things in parables, saying . . .*

*Framework Material*

Verses 1–3a are framework material, that is to say, they have been shaped by Matthew himself. A comparison with Mark shows that v. 1 stems almost entirely from the pen of Matthew. The phrase "on that day" may come from Mark 4.35, but it seems more likely that it is a Matthaean introductory idiom analogous to 3.1 and 22.23. The statement "Jesus went out of the house"[1] prefigures v. 36, where Matthew reports that Jesus "went into the house". And since the verb κάθημαι (to "sit") is one of Matthew's preferred words,[2] the only element in v. 1 that is immediately traceable to one of Matthew's sources is the expression "by the sea" (cf. Mk 4.1).

When we turn to vv. 2–3a, we notice that Matthew adheres to Mark more closely. The major changes, except for matters of word order, are Matthew's remark that the people "were standing on the shore" (cf. Mk 4.1d, "and the whole crowd was beside the sea on the land") and the substitution of ἐλάλησεν ("he spoke," v. 3a) for ἐδίδασκεν ("he was teaching," Mk 4.2a). The latter emendation must be seen in the light of Matthew's elimination of διδάσκειν (Mk 4.1a) and ἐν τῇ διδαχῇ (Mk 4.2b).

The manner in which Matthew has edited vv. 1–3a indicates that the following points deserve scrutiny: (a) the setting proper, which centres in the scene depicting Jesus sitting in the boat with the crowds standing on the shore; (b) Matthew's characterization of the actors, Jesus and the crowds; and (c) the relevance of vv. 1–3a with reference to the subject at hand, namely, Jesus' parable speech.

## The Setting: Jesus in the Boat—the Crowds on the Shore

"On that day Jesus went out of the house and was sitting by the sea." With this terse sentence Matthew begins chapter 13. His economy of language corresponds to the purpose of the statement: to place Jesus out in the open where he can meet the people. Once Jesus is in the open, Matthew, in general dependence on Mark, creates the great crowd scene which is introduced in v. 2³ and which constitutes the principal setting for the first half of chapter 13: "And large crowds gathered around him so that he got into a boat and sat down, and all the people were standing on the shore."

The significance of this setting turns on the verb κάθημαι (to "sit"), which Matthew employs twice in vv. 1–3a alone. Now the twin verbs κάθημαι–καθίζω often possess a connotation that marks the person who is "seated" as worthy of special honour or reverence.⁴ This explains why the Old Testament frequently pictures God as sitting upon a throne,⁵ an image with which Matthew, too, is familiar (5.34f; 23.22). By extension, it is to attribute honour to Jesus that Matthew describes him as sitting when he assumes the role of teacher (5.1f; 24.3), judge (19.28; 25.31), or ruler (20.21ff; 26.64).

But the express pattern Matthew is following in his use of κάθημαι in our text is apocalyptic, an example of which we find in the book of Revelation (7.9–12; cf. also 20.11f). Here God is pictured as sitting (κάθημαι) upon his throne with a great crowd (ὄχλος) of worshippers standing (ἵστημι) before him, the very sequence that Matthew, by means of redaction, has carefully reproduced: Jesus *sits* while the *crowd stands* on the shore. It would seem, then, that Matthew's intention in v. 2 is to fashion a setting that will in itself attribute honour to Jesus and underline, not merely a Rabbinic, but even a divine dignity.

Because of the vast crowds, Jesus gets into a "boat". The question is whether Matthew understands the boat in 13.1–3a in the extended sense of the Church.⁶

This is, of course, possible. If so, then Matthew, in having Jesus address the crowds from the boat, is emphasizing the fact that since the Resurrection and Exaltation, the word of Jesus comes to men from the Church.

In all probability, however, Matthew ascribes a less dramatic function to the boat in 13.1–3a. The role it plays in v. 2 is incidental. Jesus does not enter it so that he might embark upon a trip to the other side of the lake following his discourse in parables (cf. Mk 4.35). In fact, contrary to what we should expect, Matthew makes no further reference to the boat in chapter 13, neither in v. 10, where the disciples approach Jesus, nor in v. 36, where Jesus leaves the present scene to retire to the house. Furthermore, Matthew appears to conceive of Jesus as sitting alone in the boat, whereas in those pericopes in which the boat does symbolize the Church, the presence of Jesus and the disciples in it together is vividly dramatized (cf. 8.23–7; 14.22–33).

The most immediate context (13.2–3) is what is normative for determining the significance of the boat in v. 2. Apparently Matthew is making use of it in much the same way as he makes use of the mountain in 5.1 and 15.29–32a. In these two passages, Jesus is described as sitting on the mountain with the disciples and crowds assembled before him. Similarly, our text describes Jesus as sitting in the boat with the crowds standing before him on the shore. Hence, the function of the boat in 13.2 is to provide Jesus with a place where he may be seated, which is a sign of honour, and to set him apart from the crowd, thereby emphasizing that he is the focal point of attention.

## The Principal Parties: Jesus and the Crowds

We have just seen that one purpose for which Matthew employs vv. 1–3a is to create a setting that will in itself ascribe to Jesus honour and even divine dignity. A further purpose of these verses is to introduce us to the main characters in 13.1–35.

The protagonist, of course, is Jesus. In calling attention to his royal status, Matthew is conceivably alluding to him as the Messiah and most certainly as the exalted Kyrios, or Lord. On these two subjects we shall have more to say later.[7]

Noteworthy is the fact that Matthew makes no mention whatever of the disciples in vv. 1–3a. They do not appear in chapter 13 until v.10, though Matthew then has Jesus speak confidentially to them to the end of v. 23. Following v. 23, however, the disciples again give way to the crowds; this is evident from $αὐτοῖς$ ("them") in v. 24, since the antecedent of this pronoun is the crowds exclusive of the disciples (cf. 13.3, 10, 13, 34). Still, this is not to deny that Matthew makes the strongest of inferences in vv. 10, 18, and 36 to the effect that the disciples were present during the first half of Jesus' speech in parables. Therefore all indications are that in Matthew's view the disciples do indeed hear the first half of Jesus' speech; nevertheless, except for 13.10–23, it is throughout 13.1–35 the crowds to whom Jesus primarily addresses himself.

Along with the disciples, who are the intimate followers of Jesus, and the Jewish authorities, who are the implacable enemies of Jesus, the crowds (ὄχλος, ὄχλοι) form one of the three major groups which Matthew distinguishes in his Gospel. What place does Matthew give them in his document? How does he represent them? How does the role they play in chapter 13 relate to the role they play in other chapters? The answers to these questions will give us some idea of Matthew's attitude towards the Jews, which is vital to our understanding of chapter 13.

Linguistically, ὄχλος is only one of four principal terms in the first Gospel by which Matthew refers to the Jews.[8] As previous discussion implies, it is the word reserved for the Jewish masses. Yet some scholars believe that ὄχλος is elastic in meaning and can signify mixed numbers of Jews and Gentiles or even Gentiles exclusively (cf. 4.24f; 15.29ff).[9] W. Trilling, however, has proved that Matthew nowhere intends to depict Jesus as discharging his ministry among heathen, or Gentiles, but is consistent in consigning it to the "confines of Israel".[10] Accordingly, when Matthew speaks of the crowds, he is in fact thinking of Jews.

The first point to note regarding Matthew's portrait of the crowds is that he differentiates sharply between them and their leaders. In a number of instances the two groups adopt contradictory attitudes towards Jesus. The Pharisees twice accuse Jesus of casting out demons by the prince of demons (9.34; 12.24); the crowds, on the contrary, marvel at his exorcisms (9.33) and are amazed (12.23). The chief priests and the Pharisees attempt to arrest Jesus (21.45f); they refrain out of fear, however, because the crowds hold him to be a prophet (21.46). The scribes say that Jesus blasphemes (9.3); the crowds glorify God who has given such authority to men (9.8). The Sadducees attempt to confound Jesus (22.23–8); the crowds are astonished at his teaching (22.33). Finally, Matthew eclipses both Mark (12.37b) and Luke (20.45) by placing the crowds on an equal footing with the disciples as Jesus enunciates his woes against the scribes and Pharisees (23.1; cf. also 5.1 with Lk 6.20a).

This differentiation is present also in the Passion story. On the one hand, Matthew identifies the Jewish authorities as the agents responsible for plotting the death of Jesus and seeing to it that it is carried out.[11] In so doing, Matthew adheres to Marcan tradition, but he makes it plain that Mark's indictment of the Jewish leaders fully represents his own standpoint by substituting his set phrase "the chief priests and elders of the people" for Marcan phraseology in three key passages (26.3, 47; 27.1). Then, too, Matthew sharpens Mark's indictment by demonstrably exonerating the Romans of responsibility for the crucifixion of Jesus (27.24f).

Within this schema, the role of the crowds is largely that of a mob, i.e. the crowds are depicted as an instrument in the hands of the authorities, carrying out the counsel of the chief priests and the elders (cf. 26.47; 27.20). Moreover, at the height of the trial before Pilate, it is not the ὄχλος as such, but the ὄχλος as the λαός who cries out, "His blood be on us and on our children!" (27.25). In this instance λαός possesses programmatic significance,[12] for Matthew employs this term in 27.25 to show that it was not the hysterical masses who were responsible for the blood of Jesus, but Judaism in its official capacity as the chosen people of God to whom God sent Jesus as Ruler and Saviour (1.21, 2.0).

Now it would be contrary to the text to say that Matthew's use of λαός in 27.25 reveals a desire on his part to spare the crowds *per se* from the responsibility for the blood of Jesus that "unbelieving Israel" must carry. Yet the substitution of the term λαός for ὄχλος in this crucial passage at least complies with the general Matthaean tendency to place the ὄχλος as a distinct group in a neutral or even positive light.

Another striking feature in Matthew's description of the crowds is closely related to the first and has to do with the diversified role Matthew assigns them. It is noteworthy that outside the Passion story the crowd assumes a negative attitude towards Jesus only once, and that in a Marcan pericope (9.24=Mk 5.40). Otherwise, the crowds follow after Jesus,[13] witness many of his miracles and confirm them,[14] observe his clashes with the Jewish leaders,[15] and even testify positively to him,[16] particularly when they acclaim him as a prophet,[17] glorify the "God of Israel" on his behalf,[18] or acknowledge him messianically as the "Son of David".[19] But all this demonstrates not only that the crowds in general form the background of the ministry of Jesus (the chorus of ancient Greek drama), but also that Matthew is fundamentally well-disposed towards them.

The third principal factor in Matthew's picture of the crowds is that they share directly in the ministry of Jesus. Matthew tells us that Jesus teaches the crowds (4.23ff; 5.1f and 7.28; 9.35; 11.1) and heals their infirmities (4.23ff; 9.35; 14.14; 15.30; 19.2). Especially significant is the Matthaean tradition according to which Jesus makes the Jewish crowds the specific object of concerted missionary activity (9.35-8; 10.6; 15.24). Central to this tradition is the pericope of the Great Harvest (9.35-8), which in large part is a conflation of Marcan (Mk 6.6, 34) and Q (Lk 10.2) materials. If we trace these materials, we see that Mark 6.34 appears in the outline of the second Gospel *after* the return of the disciples from their missionary journey (6.7-13, 30), and that the Q passage (Lk 10:2) appears in Luke's Gospel in the pericope of the Commissioning of the Seventy, i.e. the Gentile mission. When, however, we examine the first Gospel, we find that Matthew has combined both passages, transposed them to an "earlier" position, applied them to the crowds, and affirmed in the immediate context at the Commissioning of the Twelve that the disciples are to go only "to the lost sheep of the house of Israel" (10.6). Thus, Matthew puts together a section dealing with missionary activity directed towards the Jewish masses that surpasses anything we find in Mark and Luke. Such an editorial composition leads us to believe that Matthew is here reflecting, not merely past interests[20] or just the theological necessity of having to present Jesus as the Messiah of Israel,[21] but also the intent of the Church of his day, namely, to convert the Jews.[22]

To recapitulate: that Matthew employs the term ὄχλος rather frequently,[23] that he carefully sets the crowds apart from both the disciples and the Jewish authorities, that he attributes to the crowds a relatively favourable attitude towards Jesus during his ministry and spares them at the expense of the Jewish leaders in the Passion account, that he apparently identifies them with the lost sheep of the house of Israel and expresses a missionary concern for them—these facts seem to indicate that to Matthew's way of thinking the Jewish masses, although they stand beyond the pale of the Church, are not, like the Jewish authorities, incorrigible as far as the matters of salvation are concerned, but occupy a prominent place within the universal missionary mandate of Matthew's Church.

Exactly because it is basically positive in nature, this broad portrait of the Jewish crowds is of particular interest. As it stands, it appears to contradict our findings in chapter 2, where we stated that the crowds in 13.1–35 represent the whole of unbelieving Judaism and that Jesus' speech in parables to them is essentially a scathing apology provoked by the Jews' rejection of him. But this apparent contradiction resolves itself when we observe that what Matthew in reality does in

13.1–35 is to single out and dwell on only one feature of his description of the Jewish crowds: the fact that they stand beyond the pale of the Church. Because Matthew so enlarges upon this feature in chapter 13, it is important for the sake of a proper perspective that we keep the whole of Matthew's presentation of the Jewish crowds in mind. Indeed, only by so doing will there be no occasion for surprise when, for example, Matthew unexpectedly and in seeming violation of the context alludes in the parable of the Tares to the Christian mission to the Jews.

### ". . . he told them many things in parables . . ."

Now that we have explored 13.1–3a with respect to the setting and the actors, we want to discover what these verses have to tell us about the nature of the speech in parables Jesus delivers in 13.1–35. To accomplish this, we shall focus our attention on the pivotal words λαλέω and παραβολή.

Mark conceives of Jesus' narration of parables as part of his teaching activity (4.1f). Matthew scrupulously avoids this. By systematically employing the term λαλέω (to "speak", vv. 3, 10, 13, 33, 34a–b; cf. Mk 4.33f), Matthew not only provides 13.1–35 with a more coherent structure than we find in Mark 4.1–34, but he is also able to eliminate such direct references to teaching as διδάσκειν (Mk 4.1a), ἐδίδασκεν (Mk 4.2a), and ἐν τῇ διδαχῇ (Mk 4.2b). The question is, why should Matthew studiously refrain from referring to Jesus' discourse in parables under the designation of teaching?

The answer of G. Bornkamm is that Matthew uses διδάσκω only in those contexts where Jesus is expressly characterized as a Rabbi, as a teacher of the Law.[24] W. Wilkens concurs with Bornkamm, but argues that Matthew's elimination of διδάσκω–διδαχή demonstrates his desire to have his parable chapter understood as proclamation (κηρύσσω).[25] To determine, therefore, why Matthew employs λαλέω in chapter 13, we shall embark upon a brief study of his use of the combination διδάσκω–κηρύσσω.

In a word, διδάσκω denotes for Matthew that function initiated by Jesus (22.16; 4.23; 9.35; 11.1) and carried on by the Church (28.20), whereby the "law and the prophets" are interpreted in terms of their fulfilment in him, Jesus (5.17; cf. 5.1f; 7.28f). In parallel fashion, κηρύσσω denotes the function that is first associated with John the Baptist (3.1), then Jesus (4.17, 23; 9.35; 11.1), and is likewise carried on by the Church (10.7), whereby the Gospel of the Kingdom (4.23; 9.35) is proclaimed (10.27; 24.14; 26.13), the hard core of which may be summarized in the words, "Repent, for the Kingdom of Heaven is at hand" (3.1; 4.17; 10.7).[26] While the two terms differ, there is also an underlying affinity between them.[27] The difference is that κηρύσσω emphasizes the proclamatory character of the Gospel of the Kingdom, i.e. that this Gospel confronts the individual with God's call to a new life ("Repent!") in view of the Kingdom of Heaven, whereas διδάσκω stresses that the Gospel of the Kingdom is also conditioned by the Law and the greater righteousness it demands.[28] The affinity between διδάσκω and κηρύσσω consists in that both, finally, have a common objective, namely, that men gain entrance into the Kingdom of Heaven (cf. 4.23 and 9.35 to 5.2–10, 19f), that in both there is an appeal to the will of the individual to respond to the will of God (cf. 4.17 to 7.24, 26; 15.10),[29] and that both can be referred to in a single stroke as complementary facets of Jesus' ministry (4.23; 9.35; 11.1).

On the basis of these results, Bornkamm is correct when he says that because Matthew consistently associates the teaching ministry of Jesus with the exposition of the Law, this factor alone would induce him to avoid any references to διδάσκω or διδαχή in describing the act of delivering parables. On the other hand, it would be difficult to agree with Wilkens that Jesus' speech in parables is then to be viewed as proclamation in the technical sense of κηρύσσω, for Matthew gives no indication whatever that it is a preaching of the Gospel.

In point of fact, there is a key aspect to this issue which Bornkamm and Wilkens do not discuss: the circumstance that neither to "teach" nor to "proclaim" would be appropriate in the context of chapter 13, because *within the ground plan* of Matthew's Gospel teaching and preaching, as defined above, cease as far as the Jews are concerned after the conflict-discourses of chapter 12. So it is that following 11.1, preaching is mentioned only in connection with the Church's universal missionary assignment (24.14; 26.13). As for teaching, even though the word itself occurs in several instances where Jesus is engaged in discussion with Jews, it is never used positively in the sense that Matthew provides us with an elaboration of the message of Jesus (cf. 5.2; 7.28f), nor does it ever appear in a situation where the Jews seem receptive to him. On the contrary, this term either finds its place in the scenic framework of a pericope (13.54; 21.23; 22.16; 26.55), or is employed negatively in a denunciation of Jewish doctrine (15.9; cf. 16.12), or occurs where there is debate with Jews who are manifestly obdurate already (13.54; 22.16), or merely demonstrates that Jesus has had the last word over his opponents (22.33). But once we recognize that the outline of Matthew's Gospel no longer allows for preaching and teaching to apply to the Jews after 11.1, and if we further keep in mind that 13.1–35 is apologetic in nature, we see that Matthew is following the same pattern in the first half of chapter 13 as in 23.1: in 23.1, Matthew utilizes λαλέω to introduce his "apology of woes"; in 13.1–35, Matthew utilizes λαλέω to introduce and shape his "apology in parables".

In the second Gospel the situation is different. Mark can speak of "teaching" within the framework of his parable chapter, because regardless of the extent to which the crowd is able to understand the parables of Jesus,[30] these stories are clearly envisaged as containing instruction also for the disciples (Mk 4.34b). But whereas Mark's parables are addressed as fully to the disciples as to the crowd,[31] Matthew, as we observed, consistently points out that the parables in 13.1–35 are principally addressed to the crowds and not the disciples.

The presence of λαλέω in 13.3a is thus further proof that Matthew views the first half of Jesus' speech in parables as an apology. In what way does παραβολή contribute to our understanding of the nature of this speech?

To begin with, an examination of παραβολή reveals that Matthew does not primarily employ this word, as we might expect, to alert the reader to his use of parabolic speech *per se*, for there are many parabolic units in the first Gospel that Matthew does not specifically call "parables".[32] Indeed, from the disposition of παραβολή within the first Gospel we learn that, with the exception of a single Q reference (22.1 = Lk 14.15b–16), Matthew has systematically appropriated this term from Mark. Therefore to ascertain its function in chapter 13, we must determine to what extent Matthew follows the Marcan usage of the term and to what extent he goes his own way.

Matthew's use of παραβολή seems to conform to that of Mark in two respects. Like Mark, Matthew views the parable as a type of riddle, or enigmatic form of speech.[33] Like Mark, Matthew holds that the parable is speech that is principally for outsiders, that is to say, for the Jewish crowds and their leaders. In fact, this latter attitude explains why none of the parables in the second half of Jesus' speech in parables, which is delivered to the disciples in private (cf. 13.36), is explicitly designated as such. Indeed, were it not for Matthew's statement in 13.53, "And when Jesus had finished these *parables* . . . ", we should be forced to conclude that Matthew did not at all construe 13.36–52 as a part of Jesus' speech in parables. At any rate, in that Matthew conceives of the parable as a riddle and as speech for outsiders, he complies with the Marcan tradition.

On the other hand, Matthew operates with παραβολή in his own characteristic fashion. Mark associates it with his concept of the Hidden Messiah, conveying the impression that all of Jesus' public speaking was a speaking in parables, or riddles.[34] Not so Matthew. By conspicuously deleting Mark's reference to παραβολή at 12.25 (cf. Mk 3.23), Matthew arranges for this word to occur nowhere in his Gospel before chapter 13. The end effect is that Matthew posits both a time when Jesus spoke to the Jews openly and a time when he spoke to them enigmatically.

In the second place, Matthew employs παραβολή twelve times in chapter 13 alone and only five times throughout the rest of his Gospel. As a result, he achieves for his own parable chapter a more striking and concentrated use of this term than Mark does for his. The reason behind this is Matthew's desire to emphasize that the apology in chapter 13 that Jesus directs against the Jews for having rejected him (chaps. 11–12) is distinctively *parabolic* in form.

Thus far, we have reached the following conclusions in our investigation of παραβολή in Matthew's Gospel: that Matthew regards the parable as an enigmatic form of speech directed primarily at outsiders; that he distinguishes between a time when Jesus addresses the Jews openly and a time when he addresses them parabolically; and that he emphasizes that the apology with which Jesus replies to his rejection by the Jews is distinctively parabolic in form. On the basis of these facts, we may now define the function Matthew assigns the word παραβολή in chapter 13: Matthew uses the word παραβολή and therefore his parable chapter to signal the great "turning-point" in his Gospel, and this turning-point may be described as follows: Jesus has come to the Jews preaching and teaching (4.17, 23; 9.35; 11.1) but was rejected by them; in reaction to this, Jesus addresses an apology to the Jews, yet speaks to them, not openly, but in parables, i.e. incomprehensible forms of speech, and so fashions a discourse that in form and content (a "parable apology") reveals that the Jews are no longer the privileged people to whom God imparts his revelation, but instead stand under judgement for having spurned their Messiah.

### Summary

The *function* of 13.1–3a, which constitute a Matthaean literary construction, is to establish the setting in which the first half of chapter 13 unfolds, to specify that the principals involved are Jesus and the Jewish crowds (the whole of unbelieving Israel), to underline the fact that Jesus speaks to the crowds as one who is invested with lordly dignity, and to point out that the following discourse is apologetic and stands under the sign of the parable.

## THE PARABLE OF THE SOWER (13.3b–9)[35]

(3b) *"Behold, a sower went out to sow. (4) And as he was sowing, some [seeds] fell on the road, and the birds came and ate them up. (5) But others fell on rocky ground where they did not have much soil, and at once they sprang up because they had no depth of earth. (6) But when the sun arose they were scorched, and because they had no root they withered. (7) But others fell among thorn-plants, and the thorn-plants grew up and choked them. (8) But others fell upon good soil and kept bearing fruit, some a hundredfold, others sixty, others thirty. (9) He who has ears, let him hear!"*

### The Picture-half of the Parable

The parable of the Sower takes its name from 13.18, "You, therefore, hear the parable of the sower". Matthew 13.18, in turn, stems directly from the first line of the parable, which reads appreciably the same in all three of the synoptic Gospels, "Behold, a sower went out to sow" (13.3b=Mk 4.3=Lk 8.5). Because, therefore, the traditional name of this parable has not been derived from its contents, scholars have debated throughout the years whether this parable is indeed a parable of the Sower,[36] or of the Soils,[37] or of the Seed.[38]

If we concentrate on Matthew's point of view, it would seem that the major accent in this parable lies on the seed and its fate, even though the words σπόρος or σπέρμα are not explicitly mentioned. The importance of the sower, for example, comes to bear only in terms of the seed. Of the types of soils, reference is made to that which is rocky (v. 5) and to that which is good (v. 8), but to none other.

The seed, on the other hand, is a constant throughout the story: the circumstances alter from scene to scene, but the fate of the seed is always carefully depicted. Furthermore, parables customarily reach their culmination at the end. But this parable culminates with the eye resting, not on the sower or the soil, but on the abundance of grain that the seed sown last is producing. Nor can it be a matter of chance that the most significant emendations Matthew makes of Mark's text have to do with the demonstrative and personal pronouns that refer to the seed. Where Mark applies the plural number to the seed once (Mk 4.8),

Matthew consistently does so (vv. 4, 5, 7, 8), which is in harmony with
his preference for the plural with its connotation of plenty.39 Consequently, the parable of the Sower in Matthew's Gospel is in reality a
"parable of the Seed".

Yet even though we are of this opinion, we shall, for the sake of
convention and to facilitate the discussion of the relationship between
this unit and the one known as the Interpretation of the Parable of the
Sower (13.18–23), continue to refer to it under its familiar designation
of the "parable of the Sower".

The Sower is the first of the so-called "Parables of Growth".40
Unlike the others, it is not prefixed with the introduction "The Kingdom of Heaven [God] is like [may be compared to] . . .". This is due at
once to the fact that Matthew is following his Marcan text at this
point and because the discussion on the reason for Jesus' speaking in
parables, in which Matthew first associates the parables of chapter 13
with the Kingdom of Heaven, does not follow until 13.10–17. Still,
the very presence of this story of the sower in Matthew's parable
chapter marks it as a "parable of the Kingdom".

### The Parable in Outline

The parable of the Sower may be outlined as follows: (a) the setting
(v. 3b); (b) the fourfold series of scenes in which the seeds which fall on
the road are eaten by the birds (v. 4), those which fall on the rocky
ground are scorched and wither (vv. 5f), those which fall among the
thorn-plants are choked (v. 7), and those which fall on good soil
produce fruit (v. 8); and (c) the hortatory conclusion (v. 9). If we
examine this outline, we see immediately that the fourfold series of
scenes (vv. 4–8) comprises the heart of the parable, and that these four
scenes fall into two groups: the seeds which do not produce fruit
(scenes 1–3) and those which do (scene 4).

From the standpoint of form, although the parable of the Sower
depicts an experience that was typical in ancient Palestine, it must be
classified as a fable, because it describes an event in past time. Moreover, since we shall discover that the story contains metaphors, this
parable is a mixed-form, or, more exactly, an allegorical parable.

### The Sower and the Seed

As we have observed, the two most important elements in the picture-
half of the parable are the sower and the seed. With regard to the seed,
Matthew equates it in 13.19–23 with persons.41 Yet in this same pericope he also links repeatedly the sowing of the seed to the individual's

having heard the Word (cf. 13.19a and c, 20a–b, 22a–b, 23a–b). This demonstrates that the concept of the seed as the Word is no more foreign to Matthew than to Mark and Luke (cf. Mk 4.14=Lk 8.11b). And because the seed in the parable of the Sower naturally commends itself as the Word, we shall construe it as such. With reference to the time of Jesus, the Word denotes the message of Jesus. With reference to the time of Matthew, the Word denotes the message about Jesus (Kerygma), which, in Matthaean categories, becomes the "Word of the Kingdom" (13.19).

As for the sower, scholars generally hesitate to identify Jesus with this figure. Matthew, however, seems to have done just this. The very fact that the parable speaks of a "sower", and not of a "man" ($\check{\alpha}\nu\theta\rho\omega\pi\sigma$), which is the usual designation in the Parables of Growth for the farmer who plants the seed (cf. 13.24, 31; Mk 4.26), would at least be reason for Matthew to attach special significance to the person of the sower. If the sower were then to be identified, Jesus himself would become the most logical candidate: in times past, Jesus delivered the Word as a historical personage; now, as the Kyrios, he continues to deliver the Word through his Church (28.18ff; cf. 10.5ff, 14 and 10.40, 18.20).

Support for this argument comes from Matthew's use of the genitive of the articular infinitive, $\tau\sigma\hat{\upsilon}$ $\sigma\pi\epsilon\acute{\iota}\rho\epsilon\iota\nu$ (to "sow", v. 3b). As E. Lohmeyer points out, it emphasizes that the purpose of him who "went out" was specifically to perform the one task of sowing.[42] This function is, again, reminiscent of the ongoing mission of Jesus, for he "was" and "remains" (cf. 13.37) the pre-eminent bearer of the Word. Then, too, we should also note that although the sower is mentioned only twice (vv. 3b, 4), he none the less occupies a commanding position in the whole of the narrative through his scattering of the seed (vv. 4, 5, 7, 8), a position that is intrinsically true of Jesus. On the strength of several considerations, therefore, it appears that in all probability Matthew saw in the sower a transparent symbol for Jesus.

## The Interpretation of the Parable

On the assumption that Matthew did conceive of the seed as the Word and the sower as Jesus, what was the situation to which he was relating the parable of the Sower? In simple terms, the narrative tells the story of a farmer who scattered his seed with liberal abandon, who suffered loss, but who still did not fail of a crop.

To square this with Matthew's circumstances, we must not lose sight of the fact that this parable comes immediately after chapters

11–12 but before 13.10–17, and that it is spoken to the Jewish crowds. Thus, we will recall that in chapters 11–12 the Jews reject Jesus, while the disciples are confirmed in their allegiance to him. In 13.10–17, Jesus pronounces judgement on the Jews but a blessing on the disciples. Hence, in view of the entire context of the parable of the Sower, there can be little doubt but that Matthew utilizes it to recapitulate chapters 11–12, on the one hand, and, on the other, to validate in summary fashion the denunciation and the blessing present in 13.10–17.

It would then seem that Matthew understood the parable of the Sower as follows. The sower is Jesus. At one time he delivered his message personally; after Easter, as the exalted Kyrios, he speaks through his Church. The act of sowing is the act of preaching. That which has been sown, or preached, is the Word. Just as the sower has scattered the seed with abandon, so God has not been short in his grace, and the Word has been liberally proclaimed in Israel. Just as the amount of wastage among the seed has proved to be great because of its being eaten or scorched or choked, so the incidence of failure in the preaching of the Word to the Jews has also proved to be great. But just as there are those seeds that have fallen on good soil and are producing a fine crop, so there are the disciples, or Church, who have been receptive to the proclamation of the Word, and the Word has taken hold in them and keeps producing "fruit" in them in abundance.

## The Parable in relation to the Kingdom of Heaven

At the basis of this interpretation is the twin accent on failure and success. For this reason, the parable of the Sower is a parable of contrast,[43] which is a feature common to all the Parables of Growth. To state it explicitly, the contrast is between the seeds that perish (vv. 4–7) and the seeds that produce fruit (v. 8), between the Word as proclaimed to the Jews, who have not responded to it, and the Word as proclaimed to the disciples, or Church, who have.

But this means that the culmination of the parable is to be found in v. 8a: "But others fell upon good soil and kept bearing fruit . . .". The remainder of the verse, ". . . some a hundredfold, others sixty, others thirty", merely illustrates the productivity of the seed that bears fruit,[44] the Word as it becomes effective in those who respond to it.[45]

The point is not without significance. For if v. 8b stands in the service of v. 8a, it is incorrect to view the parable of the Sower as a harvest parable signifying the reaping of the crop, i.e. the Day of the Lord.[46] Moreover, it is equally incorrect to argue that the fundamental comparison of the parable is between two distinct periods of time, namely, seedtime and harvest, the time of the historical Jesus and the future time of the fully consummated Kingdom of God.[47] The parable does not emphasize the element of time; it illustrates the fate of the seed.

To construe the parable of the Sower as a parable of the Kingdom because of an alleged reference to the eschatological harvest or Final Day is to misinterpret it.[48] In reality, the Sower is a parable of the Kingdom because it lays stress on the Word of proclamation, the vehicle by which God brings his Kingdom to men even now. And since God does bring his Kingdom to men even now, the Kingdom of Heaven, though not yet consummated, is nevertheless looked upon in the parable of the Sower as a present reality.[49]

### "He who has ears, let him hear!"[50]

The exclamation "He who has ears, let him hear!" (v. 9) is a challenge to attentive hearing, an invitation to take to heart what has been said. Towards the Jewish crowds, this cry is a warning with implications of judgement precisely because Israel has not heard in the past (cf. Jer. 5.21; Ezek. 3.7, 27; 12.2). As such, it underlines the guilt that is the Jews' for repudiating the Word of God.

Towards the members of Matthew's Church, this cry is an exhortation. It calls these Christians to make certain that they do not, like the Jews, render the Word barren. Rather, their ongoing response to it is to be such that it will always be as seed that keeps bearing fruit, enabling them to attest that they live under the eschatological rule of God.

### Summary

The parable of the Sower is the first of the *Parables of Growth* with which we shall deal. Formally, it is an *allegorical parable*.

The *contrast* inherent in it is the following: the seed that perishes is to the seed that produces grain as the Word that remains unfruitful among the Jews is to the Word that becomes productive in the disciples, or Church.

The *culmination* of the parable is found in v. 8a: "But others fell upon good soil and kept bearing fruit . . .". For Matthew, these words affirm that the Word of the Kingdom makes itself abundantly and continuously manifest in the lives of those who respond to it.

The *intention* for which Matthew employs the parable of the Sower is twofold. Inasmuch as the parable is addressed to the Jewish crowds, it is *apologetic*: through it Jesus, the exalted Kyrios, declares that although the Word calling men into God's Kingdom, or kingly rule, has been liberally proclaimed to the Jews, they have not responded to it and hence have rejected God's Kingdom. To the extent that this parable is meant for the members of Matthew's Church, it is *paraenetic*: through it Jesus Kyrios exhorts the Christians of Matthew's Church to "keep bringing forth fruit" pleasing to God, for in this way they testify that they have responded to the Word calling men into God's Kingdom and thus show themselves to be God's true people.

The *secret* this parable reveals about the Kingdom of Heaven is that the Word of proclamation, to which the Jews have not responded, is none the less the vehicle by which God confronts man even now with his rule and raises up a people that is pleasing to him.

The *function* of the parable of the Sower within its immediate context is to pave the way for the following pericope in which Matthew presents Jesus' reason for speaking in parables. The two pericopes are related to each other in at least two respects: here as there, the Jews are placed in sharp contrast to the disciples, or Church; here as there, the two groups are characterized by their divergent response to the Word of revelation.

## AN EXCURSUS
### 1. THE REASON FOR SPEAKING IN PARABLES
#### (13.10–17)

(10) *And the disciples came and said to him, "Why are you speaking to them in parables?" (11) And he answered and said, "Because to you it has been given to know the secrets of the Kingdom of Heaven, but to them it has not been given. (12) For whoever has, [more] will be given to him and he will have a great abundance. But whoever has not, also what he has will be taken away from him. (13) This is why I am speaking to them in parables, because although they look they do not see, and although they listen they neither hear nor understand. [(14) And in them the prophecy of Isaiah is being fulfilled, which says, 'In listening you will hear but you will not understand, and in looking you will see but you will not perceive. (15) For the heart of this people has become dull, and they have heard with heavy ears, and they have closed their eyes; lest they perceive with their eyes and hear with their ears and understand with their heart and turn back, and I shall heal them.'] (16) But your eyes are blessed because they see, and your ears because they hear. (17) For truly I tell you, many*

*prophets and righteous men desired to see things which you are*
*seeing and did not see [them], and to hear the things which you are*
*hearing and did not hear [them]."*

### The Text

The Reason for Speaking in Parables is a composite of disparate
materials which comprises Matthew's own literary constructions and
his appropriation and adaptation of the Marcan and Q sources. In its
composition, this unit is not unlike a multi-coloured quilt. Since
Matthew was the one who trimmed and fitted the pieces of tradition
together, it is important for us to recognize his objective in compiling it.

Matthew's objective in compiling 13.10–17 is to create a pericope in
which the disciples, or Church, are placed in stark contraposition to the
Jews. To achieve this, Matthew fits the various pieces of tradition
together, chiefly by making use of the catchword and the paraphrase,
so as to obtain a series of statements that in character are antithetically
parallel. In v. 10, the disciples ask Jesus why he is speaking in parables to
"them" (αὐτοῖς), i.e. the Jews. In v. 11, Jesus replies in words containing a sharp contrast, "Because to you it has been given . . . but to them
it has not been given." In v. 12, which Matthew links to v. 11 by means
of the catchword δίδωμι (passive voice), Jesus cites a maxim, and it, too,
displays antithetic parallelism: "For whoever has, more will be given
to him . . . but whoever has not, also what he has will be taken away
from him." In the first half of v. 13, "This is why I am speaking to
them in parables", Matthew has Jesus echo the question of the disciples
in the latter half of v. 10, "Why are you speaking to them in parables?"
Then, in vv. 13b, 16, Jesus makes a final, decisive distinction between
the disciples and the Jews in two statements that, again, are antithetically parallel to each other: "because although they look they do not see,
and although they listen they neither hear nor understand . . . but your
eyes are blessed because they see, and your ears because they hear."
This resoluteness on the part of Matthew to separate the Jews and the
disciples into two estranged camps, which has determined even the
literary structure of 13.10–17, shows us along what lines we are to
interpret this pericope.

Thus far we have omitted any reference in our discussion to 13.14f.
Verses 14f are a quotation from Isaiah (6.9f) which was most probably
interpolated into the text of Matthew's Gospel after the time of the
evangelist. The reasons for reaching this conclusion are numerous and
weighty.[51] (a) Matthew, in following Mark, makes an allusion to Isaiah

6.9 already in v. 13. It is strange, then, that he should repeat the same quotation a second time. (b) Verse 13, as we saw, is antithetically parallel to v. 16. With the intrusion of vv. 14f, this parallelism is interrupted and obscured. (c) At a glance, the introduction to this quotation appears to simulate those of the formula quotations. Yet ἀναπληρόω and προφητεία are *hapax legomena* and occur nowhere else in the Gospels or Acts. Hence, there is good reason to suppose that this introduction is non-Matthaean. (d) The quotation itself follows the LXX word for word with the exception that the first αὐτῶν in Isaiah 6.10 is omitted. Such an exact duplication of the Old Testament with reference to formula quotations is highly unusual.[52] (e) In view of the great length of the quotation, it is peculiar that it should appear again in Acts 28.26f in an identical reading. Even the same αὐτῶν is omitted in both instances. (f) Codex Bezae contains a version of v. 14 that differs appreciably from that of other manuscripts, something that is "unparalleled elsewhere in Matthew".[53] (g) The formula quotations of the first Gospel are regularly the product of Matthew's own reflection on some event in the life of Jesus. Verses 14f, however, are presented as words of Jesus.[54] (h) It is not difficult to ascertain why a later redactor should insert these passages into Matthew's text: he wanted to emphasize the fact that the hardening of Israel had been prophesied and had come to its *heilsgeschichtliche* fulfilment at the time of Jesus.[55] Though Matthew had already expressed the thought in v. 13, the redactor obviously held that this reference was not explicit enough; therefore he unfurled the quotation from Isaiah in its full breadth.

There is one additional remark to make. Should the reader discount the evidence cited above and choose to retain vv. 14f as a genuine part of Matthew's text, the antitheses between the disciples and the Jews, which characterize 13.10–17, would prohibit any amelioration of μήποτε (v. 15) in the sense of allowing for the repentance and forgiveness of the Jews as "Israel".[56] As we shall observe, at this point in his Gospel Matthew portrays the Jews exclusively as being under the judgement of God.

## A Temporary Change of Setting

In vv. 10–11a, Matthew constructs a scene in which Jesus speaks to the disciples apart from the crowds. This scene extends to v. 23 and temporarily disrupts the setting Matthew established in the opening verses of chapter 13, where all attention was focused on Jesus and the crowds.

It is noteworthy that Matthew tells us explicitly neither how nor where we are to conceive of the disciples' coming to Jesus. This is somewhat surprising, especially in view of the fact that according to 13.2 Jesus is apparently sitting out on the water in the boat alone. Such paucity of detail, however, is in keeping with the way in which Matthew customarily deals with matters of this kind, for nowhere in his Gospel does he appear to go beyond the chronological and geographical data supplied him by his sources.[57]

Since Matthew reverts to the crowd scene already in 13.24, at which point Jesus resumes his speech in parables to the Jews, we have an indication that Matthew considers the section 13.10–23 rather like an "aside" or "excursus". To say this is not, of course, to depreciate the importance of the material.

### The Partners in Discussion: Jesus and the Disciples

In v. 10a, we read that "the disciples came and said to him . . .". This introductory statement betrays the hand of Matthew on two counts: because it is characteristic of him to combine προσέρχομαι with λέγω to form a more or less stereotyped formula by which to introduce direct discourse,[58] and because προσέρχομαι is overwhelmingly peculiar to his Gospel.[59] Since v. 10a is a Matthaean formula, we ask whether it does not have a function beyond that of merely evoking the commonplace picture of Jesus engaging in discussion with his disciples.

The significance of this formula lies in the cultic overtones προσέρχομαι can acquire.[60] In Hellenistic Greek literature, it is often used in the sense of coming before a deity;[61] in the LXX, it frequently denotes the act of approaching God or of coming for sacrifice or worship;[62] and in the writings of Josephus, it appears in connection with stepping before a king.[63]

In the first Gospel, of the fifty-two instances in which προσέρχομαι occurs, in no less than forty-nine it signals the approach of others to Jesus.[64] On three occasions, those who approach Jesus address him directly as Kyrios (8.25; 17.14f; 18.21), which even in the vocative case is a christological predication in Matthew's Gospel.[65] What is more, on two of these three occasions the salutation is followed by a prayer for deliverance (8.25; 17.14f). In other respects, Matthew often couples προσέρχομαι with verbs that themselves have a cultic colouring, such as προσκυνέω (to "[fall down and] worship"; 8.2; 9.18; 20.20; 28.9), διακονέω (to "serve", 4.11), παρακαλέω (to "beseech", 8.5). and γονυπετέω (to "kneel down before", 17.14).

Matthew's use of προσέρχομαι suggests that for him, too, it has acquired a cultic connotation. Indirectly it ascribes a lordly dignity to Jesus, for people approach him with the same reverence that would be

due to a king or deity. Accordingly, when Matthew states in v. 10a
that "the disciples came . . . to him", he provides us with a thumbnail
sketch of Jesus by portraying him as a person of royal dignity whom the
disciples approach in full awareness of his majestic status.

Jesus' partners in discussion are the disciples ($\mu\alpha\theta\eta\tau\alpha\acute{\iota}$), who constitute another of the major groups in Matthew's Gospel. What image
does Matthew give us of them?

Throughout the first Gospel, the term "disciple(s)", where it refers to
followers of Jesus, is synonymous with those who are otherwise familiar
to us as the Twelve. Matthew indicates this by referring to Jesus' closest
associates as "his [the] twelve disciples",[66] and by using the words
"twelve" ("eleven") and "disciples" interchangeably.[67] In those cases
where Matthew employs "disciple" impersonally (10.24f, 42), or to denote the followers of John the Baptist (9.14; 11.2) or those of the Pharisees (22.15f), he regularly makes this clear. In only one passage is Matthew
somewhat ambiguous regarding the antecedent of this noun (8.21).

Commentators have long pointed out that when Matthew discusses
the disciples, he consistently, though by no means rigorously, casts
them in a favourable light either by minimizing their faults or over-
looking them altogether.[68] This tendency on the part of Matthew gives
rise to an important strain of material in his Gospel which describes the
disciples as the recipients and bearers of special insight and revelation.[69]
Nowhere is this more prominent than here in 13.10–17, for Matthew
pictures Jesus as telling the disciples that it has been given to them to
know the secrets of the Kingdom of Heaven (13.11 = Mk 4.11), that
their eyes and ears are blessed because they see and hear (13.16 = Lk
10.23b), and that they have been eye- and ear-witnesses to things that
not even prophets and righteous men were privileged to experience
(13.17 = Lk 10.24).

Of course Matthew can also state that the disciples are without understanding (15.16f = Mk 7.18),[70] or he can depict them as reluctant to
accept one of Jesus' precepts (19.10ff). But when Matthew, by reason of
his sources, is confronted with situations in which ignorance on the
part of the disciples is somehow intimated (13.36; 16.8–11; 17.10ff), his
customary procedure is either to spare them permanent embarrassment
by appending a statement to the effect that they did finally understand
the words of Jesus (13.51; 16.12; 17.13), or to modify his draft of the
text so that no mention of their lack of comprehension remains (17.23 =
Mk 9.31f), or simply to pass over such passages completely (Mk 6.52;
9.6, 10; Lk 12.41). In one instance, Matthew even goes so far as to substitute a benediction for an admonition (13.16f = Mk 4.13).

The net effect of Matthew's editorial activity as regards the capacity of the disciples for understanding is clearly to project on to them the image of being the enlightened followers of Jesus. With respect to chapter 13, this means that the disciples of Jesus are fully capable of comprehending his parables. With respect to the whole of the Gospel, it means that Matthew endows the disciples before Easter with insight that, according to Mark, Luke, and John, they do not attain until after Easter.[71] The result is that the correlation in the first Gospel between the disciples of Jesus and the Christians of Matthew's day is so close that the disciples of the text simply become the representatives of the Christians, or Church, of this later age.[72] This fact, too, is of paramount importance in interpreting Matthew's parable chapter.

### The Message of Jesus: (1) The Disciples are of Privileged Status

(a) The climax of the message of Jesus in 13.10–17, which has to do both with the disciples and the Jews, is the pronouncement in vv. 16f (=Lk 10.23f) that the disciples are of privileged status by reason of the quality of the time in which they live: their age is the Age of the Messiah, the goal of Heilsgeschichte.

In their original form, the force of vv. 16f lay in the recognition that he who spoke these words, the earthly Jesus, was in truth Israel's long-awaited Messiah. Matthew not only transmits this idea, but stresses it still more by placing the particle ἀμήν ("truly") at the head of v. 17, the purpose of which is to underline the messianic authority of this saying of Jesus.[73]

The corollary in vv. 16f to the fact that Jesus is the Messiah is the thought that the disciples have been given to understand this and thereby to share in the joyous events of salvation which he has inaugurated. This point is likewise accentuated by Matthew. Jesus, for example, calls the disciples "blessed" (μακάριος) and thus imputes to them the joy that is distinctive of the person who participates in the salvation associated with God's eschatological rule.[74] The disciples are furthermore said to "see" and "hear", that is to say, they are the intelligent eye- and ear-witnesses to the words and work of Jesus which comprise the dawn of the Messianic Age (11.4ff). Indeed, the disciples are even declared to be more honoured than "prophets and righteous men", all those in the history of Israel, namely, who longed in vain to experience the breaking in of the Messianic Age.[75] Accordingly, throughout vv. 16f, the disciples are described as of privileged status because their age is the Age of the Messiah.

There is, however, a problem in this connection. Historically speaking, vv. 16f apply only to the twelve disciples of Jesus. Yet from the context we know that Matthew applies these verses equally well to the Christians of the Church to which he belongs. How is this possible?

The answer is that Matthew considers vv. 16f to be as relevant to the Christians of his Church as to the initial Twelve. Because these Christians possess a tradition of the words and deeds of Jesus, Jesus speaks also to them, for as Jesus Kyrios he resides in their midst (18.20; 28.20). In addition, like the Twelve, these Christians, too, as we shall presently see, have been given by God to know and understand the secrets of the Kingdom of Heaven. Hence, the very fact that Matthew relates vv. 16f to his Church, serves to document the keen eschatological consciousness of this community: it traces the reason for its existence directly to the Messiah himself and aligns itself squarely within the tradition of the Apostles.

(b) The privileged status of the disciples further extends to the quality of the revelation they have received: "Because to you it has been given (δέδοται) to know (γνῶναι) the secrets of the Kingdom of Heaven (τὰ μυστήρια τῆς βασιλείας τῶν οὐρανῶν) . . ." (v. 11b).

To get some idea of the nature and content of the revelation bestowed upon the disciples, or Church, we will want to look closely at v. 11b. It confronts us with several matters of fundamental importance for our understanding of chapter 13 and the theology of Matthew. For example, what is the significance of the verb δέδοται and the infinitive γνῶναι? How is one to define the phrase "the secrets of the Kingdom of Heaven"? Why does Matthew render the word "secret" in the plural? What exactly do the secrets of the Kingdom comprehend?

The verb δέδοται is in the passive voice, the use of which in this instance was originally dictated by the Jewish custom that one should refrain from uttering the divine name. Consequently, the expression "it has been given to you" is a circumlocution for the statement "God has given to you".[76]

The disciples have been given by God "to know". The purpose of the infinitive γνῶναι is to emphasize what we have already observed, namely, that "knowledge" is a distinctive mark of the disciples of Jesus. Moreover, by standing in juxtaposition to δέδοται, γνῶναι characterizes the knowledge of the disciples as a gift of God (cf. 11.27; 16.17).

The substance of the knowledge given by God to the disciples is "the secrets of the Kingdom of Heaven", or better, the secrets about the Kingdom of Heaven. That Matthew substitutes "Heaven" for "God" (cf. Mk 4.11; Lk 8.10) is probably due more to his desire to utilize his own idiom than to any reluctance on his part to mention the divine name explicitly.[77]

To arrive at a summary definition of the secrets of the Kingdom of Heaven, we should take into account all of the following factors: that Matthew has rendered μυστήριον in the plural, that these secrets are, again, a gift of God, that the Kingdom of Heaven denotes God's kingly rule, that according to Matthew these words come from the mouth of Jesus, and that Matthew has Jesus address these words specifically to the disciples. In line with these considerations, we may define "the secrets of the Kingdom of Heaven" as those insights (knowledge) concerning God's kingly rule which God reveals to the disciples, or Church, in and through Jesus.

That Matthew should employ the plural of μυστήριον ("secrets") in referring to the knowledge that God reveals to the disciples, or Church, is not a foregone conclusion.[78] Mark, by contrast, contents himself with the singular (cf. Mk 4.11). What, then, could have induced Matthew to choose the plural?

It is possible that Matthew's adoption of the plural was the immediate consequence of his dependence upon a source.[79] Nor should we overlook the fact that we have a use of the plural in v. 11b which is completely typical of the Matthaean idiom both editorially, since Matthew displays a preference for the plural number in all parts of his Gospel,[80] and compositionally, since Matthew arranges his parable chapter in such a manner that it takes on the form of a rather long discourse in parables concerning numerous mysteries of the Kingdom of Heaven. But in the last analysis, Matthew's preference for the plural was most likely determined by the broad application he gave the word μυστήριον.

To illustrate this, we should observe that v. 11b–c is absolute in character. Formally, the very structure of the verse endows it with an absolute character. Materially, it is related to parabolic speech only by way of its context. By itself it deals, not with parables, but with the revelatory act of God both with reference to the disciples, or Church, and Jews.

The circumstance that v. 11b–c is absolute in character is of importance because it indicates that the scope of the secrets of the Kingdom of Heaven is not to be restricted, let us say, to the parables of chapter 13 or even to the whole complex of the parables of the Kingdom.[81] Instead, the secrets of the Kingdom, or revealed knowledge, must be defined comprehensively.

Once this is recognized, it becomes apparent that there is a substan-

tial affinity between our phrase and the declaration of the enthroned
Kyrios in 28.20a: ". . . all that I have commanded you" (cf. 11.25ff).
These latter words, as O. Michel remarks, are not to be interpreted
solely in terms of Matthaean pronouncements on the Law.[82] On the
contrary they too are to be defined comprehensively, for they denote
the "binding, authoritative Word" that Jesus has delivered to the disciples,[83] which, in the case of Matthew's Church, is nothing less than
the first Gospel itself.

But if we are correct in believing that 28.20a is an authentic interpre-
tation of 13.11b, it follows that the singular form of $\mu\nu\sigma\tau\acute{\eta}\rho\iota\sigma\nu$, which
Mark employs, would be too narrow a concept for Matthew, all the
more so because Mark's term is eschatological and christological in a
very strict sense, proclaiming that "the kingdom of God has come in
the person and words and works of Jesus".[84] Matthew, for his part, is
thinking in broader categories. He envisages not only eschatology, but
ethics as well, and he expresses this with the plural number $\mu\nu\sigma\tau\acute{\eta}\rho\iota\alpha$.

Confirmation of this thesis comes from Matthew himself. Within
his Gospel are certain parables, which he explicitly designates as
parables of the Kingdom, the major thoughts of which do not directly
delineate eschatology in the sense of God's plan of salvation in Jesus or
the series of events that mark the last times, but enjoin the disciples
variously to commit themselves totally to the doing of God's will
(Hidden Treasure, Pearl), or to forgive the brother (Unforgiving
Servant), or to be generous as the heavenly Father (Labourers in the
Vineyard), or to order their lives in the attitude of readiness (Ten
Virgins). In other words, in these parables the accent is squarely on
matters of ethics.

Yet once it becomes clear that Matthew does attribute to the secrets
of the Kingdom a dual emphasis incorporating ethics and eschatology,
we are faced with the question of his reason for doing so.[85] The
answer lies in Matthew's view of, and experience in, history. As a
Christian, Matthew is firmly convinced that the eschatological rule of
God has already come in Jesus. However, this rule has not brought
about an end to history, as Jewish expectation would have it. In taking
account of these two factors, Matthew affirms that the secrets of the
Kingdom, knowledge about the kingly rule of God, have to do with
those matters of both faith (eschatology) and life (ethics) that together
constitute the Christian existence between the Resurrection and the
Parousia as it is governed by the rule of God.

To sum up, in v. 11b Jesus tells the disciples, or Church, that they
are of privileged status as regards the quality of revelation they have

received. This revelation comes to them as a gift of God through him, Jesus. It consists of knowledge of the secrets of the Kingdom of Heaven, and as such it embraces the whole of ethics and eschatology, the faith and life of the disciple living under God's kingly rule.

(c) Finally, the privileged status of the disciples also results from the promise that is theirs: "For whoever has, [more] will be given to him, and he will have a great abundance" (v. 12a).

This logion appears in a correspondingly later section of Mark's parable chapter (Mk 4.25). Matthew transposes it to this position so that it will reinforce and elucidate the dictum laid down in v. 11b. The catchword δίδωμι facilitates this transposition, particularly since both δέδοται (v. 11b-c) and δοθήσεται (v. 12b) are in the passive voice and represent the now familiar circumlocutions for the divine name.

Matthew recognizes in the words of Jesus in v. 12a a divine principle[86] that applies to the disciples, or Church. Accordingly, the disciples and their God-given capacity to receive divine revelation is what is meant by "whoever has". In this respect v. 12a presents no problem.

But the logion goes on to speak of a certain "more" that the disciples will receive. Most scholars construe this "more" as ever greater insights into the Kingdom of Heaven.[87] It is doubtful, however, that Matthew was of this opinion, because it does not do justice to the absolute character of v. 11b. Verse 11b does not say that the disciples are given some portion, however large or small, of the secrets of the Kingdom of Heaven; it proclaims with no qualification whatever that the disciples receive the secrets of the Kingdom.

In point of fact, the idea Matthew advances in v. 12a is thoroughly eschatological. He discloses this in the parable of the Talents (25.14-30), to which he has appended the very logion we are attempting to interpret (25.29). In this parable, "he who has" is, above all, the "good and faithful slave" (25.21) who has earned five talents for his master (25.16, 20). The "more" this slave receives is a double gain. It is at once the additional talent given him (25.28) and the master's promise and invitation: "I shall set you over much; enter into the joy of your Lord (Kyrios)" (25.21).

Against this background, Matthew's argument in v. 12a takes on firm lines. The "more" the disciples will receive and the "great abundance" they will then have is, in the last analysis, the Kingdom itself: "enter into the joy of your Lord". Hence, Lohmeyer is correct when he terms v. 12 an "eschatological statute",[88] for through it Jesus declares to the disciples that inherent in the capacity granted them by God to comprehend divine revelation is the promise of inheriting God's latter-day Kingdom.

To conclude this discussion, the message of Jesus in 13.10–17, as it concerns the disciples, is one that emphasizes their privileged status. This status results from the unique time they live in, the divine revelation imparted to them, and the glorious promise they are given. This is the joyful side of the message of Jesus in this pericope. The other, sombre side concerns the Jews.

### The Message of Jesus: (2) The Jews are a People under Judgement

We began our examination of 13.10–17 by pointing out that Matthew has constructed this pericope mainly on the principle of antithetic parallelism.[89] With the aid of this literary device, he starkly contrasts the disciples with the Jews. In terms of the message of Jesus, this means that as he talks with his disciples in private audience away from the Jewish crowds, he tells them not only of their own privileged status but also of the judgement befalling the Jews.

In contradistinction to the blessing that Jesus pronounces upon the disciples (vv. 16f) stand the oft-repeated references to the Jewish crowds throughout the whole of 13.1–35 as "them" ($a\dot{v}\tau o\hat{\iota}s$; vv. 3, 10, 13, 24, 31, 33, 34). By providing for this, Matthew, as we previously mentioned, effectively makes of $a\dot{v}\tau o\hat{\iota}s$ a *terminus technicus* designating the Jews.[90] As the antonym of "you", which denotes the disciples (cf. vv. 11, 16, 17, 18), and the synonym of $\dot{\epsilon}\kappa\epsilon\dot{\iota}\nuo\iota s$ (cf. vv. 10b, 13a to v. 11c), $a\dot{v}\tau o\hat{\iota}s$ possesses the connotation of "apartness" or "alienation". By means of it, Matthew pictures the Jews as a people who stand outside the circle of those who participate in the joy and salvation of the Messianic Age.

Whereas Jesus states that it has been given to the disciples to know the secrets of the Kingdom of Heaven (v. 11b), he says of the Jews, "but to them it has not been given" (v. 11c). Matthew's purpose with these antithetically parallel statements is that Jesus, in compliance with Israel's tradition, should refer both the granting of knowledge and the withholding of knowledge to the divine resolve of God.[91] In this way, Matthew introduces the twin categories of grace and judgement, applying the former to the disciples and the latter to the Jews.

The "eschatological statute" Jesus cites in v. 12 maintains this pattern. While the disciples are described as those who have and will receive more, until at the last they will enjoy a great abundance, the text reads with regard to the Jews, "But whoever has not, also what he has will be taken away from him". For Matthew, the clause "whoever has not" is a clear reference to the inability of the unbelieving Jews to grasp the secrets of God. They are like the "wicked and slothful slave" in the parable of the Talents who has earned nothing for his master (25.25f). This slave, because he "has not", loses also "what he has" (25.29), the talent with which his master initially entrusted him (25.28), and the master's fellowship: "Cast the worthless slave into the outer darkness; in that place there will be weeping and gnashing of teeth" (25.30). By analogy, so also the Jews, because they "have not", lose even what they have, namely, the prerogatives connected with being the chosen people of God.[92] This means that their loss is, ultimately, nothing less than that of the Kingdom itself and of eternal fellowship with God (25.29f; cf. 8.12).

Since the antithetical character of the message of Jesus in 13.10–17, according to which the disciples are of privileged status but the Jews stand under God's judgement, has now been sufficiently demonstrated, we are in a position to consider the place in this unit of vv. 10b, 13, the passages regarding parables.

### The Reason for Speaking in Parables

Verse 13 has been edited by Matthew. The statement of Jesus in the first half of the verse, "This is why I am speaking to them in parables . . .", has been assimilated to v. 10b, where the disciples ask him, "Why are you speaking to them in parables?"[93] The second half of the verse, ". . . because although they look they do not see, and although they listen they neither hear nor understand", is an adaptation of Mark's quotation of Isaiah 6.9: Matthew has replaced Mark's ἵνα, which denotes purpose, with ὅτι, which denotes cause, while at the same time changing the mood of the primary verbs from the subjunctive to the indicative.

If we take Mark's text (Mk 4.11b–12) at face value, at least two things stand out: Mark states that the parable as such is an enigmatic form of speech; and ἵνα can only mean that Jesus speaks to the Jewish crowd *in order to* conceal from them the revelation he otherwise makes known to his disciples (Mk 4.11f, 34).[94]

Matthew confronts us with a slightly different picture on both counts. To begin with, he does not say that the parable is enigmatic *per se*. What he says is that to comprehend a parable one must have received from God the capacity to grasp revelation (vv. 11, 16f). Hence, we have the following two viewpoints. According to Mark, the *unexplained* parable is every bit as much a riddle for the disciples as for the Jewish crowd (Mk 4.13). Because of this, Jesus interprets his parables for the disciples (ἐπιλύω, Mk 4.34), and thus imparts to them the secret of the Kingdom of God. According to Matthew, the parable is a riddle only for the crowds, not for the disciples, because the latter, by virtue of the very fact that they have been made disciples, have also been made the recipients of divine insight and therefore comprehend the parables of Jesus as a matter of course.[95]

In the second place, Matthew, again in contrast to Mark, does not say that Jesus speaks to the crowds in parables *in order to* make them blind, etc., but *because* they are blind, deaf, and without understanding. For Matthew, the fact that Jesus speaks to the crowds in parables substantiates the circumstance that they have already proved themselves to be hardened towards the Word of revelation.[96] Still, in the one decisive point Matthew and Mark agree: the parables of Jesus strike the Jews as enigmas.

The emendations Matthew makes to v. 13 serve his context well. In vv. 10–13, the following argument emerges. Because the Jews have rejected the Word of proclamation and consequently demonstrated that they are an obdurate people (v. 13b), God has resolved not to impart to them the secrets of the Kingdom (v. 11). In fact, the Jews have become a people under judgement (v. 12). In recognition of this, Jesus now addresses them only in parables, i.e. in speech they cannot understand (vv. 10, 13).

## Does Matthew develop a Theory of Parables?

Over the years, scholars have vigorously debated the question as to whether 13.10b, 13 admit of a Matthaean theory of parables. In our opinion, this is not the case. The best indication of this is the fact that if we examine the whole of the first Gospel, we find that Matthew has incorporated a double tradition into his book regarding the perspicuity, and therefore the nature, of the parables of Jesus.

The one tradition is found here in chapter 13, where Matthew argues that while the disciples, i.e. his Church, can comprehend the parables of Jesus, the Jews cannot, for they stand before them as before riddles. At the same time, Matthew records elsewhere in his Gospel that the Jews are able to master parables of Jesus. For example, Matthew stipulates that the parable of the House Built upon the Rock (7.24–7=Lk 6.47ff) is as fully directed to the crowds as to the disciples (5.1; 7.28f). Moreover, he points out in the context that the crowds perfectly well understand this illustration for what it is, a clear admonition to hear and do the teaching of Jesus as set forth in the Sermon on the Mount (7.28f). Again, following the narration of the parables of the Two Sons

(21.28–32) and of the Wicked Husbandmen (21.33–46), Matthew reports that "when the chief priests and the Pharisees heard his *parables*, they perceived that he was speaking about them" (21.45). Accordingly, in these passages, particularly 21.45, we have a parable tradition that openly conflicts with that of chapter 13.

But since we find two traditions in the first Gospel with respect to the intelligibility of the parables of Jesus, we conclude that Matthew does not reduce his views on this matter to any unified concept. Yet this is something we should certainly expect were Matthew's remarks concerning parables subject to a fixed theory of parables.

That Matthew does not propound a formal theory of parables is also evident from the *Sitz im Leben* which the statements about parables in 13.10–17 are intended to serve. We noted above that the pericope on the Reason for Speaking in Parables is an integral part of the apology Matthew develops in 13.1–35. The logical *Sitz im Leben* for such an apology, and therefore also for the Reason for Speaking in Parables, is the intense conflict that characterizes the relationship between Matthew's Church and Pharisaic Judaism. Hence, the statements on parables in chapter 13 which Matthew makes cannot be attributed to anything like abstract reflection on his part with reference to the nature and purpose of parabolic speech. In fact, these statements actually have nothing at all to do with parabolic speech *per se*, since their purpose is to portray the judgement that has overtaken the Jews for having responded so negatively to the Word which first Jesus and then the Church have proclaimed to them.

The most striking thing about Matthew's use of the parable is that it is governed, not by an abstract theory or dogmatic principles, but by eminently pragmatic interests. Matthew's intent is to take the parables of Jesus, which, of course, had originally been spoken in a totally different context and subsequently exposed to the influences of both an oral and a written tradition, and to apply them to the circumstances of his own day so that they speak for the needs of his Church. In this way, Jesus, who presides over and resides in Matthew's Church as Kyrios, once more brings God's kingly rule to bear on the life-situations of a later generation.

Matthew's pragmatism in relation to parables further reflects itself in the way he makes each parable totally subservient to the context into which he inserts it. This explains why Matthew can attribute an enigmatic quality to the parables in chapter 13, yet state in chapter 21 with Mark that the chief priests and Pharisees can very well perceive the meaning of parables of Jesus. This procedure discloses more than that Matthew adheres to Mark at this point; it demonstrates that Matthew is willing to sacrifice conceptual consistency in dealing with parables in order to gain greater latitude in utilizing them to develop the topic at hand.

Finally, as to the relationship between Jesus and Matthew as far as parables are concerned, it should go without saying that it is misguided to attempt to determine on the basis of the Matthaean text how Jesus must have employed parables in his ministry. Nor are we authorized to postulate, simply on the basis of 13.10–17, a conflict between an alleged Matthaean parable theory[97] and the will of Jesus that all men should be saved.[98] Since Matthew's statements on parables are geared to the immediate situation he faces, one can rightly say that, just as Jesus used his parables as he saw fit within his own ministry, so Matthew has done the same thing with them in his Gospel.

### Summary

In our analysis of this pericope on the Reason for Speaking in Parables, we have witnessed repeatedly how Matthew has edited the material to serve the theological interests of his own situation. This situation is characterized by the disappointing results of the Christian mission to the Jews and the attendant debate between the Church and Pharisaic Judaism over which of these two communities was the true people of God.

As spokesman for his Church, Matthew develops in 13.10–17 a series of antitheses that mark the disciples, or Church, as the recipients of God's divine mysteries, but the Jews as living under God's disfavour. Specifically, Matthew establishes his argument as follows. Formally, he underlines the cleavage between the Jews and Jesus and his disciples by referring to the Jews as "them" (v. 10). Materially, he shapes the words of Jesus, so that through this pericope Jesus Kyrios might declare that God reveals the secrets of the Kingdom of Heaven to the disciples, or Church, but withholds them from the Jews (v. 11); that the situation of both the disciples and the Jews may be described by means of an eschatological statute according to which the disciples are promised participation in God's final, glorious Kingdom, while the Jews are threatened with eternal rejection (v. 12); and that because the Jews are obdurate, God's revelation in and through Jesus comes to them in parables, i.e. speech that they cannot comprehend (v. 13), whereas the disciples, because they see and hear, are blessed with the privilege of being intelligent eye- and ear-witnesses to the words and deeds that are indicative of the Messianic Age (vv. 16f).

When we review this argument, we see that the *intention* for which Matthew employs the Reason for Speaking in Parables is twofold. As a word about the Jews, this pericope is *apologetic*, for through it Jesus Kyrios, by accusing the Jews of being blind, deaf, and without understanding as far as God's revelation to them is concerned, disputes their claim that would make of them the chosen people of God. As a word directed to the Christians of Matthew's church, this pericope is *paraenetic*, for through it Jesus Kyrios fortifies these Christians in their conviction that they are the eschatological community of God that will one day inherit the magnificent Kingdom.

In terms of its immediate context, the *function* of the Reason for Speaking in Parables is to complement the argument laid down in the parable of the Sower. There we learned that the Word preached to the Jews was unfruitful, and that only the disciples, or Church, responded to it. Here we learn that God imparts his revelation to the disciples, or Church, but not to the Jews, a hardened people that stands under judgement.

## AN EXCURSUS
## 2. THE INTERPRETATION OF
## THE PARABLE OF THE SOWER
### (13.18–23)

(18) *"You, therefore, hear the parable of the sower. (19) Whenever a person hears the Word of the Kingdom and does not understand [it], the Evil One comes and snatches away what has been sown in his heart. This is the [seed] which was sown on the road. (20) As for the [seed] which was sown on the rocky ground, this is the person who hears the Word and immediately receives it with joy. (21) Yet he has no root in himself but lasts only for a time, and when affliction or persecution comes on account of the Word, he immediately falls away. (22) As for the [seed] which was sown among the thorn–plants, this is the person who hears the Word, and the worry which is of the world and the seduction which comes from wealth choke the Word, and it proves to be unproductive. (23) As for the [seed] which was sown on the good soil, this is the person who hears the Word and understands it, who indeed bears fruit and produces, one a hundredfold, another sixty, another thirty."*

## The Text: Authenticity and Redaction

In the course of the last century, there has been considerable discussion among scholars as to the authenticity of the Interpretation of the Parable of the Sower. On the one hand, many commentators, such as C. E. B. Cranfield, stoutly maintain that at least the general lines of the Interpretation probably go back to Jesus and that it is "premature" to regard the unauthenticity of this explanation as "an assured result of modern criticism".[99] On the other hand, other commentators, such as Jeremias, contend that the Interpretation must be construed as a product of the early Church.[100] For us, this debate is of interest only to the extent that almost all scholars agree that, from the standpoint of transmission, Matthew's text is secondary to that of Mark.

Matthew appropriates Mark's text (4.13-20) in a notably literal fashion. In fact, if we ignore for the moment any insertions and the less significant alterations, we discover that Matthew emends only one feature of the Marcan pericope: he attempts to rectify the apparent confusion Mark instigates by referring the seed that is sown now to the Word (Mk 4.14f) and now to the people who hear the Word (Mk 4.15, 16, 18, 20).

To eliminate this ostensible inconsistency, Matthew passes over Mark 4.14 for the most part and introduces each subsection of the Interpretation of the Parable of the Sower with a fixed formula that should be translated as follows: "Just as in the case of that which was sown (on the rocky ground, etc.), so it is with the person who hears the Word (and immediately receives it, etc.)" (cf. vv. 19a, c; 20a-b; 22a-b; 23a-b). In this way, the attributive participle ὁ σπαρείς ("that which was sown"), even though grammatically it could denote either the individual, or the "Word" (ὁ λόγος), or the "seed" (ὁ σπόρος), can, from the intention of the text, be seen to refer to the seed. Hence, to capture the intended meaning of Matthew's formula, we must revise it in the following manner: "Just as in the case of the *seed* which was sown . . . , so it is with the person who hears the Word . . .". But once this translation has been established, it reveals that the way in which Matthew actually overcomes the apparent confusion of Mark's text is by dropping any direct reference to the Word and referring the seed exclusively to the hearers (cf. 13.38).

## The Pericope in Outline

From a technical point of view, Matthew's fourfold use of the stereotyped formula just discussed demonstrates that each of the subsections of the Interpretation of the Parable of the Sower is a miniature parable in its own right. Specifically, the larger unit is a composite of four independent similitudes, so that it neatly divides itself along the following lines: (*a*) the transitional statement, v. 18; and (*b*) the four similitudes depicting the man who loses the Word because he does not understand it (v. 19), the man who falls from faith in the face of affliction or persecution (vv. 20f), the man who succumbs to the stresses and pleasures of the world (v. 22), and the man who is productive for God because he hears the Word and understands it (v. 23).

### The Significance of the Transitional Statement

Verse 18, the transitional statement, stems from the hand of Matthew. Formally, the expression "You, therefore, hear . . ." consists of a combination of catchwords ("you", "hear") that link v. 18 to preceding verses (cf. 13.11, 16f). The Interpretation of the Parable of the Sower is thus firmly bound to the Reason for Speaking in Parables.

The words "you" and "hear" are of prime theological significance. By their very position of stress they reinforce the distinction Matthew makes between the disciples as the recipients of revelation and the Jews from whom such revelation is withheld (cf. 13.10–13, 16f). So it is that Jesus explains the parable of the Sower solely to the disciples, and the disciples receive this explanation, not as in Mark, to combat their ignorance, but as a testimony to the fact that they do possess the God-given capacity to understand the true intention of Jesus' words.[101]

Finally, the circumstance that Matthew adroitly changes Mark's bold statement "The sower sows . . ." (Mk 4.14) into a pericopal heading, ". . . the parable of the sower", is of the utmost importance. With just this redactional turn Matthew successfully removes the sower from the field of action and focuses all attention on the respective persons who hear the Word (vv. 19a, 20b, 22b, 23b).[102] To put it another way, Matthew circumvents a potential christological allusion in order to give the Interpretation of the Parable of the Sower an unmistakably ecclesiological character.

### The Recipients: Converts or the Whole Christian Community?

Before we take up each of the several similitudes, we should be clear about the situation presupposed by the Interpretation of the Parable of the Sower. The reference in v. 18 to "the parable of the sower" and the fourfold refrain concerning "the person who hears the Word" (vv. 19a, 20b, 22b, 23b) convey the impression that the Christian mission provides the point of orientation.[103]

In reality, the Christian mission is only the point of departure, the external framework, for an address that is aimed at the whole body of Matthew's Church. A look at Matthew's use of the word ἀκούω will substantiate this.

In the case of the unbelieving Jews, Matthew does not even allow that the Word in any real sense is heard by them, for he writes that "although they listen, they neither hear nor understand" (13.13; cf. Mk 4.12). In v. 19, however, Matthew reports unconditionally that the person "hears the Word of the Kingdom". This is tantamount to saying that he becomes a Christian. Indeed, that this hearing is more than a superficial listening is indicated by two factors: the hearing is such that the Word penetrates to the very seat of the personality, a matter that Matthew emphasizes more than either Mark or Luke by stating that the Word "has been sown" (v. 19b=Mk 4.15c) "in his heart" (v. 19b= Lk 8.12b); and in describing the loss of the Word, Matthew employs the forceful verb ἁρπάζω (to "rob", "steal") in place of the more conventional verb αἴρω (to "take", Mk 4.15c and Lk 8.12b). Accordingly, the man of v. 19 does not represent a class of people who reject missionary preaching out of hand and who never cross the threshold of the Church. He is the archetype of a certain class of people who do become Church members. Moreover, what is true of v. 19 is equally true throughout the whole of the Interpretation of the Parable of the Sower. To repeat, the Interpretation is aimed at the members of Matthew's Church, and the text does not even intimate that this circle is to be restricted to converts.[104]

## The Similitude of the Seed sown on the Road (v. 19)

The first thing to note in this similitude is that Matthew, unlike Mark, does not employ the term "Word" in an absolute sense. He modifies it with an objective genitive, so that a typically Matthaean idiom emerges: "the Word of (about) the Kingdom". For Matthew, the Word about the Kingdom is the Church's total message regarding Jesus. It is, to be sure, Kerygma, in which God's kingly rule comes to men, but it is also διδαχή, the word that sustains the Christian in fellowship and guides him through life.

Matthew records that the man who hears the Word "does not understand it". The verb "understand" (συνιέναι) is a Matthaean interpolation into the Marcan text both here and in v. 23. If we compare v. 19 with v. 23, we find that of the two individuals, the one is the opposite of the other. There we read that the man "hears" the Word, "understands" it, and "indeed bears fruit and produces (ποιέω)". This is an oblique way of saying that this man knows the will of God and does it, a concept in which one should observe that the doing of the will of God is the factual proof that the will of God has, in truth, been understood.

If this is a correct interpretation of v. 23, the man in v. 19 who does not understand the Word must necessarily be an example of one who does not know and do the will of God. But not knowing and doing the will of God is never a passive or neutral thing in Matthew's Gospel. It is, in fact, disobedience to the will of God, i.e. "lawlessness".[105] Consequently, when Matthew declares that a Christian does not understand the Word of God, he is saying that that Christian has proved himself to be in some sense guilty of lawlessness.

Matthew goes on to say of this man that "the Evil One comes and snatches away what has been sown in his heart".[106] Of interest is the circumstance that the "Evil One" (ὁ πονηρός) represents a Matthaean substitution for the Marcan term "Satan" (Mk 4.15c). The reason for this substitution lies in Matthew's concept of evil.

The word "evil" (πονηρός) enjoys a preferred status in the first Gospel.[107] Whereas Matthew uses it some twenty-six times, it occurs but twice in the second Gospel and only thirteen times in the third. Matthaean usage of it reveals a dualistic bent. On the one hand, Matthew establishes a fundamental dualism between God and man according to which God alone is good (19.17=Mk 10.18) and mankind in toto is evil (7.11).[108] On the other hand, Matthew can also apply the categories of good and evil solely to men (5.45; 22.10). The basis for any such classification, however, is never institutional in nature, with good becoming synonymous with the Church and evil with the world. Instead, the norm is exclusively the will of God as expressed in his commandments and interpreted by Jesus (19.17b–19; 22.37–40; chaps. 5—7). Thus, "evil" is an eminently moral and ethical term in Matthew's Gospel. It basically denotes contrariety to the will of God regardless of whether the object so designated is a being, person, deed, or thing.[109] When, therefore, Matthew characterizes Satan as the Evil One, he does so because he sees in Satan the very personification of all "lawlessness".[110]

To pick up our former train of thought, we will recall that the man who does not understand the Word is one who is guilty of lawlessness. But we have just seen that, according to Matthew, the fountainhead of all lawlessness is Satan. Hence, Matthew's argument in the similitude of the Seed sown on the Road is the following: when a Christian proves himself guilty of lawlessness, he falls into the power of the Lawless One who, in turn, robs him of the Word and consequently makes of him a son of lawlessness. Understood in this manner, this similitude assumes the character of an admonition: Jesus Kyrios, who speaks these words, exhorts the members of Matthew's Church to show that they have heard the Word aright, which in this case means that they must not, through lawlessness, prove themselves ignorant of the Word and thus become sons of the Lawless One, losing the very thing that has called them into God's kingly rule.

On the practical level, this admonition squarely meets the state of affairs in Matthew's Church, for Matthew belongs to a community which is very much engaged in a struggle with lawlessness. The threat comes both from without, for example, on the part of Jewish persecutors (5.11f, 39), especially since they represent a different understanding of God's Law from that of Matthew's Church (cf. 9.4; 12.34, 39; 16.4), and from within, where the Church is troubled by the heresy of the false prophets (cf. 7.15–23; 24.11, 24), or by those whose behaviour presents a threat to the faith of others (σκάνδαλον, ἀνομία), or by just any number of sins that either conflict with the ethic laid down in the law of love (cf. 15.19; 18.32; 20.15) or reflect a lack of single-hearted devotion to God (cf. 6.23; 25.26, 30).[111] The admonition in 13.19, then, is wholly relevant for the Christians of the first Gospel.

### The Similitude of the Seed sown on Rocky Ground (vv. 20f)

Linguistically, vv. 20f reproduce the Marcan text almost exactly (cf. Mk 4.16f). This textual dependence, however, can be deceptive. Close examination proves that these verses are deeply rooted in the experience and theology of Matthew's Church.

The protagonist of this second similitude is characterized as one "who hears the Word and immediately receives (λαμβάνω) it with joy" (v. 20b). That Matthew speaks of "receiving" the Word in place of "understanding" (συνιέναι) it (cf. vv. 19, 23) is by no mean fortuitous. The reason for this is that, in Matthew's eyes, understanding is the mark of the true disciple, the disciple in whom the Word roots itself so firmly that he bears fruit (v. 23). But since the man described here is said to have "no root in himself but lasts only for a time" (v. 21a), he, like his predecessor (v. 19), will not have been considered by Matthew to have understood the Word in the true sense of the term.[112]

Matthew states that the second man encounters "affliction" (θλῖψις) and "persecution" (διωγμός) on account of the Word (v. 21b). If we investigate each of these terms, we find that "affliction" occurs four times in the first Gospel: in three instances, Matthew has appropriated it from Mark; but once Matthew has himself inserted it into the text (24.9).

As to its signification, Matthew, in contrast to Paul, who knows of affliction also as mental and spiritual anguish (2 Cor. 2.4; 7.5; Phil. 1.17), seems to employ this word solely to specify "distress that is brought about by outward circumstances".[113] At any rate, θλῖψις is so variegated in meaning that it can encompass tribulations as diverse as death, enduring the hatred of enemies, apostasy, betrayal, the agitation of false prophets, lawlessness, and lovelessness (cf. 24.9–12). Moreover, it is noteworthy that while Christians are put to death and hated "by all nations" (24.9), the other vicissitudes we have just listed arise from within the Church itself. This gives us further insight into the turbulent and disturbed conditions of Matthew's Church.[114]

Paradoxically, the occurrence of such afflictions strengthens Matthew's Church in its eschatological consciousness. In principle, the Christians of Matthew's Church view all manner of affliction in terms of the Messianic Woes (24.8 = Mk 13.8), which signal the End of the Age and prefigure the coming of the Son of Man (24.3, 30f). Affliction is misfortune born of divine necessity (24.6 = Mk 13.7), the endurance of which marks the individual as belonging to the eschatological community of God, the company of the saved (10.22 – 24.13 – Mk 13.13), the band of the elect (24.22, 24 = Mk 13.20, 22). Hence, from Matthew's standpoint, we may summarily define "affliction" as divinely ordained distress that is external to the Christian but of the very essence of discipleship, something that strikes at the Church in the latter days both from within and without and must be endured by him who will be saved.

The word "persecution" (διωγμός) is, as we might expect, very similiar in meaning to "affliction". As a substantive, "persecution" appears in Matthew's Gospel only here in v. 21. By contrast, the verb "persecute" (διώκω) occurs six times and occupies a special place in Matthew's vocabulary.

On the basis of Matthew's use of the verb, "persecution" denotes injury of some nature inflicted through physical or verbal abuse. It may designate that one is the victim of perjured testimony offered in a court of law (5.11), or that one suffers verbal or physical assault which apparently can, under circumstances, attain such severity as to make it comparable to being scourged or even killed or crucified (5.11f; 10.17–23; 23.34).[114a]

The first Gospel contains strong evidence to the effect that Matthew's Church experienced both Jewish and Gentile persecution,[115] though the former seems to have predominated (10.17–23, 28, 38f; 23.34). Furthermore, while Matthew speaks pointedly of the members of a

household delivering up one of their own to be persecuted (10.21, 35f),
there is only scanty and indirect evidence that Christians may likewise
have turned on one another in this way (cf. 24.10b–c).

But as in the case of affliction, Matthew's references to persecution
disclose that it, too, has an eschatological accent.[115a] For the most part,
Matthew's Church is persecuted on religious grounds (5.10f). Such
religious persecution is considered by this body of Christians to be
divinely ordained and therefore to be expected (5.11, 44; 23.34f; 10.22f).
Indeed, it is to be endured with joy (5.11f), for it is the very hallmark of
discipleship (10.22ff, 5.11) and designates him who has to submit to it
as standing squarely in the way of Jesus and the Old Testament prophets (5.12). What is more, persecution for the sake of discipleship
carries with it the promise of inheriting the Kingdom of Heaven
(5.10).

To sum up, "persecution" in the first Gospel is defined principally as
physical or verbal abuse, which the Christian must be prepared to
suffer at the hands of hostile Jews, Gentiles, members of his own
family, and even other apostate Christians because of his allegiance
to Jesus, his Lord. If the personal cost for the Christian is high, so
is his reward; the knowledge that he is sharing in the lot of Jesus
and the prophets and the promise that he will inherit the Kingdom
of Heaven. Then, too, when "persecution" is mentioned in the same
breath as "affliction", as here in v. 21, the latter term, which denotes
the broad spectrum of all manner of distress which enemies may inflict
upon the Christian, and the former, which denotes a specific type of
such distress, namely, physical or verbal assault, combine to form a
hyperbolic expression signifying every external misfortune which can
befall a Christian in the time before the end by reason of his allegiance to
Jesus Kyrios.

Matthew reports that the second man, as a result of the affliction and
persecution he encounters, "falls away" (σκανδαλίζεται, v. 21c). The
word family σκάνδαλον–σκανδαλίζω–σκανδαλίζομαι is typical of the
first Gospel: it occurs nineteen times in Matthew, eight times in Mark,
and only three times in Luke.

Because the fundamental concept which always lies at the basis of
σκάνδαλον–σκανδαλίζω has to do with the hindrance or the lack or
loss of faith,[116] this word-group takes on highly eschatological overtones. We see this particularly in those places where Matthew utilizes
one of these terms in conjunction with the crass alternatives of salvation and perdition.[117] Accordingly, eschatologically coloured as
σκανδαλίζομαι is, it goes without saying that it exhibits a close affinity

to affliction and persecution. Without dealing at all in v. 21 with the problem of the readmittance to the Church of the lapsed, Matthew, through the words of Jesus, brands the second man who "falls away" in the face of affliction or persecution as an apostate whose final lot is certain damnation.

Before we leave vv. 20f, we wish to consider briefly the statement that affliction or persecution "comes on account of the Word" (v. 21b). This concise remark admirably reflects post-Easter theology. In the course of the ministry of Jesus, Jesus himself was the rock of decision that was set in Israel for the rise or fall of many (Lk 2.34), a thought that Matthew ideally expresses in those passages in which Jesus speaks of "falling away because of me" (26.31, 33; cf. 11.6; 13.57).[118] After Easter, the rock of decision and therefore also of offence becomes, in one respect, the Word as the Church's missionary proclamation (v. 20), and, in another respect—for those who respond to this proclamation and become Christians—the Word as the Church's credo, which is what we have here in v. 21b. When, therefore, Matthew's text reads that affliction or persecution comes on account of the Word, this reveals the natural tendency, in fact the necessity, for the Church to supplant the person of Jesus with the Word about him. During the ministry of Jesus, the issues of salvation and damnation were determined for men in confrontation with his physical person. In the time of the Church, they are determined by the Kerygma, in which Jesus Kyrios calls men into his kingly rule, and by credo, in which the disciples of Jesus Kyrios profess their continued allegiance to him. Once Jesus himself provoked controversy; now the Word of allegiance to him provokes the far more severe affliction and persecution.

To recapitulate, the similitude of the Seed sown on Rocky Ground provides us with added insight into the conditions within Matthew's Church. The picture it mediates is that of a suffering community physically threatened from without by both Jews and Gentiles and troubled from within by false doctrine, serious ethical offences, and even apostasy. Against this background of peril and dissension, Matthew sees in this similitude an admonition of Jesus Kyrios to the Christians of his community: Jesus Kyrios exhorts these Christians to be disciples who have heard the Word aright, which means that they are to show that the Word by which they have been called into God's kingly rule is so firmly rooted in their hearts that no affliction or persecution they may be called upon to endure as a result of their professed allegiance to him (Jesus) will cause them to lose their faith and thus effect their spiritual ruination.

### The Similitude of the Seed sown among Thorn-plants (v. 22)

This third similitude takes us into the sphere of the Christian's struggle
with worldly influences. Linguistically, Matthew is totally dependent
upon Mark (cf. Mk 4.18f). Yet even in this case the matter at hand
enjoys a broad base in Matthew's Gospel.

G. D. Kilpatrick has sketched the character of the community in
which Matthew's Gospel held sway.[119] By examining the word "city"
as well as Matthaean references to money and economic conditions,
Kilpatrick comes to the conclusion that Matthew's community must
have been rather "well-to-do", that it was little concerned about
"poverty", and that, in comparison with the Church for which
Mark wrote, it was "accustomed to a much wider financial range".[120]

If we apply the results of Kilpatrick's investigation to this similitude
of the Seed sown among Thorn-plants, it takes no imagination to see
why Matthew should be interested in having the members of his
Church warned against the "worry which is of the world" and the
"seduction which comes from wealth" (v. 22c). For if these Christians
did indeed live in a wealthy city, such temptations would constantly be
present to "choke the Word" and render it "unproductive" in their
lives (v. 22c; cf. 6.25–34). In recognition of this danger, Matthew
employs this similitude so that Jesus Kyrios might exhort the Christians
of this urban Church to be disciples who have heard the Word aright,
which means that they must not allow involvement with the world to
keep them from being productive for God, i.e. from doing his will.

### The Similitude of the Seed sown on Good Soil (v. 23)

We come now to the last of the four similitudes. With the insertion of
συνιέναι into vv. 19a and 23b, Matthew discloses that "understanding"
is the principal theme of the Interpretation of the Parable of the
Sower.[121] This means that the four "case histories" which Matthew
records, fall fundamentally into two categories: either the person
understands the Word and demonstrates this in his life (v. 23), or he
does not understand it and remains unproductive (vv. 19–22). Then,
too, by placing the Interpretation of the Parable of the Sower under the
heading of "understanding", Matthew gives this pericope an ethical
accent[122] not found in either Mark (cf. 4.20) or Luke (cf. 8.15).

Matthew is exact in defining his concept of "understanding".[123]
On one level, understanding can denote intellectual comprehension,
such as knowing the teaching of the Pharisees and Sadducees (16.12) or
being aware of the role of John the Baptist as the forerunner of Jesus

(17.13). In its deepest significance, understanding is closely linked in particular to hearing (13.13, 19, 23; 15.10). What is to be heard and understood is the Word of the Kingdom, the Church's Kerygma (13.19, 23). True understanding takes place when what is heard (or "seen" [5.28; 13.13]) and therefore grasped by the mind touches the heart of the individual (13.19),[124] i.e. his complete inward being (15.18), which comprises both the emotional (5.28; 6.21; 15.19) and the rational self (9.4; 12.34; 24.48). When this occurs, the individual undergoes a spiritual renewal, and the necessary result (cf. "indeed", 13.23c) is that he does (cf. ποιεῖ, v. 23c) the will of God, i.e. he "bears fruit" pleasing to God (13.23; 7.16, 20). Hence, according to Matthew the concept of understanding describes the nature of the Christian man.[125]  *Barth in Tradition + Interpretation pp 112-116*

With the similitude of the Seed sown on Good Soil, the Interpretation of the Parable of the Sower reaches its culmination. Coming as it does at the end of the unit, this similitude occupies the position of stress. But what is more decisive, while the other three are negative in outlook, thus exhorting the members of Matthew's Church to hear the Word aright by reverse example, this one is positive in outlook. In it the members of Matthew's Church are confronted with the ideal Christian, and thus exhorted to hear the Word aright as exemplified by the man who knows and does the will of God. This final similitude, therefore, is an appeal of Jesus Kyrios to all segments of Matthew's Church, particularly to those who may have made themselves guilty of the offences touched upon in the previous subsections.

### This Pericope in relation to the Parable of the Sower

If we compare the Interpretation of the Parable of the Sower with the parable itself (13.3b–9), we find that each pericope stresses a different aspect of the same matter. In both, the common denominators are the seed and the soil, the Word and the person. But whereas the emphasis rests on the Word in the parable of the Sower, it rests on the person in the Interpretation. Hence, the two pericopes are at best complementary, but it is not in keeping with their actual character to regard the one as an explanation of the other. This confirms our thesis that the parable and the Interpretation are to be treated independently of each other.

### Summary

Through editorial technique Matthew gives the Interpretation of the Parable of the Sower a specific ecclesiological orientation and invests it with an ethical quality. Consequently, he demonstrates that the *intention* for which he employs it is *paraenetic*: through it Jesus, the exalted Kyrios, exhorts the members of a Church that was beset by lawlessness, persecution and affliction, secularization and materialism, to make certain that they are disciples who are hearing the Word aright, i.e. that their response to the Word by which they have been called into God's kingly rule is a hearing with understanding, a knowing and a doing of the will of God.

The *function of this pericope* within its immediate context is to expand through illustration on the topic of "hearing and understanding", a subject Matthew has already broached with reference to the Jews and the disciples in the preceding unit on the Reason for Speaking in Parables (13.10–17). But if in the previous unit the disciples, or Church, are pronounced blessed because they "see and hear" (cf. 13.10–17), in the Interpretation of the Parable of the Sower they are warned against the moral problems that are acute in their circles. In unequivocal terms they are reminded that "seeing and hearing" imply "knowing and doing" the will of God. In other respects, to the extent that the Reason for Speaking in Parables and the Interpretation of the Parable of the Sower are directed exclusively to the disciples, or Church, and not at all to the crowds, or Jews, these two units stand in relative isolation within their immediate context.

## THE PARABLE OF THE TARES (13.24–30)

(24) *Another parable he put before them, saying, "It has been the case with the Kingdom of Heaven as with a man who sowed good seed in his field. (25) But while his men were sleeping, his enemy came and sowed darnel among the wheat and went away. (26) And when the stalk[s] began to bud and produce fruit, then the darnel appeared also. (27) And the slaves of the master of the house came and said to him, 'Sir, did you not sow good seed in your field? From what source then has it [got] darnel?' (28) And he said to them, 'An enemy has done this.' And the slaves said to him, 'Do you want us then to go out and pick [them]?' (29) And he said, 'No, lest in picking the darnel you might uproot the wheat along with them. (30) Let both grow side by side until the harvest. And at the harvest time I shall say to the reapers, "Pick first the darnel and tie them up in bundles to burn them, but gather up the wheat into my storehouse." ' "*

*This Parable in relation to that of the Seed Growing Secretly*     ·

One of the great anomalies in the study of the relationship of the synoptic Gospels to one another is the absence of Mark's parable of the Seed Growing Secretly (Mk 4.26–9) from both Matthew and Luke. This is particularly surprising in the case of Matthew, for in 13.1–35 he otherwise follows his Marcan source rather closely. Scholars have advanced a number of theories to explain this curiosity, but only one has come to enjoy a fair measure of recognition.[126]

B. W. Bacon,[127] T. W. Manson,[128] and C. W. F. Smith[129] hold that it is inaccurate, strictly speaking, to say that the parable of the Seed Growing Secretly has been passed over by other synoptists. Matthew, for example, or an editor before him, has freely adapted and expanded Mark's parable, so that it appears in the first Gospel in the form of the parable of the Tares. In this way, Manson and Smith contend, one can account both for the location in chapter 13 of the parable of the Tares and for the linguistic similarities between Matthew 13.24ff and Mark 4.26ff.[130]

This is an ingenious, though unlikely, conjecture. That linguistic similarities exist between the two parables comes from the fact that both deal with agricultural life and culminate in a harvest scene.[131] Moreover, if Matthew were to substitute another parable for that of the Seed Growing Secretly at precisely this place in his parable chapter, he would be compelled to introduce one that would tie in as neatly with the parable of the Sower as does the story of the Seed Growing Secretly. But the parable of the Tares meets all the requirements. Then, too, to view the parable of the Tares as deriving from the parable of the Seed Growing Secretly is to postulate such a thorough recasting of the latter that the only thing the two parables would still have in common is a scant terminological affinity. But in this case there is no longer any justification for the thesis.

In the last analysis, it is impossible to divine exactly why Matthew has not incorporated the parable of the Seed Growing Secretly into his Gospel. Of course it may have been absent from his Marcan source,[132] but this does not seem probable, since W. Marxsen points out that the transitional clause "And he said" (Mk 4.26a) proves that it had been firmly linked to the parables of the Sower and of the Mustard Seed already at a very early date.[133] Some scholars believe that Matthew omitted Mark's parable because of its cryptic character.[134] Our suggestion is that Matthew found the parable of the Seed Growing Secretly inadequate for his objective, which is to develop in 13.1–35 an apology against "unbelieving Israel". Be that as it may, one thing appears certain: the relationship between the parable of the Seed Growing Secretly and that of the Tares is best explained in terms of substitution.

## An Allegory of Later Date?

Similar to the preceding theory is the view that the parable of the Tares did not originate with Jesus, but is an allegory composed at a later date, perhaps even by Matthew, for the sake of its explanation, 13.36b–43.[135]

If there is any truth to this, it lies in the fact that a literary analysis of the parable of the Tares does allow for the cogent argument that Matthew has edited it rather extensively. Both the introduction of the parable (v. 24a) and its conclusion (v. 30) stem from the pen of Matthew.[136] The dialogue in vv. 27–8a merely reproduces in direct speech, a literary device of which Matthew is very fond,[137] the narrative of vv. 24b–6. The function of the question, v. 28b, is to introduce the answer, vv. 29f, and the subject matter in vv. 28b–30 harmonizes well with the circumstances of Matthew's day.

The conclusion we may readily draw from the foregoing is that vv. 24b–6 represent the core of an original parable that Matthew has appropriated and revised to suit his purposes. This supposition is strengthened by the observation that it is precisely in these passages, specifically in v. 26, that we discover the feature that not only dominates the parable of the Tares but would have been equally prominent in its probable precursor: the presence of wheat and darnel side by side in the same field. Accordingly, while there is no compelling reason to deny that the parable of the Tares comes in substance from Jesus, one can find numerous traces of editorial activity which are very possibly the work of Matthew himself.

## The Parable of the Tares in relation to its Alleged Interpretation

In order to achieve an adequate understanding of the parable of the Tares and the unit known as the Interpretation of the Parable of the Tares (13.36b–43), it is necessary to determine how the two pericopes are related to each other. This, in turn, is essentially a question of the widely diverse positions they occupy in chapter 13. Some scholars would explain this on the basis of source-criticism.[138] We have already shown, however, that Matthew, not tradition, is responsible for the arrangement of the materials in 13.24–52 and therefore of these two pericopes.[139]

Since this is the case, that the two pericopes do not, for instance, stand in juxtaposition to each other can only be due to deliberate planning on the part of Matthew. If we ask why Matthew planned in this manner, the answer is that he conceived of each of these pericopes as independent in its own right, with the result that he assigned each one to that place where it would best serve its intended function. This means that the interpreter should not, as almost invariably happens, treat the parable of the Tares and its ostensible interpretation as two halves of the same whole.[140] The "Interpretation" of the Parable of the Tares is only apparently, not really, an explanation of the parable of the Tares. Once this is recognized, there are data the exegete need not (as is the rule) ignore, but can deal with seriously, such as the following: that the parable is located in the first half of chapter 13 (vv. 1–35) but the Interpretation in the second half (vv. 36–52); that the parable is spoken to the crowds (13.24) but the Interpretation to the disciples (13.36b); that the setting of the parable is the lake (13.1–3a) but that of the Interpretation is the house (13.36a); and that whereas the heart of the parable is found in the master's dialogue with his slaves (13.27–30), the Interpretation presupposes only the first and last portions of the parable (13.24f; 30b–d), with the consequence that the Interpretation contains not even an echo of the climax of the parable (13.30a). The upshot of our argument, therefore, is that despite an external similarity of language, the dissimilarity between the parable of the Tares and its alleged interpretation is so great as to require that the two pericopes be examined apart from each other.

## The Parable in Outline

In analysing the parable of the Tares, scholars often draw up an outline that is based upon formal and stylistic considerations (narrative, vv. 24b–6; dialogue, vv. 27–30).[141] A more preferable division, however, is one that adheres to the inner logic of the story, as follows: (a) the situation, vv. 24b–8a; (b) the slaves' reaction to the situation, v. 28b–c; and (c) the master's directive to the slaves, vv. 29f.

Formally, the parable of the Tares is a story narrated in past time and interspersed with dialogue. In Jülicher's terminology, it is a fable, or parable in the strict sense of the word. But since the story likewise contains a series of metaphors, this unit is more properly a mixed-form, or, specifically, an allegorical parable.

## The Introduction

Verse 24b is a Matthaean literary construction, as is evident from the idiom "the Kingdom of Heaven" and from the presence of both the introductory dative (ἀνθρώπῳ)[142] and the aorist passive ὡμοιώθη. This form of the verb ὁμοιόω is peculiar to the first Gospel (cf. also 18.23; 22.2).

The significance of ὡμοιώθη is disputed. Jeremias, for one, translates it in the same manner as the other Matthaean idiom, ὅμοιός ἐστιν, on the grounds that both forms are derived from the Aramaic *lᵉ*.[143] But since Matthew wrote in Greek and was a careful editor, it is doubtful whether he regarded the matter so simply. We are better advised to assume that just as ὁμοιωθήσεται clearly points to the future (25.1; 7.24, 26), so ὡμοιώθη clearly points to the past.[144] If this is the case, Matthew has utilized this aorist passive to indicate that the Kingdom of Heaven, from his vantage point, is a present reality and already has a certain history behind it. This recognition is of the utmost importance for interpreting the parable of the Tares.

There is one other feature in v. 24b that must be mentioned. The text, when taken literally, reads that the Kingdom of Heaven may be compared to a "man". This is manifestly not the focal point of the parable. There is a measure of ambiguity in this introduction which P. Fiebig calls "*Inkonzinnität*",[145] or incongruence. This incongruence, together with the introductory dative and the aorist passive of ὁμοιόω, suggests that the opening words of the parable of the Tares are best translated as follows: "It has been the case with the Kingdom of Heaven as with a man . . .".[146]

## The Setting of the Story

The setting for the action that takes place in the picture-half of the parable is "his field" (v. 24b), i.e. the field belonging to the "master of the house" (v. 27a). In 13.38, the "field" is interpreted as the "world". But as we pointed out above, the situation there is different from here. There Jesus is addressing the disciples didactically in the house; here he is addressing the Jewish crowds apologetically beside the lake, and between vv. 24 and 38 lies the conclusion to the first half of chapter 13. In view of these facts, the context indicates that the field is "Israel",[147] and by this we mean the people of Israel, not a geographical area. The obvious strength of this interpretation is that we then take Matthew's statement in v. 24a at face value: Jesus spoke another parable to "them", i.e. the Jews.

## The Characters: (1) The Man, the Reapers, the Slaves

A review of the characters we encounter in the story of the Tares reveals that this parable possesses an inherent, though not perfectly balanced, dualism.

The "man" in v. 24 who supervises the sowing is identified in v. 27 as the "master of the house" ($oi\kappa o\delta\epsilon\sigma\pi\acute{o}\tau\eta\varsigma$). This term is genuinely Matthaean;[148] it is applied to Jesus (10.25), God (20.1, 11; 21.33), and even Christians (13.52; 24.43). Here in v. 24, the context shows that the man, the master of the house, is a transparent symbol for Jesus, who at the time of Matthew is the exalted Kyrios: the man is addressed as "Sir" (v. 27), i.e. Kyrios (cf. 25.20f, 22f); the term "slaves", as we shall see, is a common Matthaean symbol for the disciples, or Church;[149] and the word of the man is authoritative and governs both the direction and the climax of the parable (vv. 29f).

Towards the end of the parable Matthew informs us that the master of the house has "reapers" ($\theta\epsilon\rho\iota\sigma\tau\alpha\acute{\iota}$, v. 30b) at his disposal. Elsewhere in Matthew's Gospel, the reapers symbolize angels (cf. 13.39), i.e. heavenly beings who are to accompany Jesus Son of Man on the Last Day[150] and, as agents[151] under his command,[152] act both with him[153] and for him[154] in carrying out the Great Assize.

Last, the master of the house also possesses "slaves" ($\delta o\hat{u}\lambda o\iota$, vv. 27a, 28c), who, it must be observed, are noticeably differentiated from the reapers. From Matthew's standpoint, there is good reason to believe that the "slaves" refer to the disciples of Jesus in the comprehensive sense of the Church.

Broadly speaking, a slave in terms of the New Testament is one who possesses no personal autonomy and is totally subject to the will of another,[155] be it that of God, man, or other forces. For the most part, Matthew, in harmony with other New Testament writers, applies a religious connotation to the word "slave". In 20.27, he borrows a Jesus-logion from Mark (10.44) to designate the disciple, like the Son of Man, as a slave. In 10.24f, Matthew places the disciples of Jesus in the same relationship to him, their teacher, as a slave to his master.

When we turn to certain of the parables in Matthew's Gospel, which are often Q pericopes and where $\delta o\hat{u}\lambda o\varsigma$ occurs no less than twenty-five times, the religious colouration of this word is very much in evidence. In the parable of the Wicked Husbandmen (21.33–46=Mk 12.1–12), the slaves (vv. 34ff) refer to the Old Testament prophets;[156] perhaps a distinction is even made between the earlier and later prophets.[157] In the parable of the Great Supper (22.1–14=Lk 14.15–24), the Old Testament prophets again appear as slaves (v. 3), but so do the Apostles (v. 4), early martyrs (v. 6), and the first Christian missionaries to the heathen (vv. 8, 10).[158] In the parable of the Good Servant and the Wicked Servant (24.45–51=Lk 12.41–6), the slave could conceivably be a transparent symbol for the Apostles and, by extension, the leaders of Matthew's Church,[159] but it is more likely that the entire body of Matthew's Church is expected to identify itself with the slave.[160] This is certainly the case with the three slaves in the parable of the Talents (25.14–30=Lk 19.11–27). The same holds true for the parable of the Unforgiving Servant (18.23–35), though in this instance the Christian is made to realize the meaning of forgiveness by reverse example, i.e. in the confrontation with one slave who refuses to forgive a fellow slave (cf. 18.21f, 35).

This use of the term slave both in Matthew's own material and at those places where he has edited his sources[161] discloses that it is undergoing a process of "christianization" in his Gospel. Matthew never designates contemporary Jews as slaves. Where the word slave refers to a body of Jews as such, it signifies the prophets of the Old Testament. Otherwise, it is reserved for the Apostles, martyrs, missionaries, and members of the Church. Hence, one can assert with ample corroboration that in the parable of the Tares it is the Church that is speaking through the mouth of the slaves (vv. 27f). Indeed, the parable calls for this identification when we recall, again, that Jesus is the master of the house and that v. 30 sharply distinguishes between the reapers and the slaves when it comes to the burning of the darnel and the gathering of the wheat into the storehouse.

### The Characters: (2) The Enemy

Of the two fronts in the parable of the Tares, we have just seen that the one is made up of Jesus (who is the master of the house), the angels at his command (who are the reapers), and his disciples (who are the slaves). In opposition to this group stands "his enemy" ($a\dot{v}\tau o\hat{v}$ $\dot{o}$ $\dot{\epsilon}\chi\theta\rho\acute{o}s$, vv. 25, 28b), i.e. the personal adversary of the master of the house.

The "enemy" is an allusion to the Devil, or Satan (cf. 13.39).[162] That the Greek reads $\dot{\epsilon}\chi\theta\rho\acute{o}s$ and not, as we might expect, $\pi o\nu\eta\rho\acute{o}s$, simply attests to the fact that $\dot{\epsilon}\chi\theta\rho\acute{o}s$ was already firmly anchored in this parable by the time Matthew adopted it.[163]

In conformity with the whole of Jewish tradition,[164] Matthew's concept of $\dot{\epsilon}\chi\theta\rho\acute{o}s$ is eminently religious in tenor. At 10.36, he reveals how he understands this word: "and a man's enemies are the members of his household". The immediate context deals with the nature of discipleship. The argument is that the disciple's salvation hinges upon his professed allegiance to Jesus (10.32f). But as a direct result of such allegiance, the disciple may well find himself at odds with his own relatives (10.34f). Hence, according to 10.36, an enemy is that person with whom the disciple comes into conflict because of his allegiance to Jesus.

This indicates what Matthew has in mind when he designates the Devil as the Enemy. As the personification of a will that is inimical to all for which Jesus stands, the Devil makes the calculated attempt to destroy the allegiance of Christians to their Lord. In this sense, the Devil is the arch-enemy of both Jesus and his Church (13.25, 28, 39). Still, in that the object of the enemy's attack in the parable of the Tares is what belongs to the master rather than the master himself, we learn that when the Devil is depicted as the Enemy, he properly belongs less to the christological sphere of the Gospel than to the ecclesiological sphere.[165]

*The Interpretation:*
(1) ". . . a man who sowed good seed in his field"

Matthew tells us in v. 24b that the man, the master of the house, sowed good seed in his field. The emphasis in this statement is plainly on the circumstance that the "seed" (σπέρμα) was indeed "good" (καλόν). What is meant by this?

The force of σπέρμα is that it can denote not only seed that is sown, but people as well.[166] Therefore, linguistically, it is capable both of conforming to the agrarian scene depicted in the picture-half of the parable and of referring beyond this to the Word or to individuals in whom the Word is rooted (cf. 13.38, "sons of the Kingdom").

As in the parable of the Sower, the seed most likely alludes to the Word.[167] The relationship between the good seed that is sown and the stalks of wheat that bud and produce fruit (v. 26) is the relationship that exists between the Word of proclamation and the person in whom the Word has taken hold and exercises its influence.[168] Matthew has described this for us already in 13.23 (cf. Mk 4.14ff, 18, 20).

The seed is said to be "good" (καλόν, masc. καλός) both in v. 24 and in v. 27. While Matthew invariably employs καλός to describe deeds or things, it is none the less a synonym of ἀγαθός (7.17f; 12.33–7) and has the corresponding moral and ethical implications.[169]

For Matthew, καλός designates a man as a son of the Kingdom (13.38) in contrast to him who stands under the dominion of the Devil (13.38). But "good" is not an inherent or static quality that the individual has by nature or can possess. It is dependent upon the Word that calls to repentance and to life under God's kingly rule (3.10ff; 13.23). That person is good, therefore, who hears the Word, understands it, and, what Matthew particularly emphasizes (δή), gives evidence of this by bearing fruit (13.23), i.e. by performing works that glorify the heavenly

Father (5.16). These works are the works of love directed towards the brother and therefore towards Jesus himself (25.34-40). Consequently, the man who is good is numbered among the righteous (13.48ff; 13.43), he escapes condemnation and the fire of judgement on the Last Day (3.10; 7.19; 12.33–6; 13.48ff), and he inherits the Kingdom the Father has prepared for him (13.43; 25.34).

On the basis of the preceding, we can now attempt to pin down the line of thought in v. 24b. We will remember that the man, the master of the house, is Jesus, that the field is Israel, and that the seed is the Word, which, moreover, is good in the sense that it is intended to beget a people who will live under God's kingly rule, conforming to his will in works of obedience and love. With these factors in mind, it is evident that behind the statement in v. 24b that the man sowed good seed in his field is the idea that Jesus has come, and, through the vehicle of his own message (as Jesus Messiah) and the Kerygma of his Church (as Jesus Kyrios), he has preached the Word in Israel, a Word designed to produce a nation living under and doing the will of God.

*The Interpretation:*
(2) ". . . his enemy came and sowed darnel among the wheat . . ."

Once the sowing has been completed, the master's men take their rest. But while they are sleeping, the master's enemy comes, sows darnel (tares) among the wheat, and steals away (v. 25). What meaning would this episode have had for Matthew?

Since we have already identified the master's enemy as the Devil, the key concept in this attack by night has to do with the "darnel" (ζιζάνια). Darnel (*Lolium temulentum*) is a Palestinian weed that is botanically related to wheat and all but indistinguishable from it until the individual plants begin to mature.[170] Interestingly enough, the Rabbis looked upon darnel as a degenerate form of wheat, the product of the sexual excesses that took place even in the plant world at the time before the flood (cf. Gen. 6.12).[171] This view of the Rabbis is best reflected in haggadic etymology, according to which the Aramaic word for darnel, *zunin* (plural of *zun*), is derived from the verb *zanah*, which means to "commit fornication".[172]

There are two places in the first Gospel (12.39; 16.4) where Matthew has inserted the word "adulterous" into his Marcan text. In both instances, Jesus is entangled in debate with the leaders of the Jews ("scribes and Pharisees", 12.38; "Pharisees and Sadducees", 16.1). These interpolations are thinly veiled allusions to such Old Testament prophets as Hosea, Jeremiah, and Ezekiel, for they openly denounced the Israel of their time for being religiously unfaithful to God.[173] This is the very charge that Matthew, in turn, takes up against the contemporary Judaism with which he has to do (cf. 8.11f; 21.43).

Now if we project v. 25 of our parable on to this background, the point that is made in connection with the enemy's sowing darnel in the master's field of wheat would seem to be the following: even as Jesus, first in his own person as Messiah and subsequently through his ambassadors as Kyrios, has come to Israel and proclaimed a message designed to raise up a people who would do the will of God (v. 24b), so Satan, too, has been at work in Israel, and he has made it his objective to usurp the allegiance rightly belonging to Jesus in order to raise up a people that is unfaithful to God and to the doing of his will (v. 25).

*The Interpretation:*

(3) *"And when the stalks began to bud . . . the darnel appeared also"*

Because wheat and darnel look alike until their respective stalks begin to ripen, the words of stress will be found in the latter half of v. 26: "then the darnel appeared also". With this brief statement, Matthew brings us face to face with the situation of moment in the parable of the Tares: the presence of wheat and darnel side by side in the same field. In terms of the circumstances of Matthew's Church, v. 26b becomes a very apt description for the presence of two quite different bodies of "Israelites" existing side by side but in opposition to each other. As we shall see, v. 29 cautions us against making the wheat *per se* fully coterminous with the Church. Yet off-hand this is, in fact, the situation we have: the Church, or "true Israel",[174] existing side by side with, but in opposition to, Pharisaic Judaism, or "unbelieving Israel".

This thesis is confirmed by vv. 27–8a, in which the literary style of the parable abruptly switches from narrative to dialogue to permit Jesus, the exalted Kyrios who lives in the circle of his followers (18.20; 28.20), to enter into conversation with them and in this way deliver to them his authoritative Word: "And the slaves of the master of the house came and said to him, 'Sir, did you not sow good seed in your field? From what source then has it [got] darnel?' (28) And he said to them, 'An enemy has done this'. "

The two questions asked by the slaves reinforce v. 26b, for they reflect two aspects of the same concern: disquietude over the fact that in spite of the coming of the Messiah and the missionary efforts of the Church, there was such a large segment of the chosen nation that had not responded to the Word in obedience and faith;[175] and a genuine desire that the whole of Jewry should be won to the Way that finds its centre in Jesus (cf. 13.29b; 10.6; 15.24). Nevertheless, the failure to convert the Jews did not lack an explanation in the eyes of Matthew and his Church. As far as they were concerned, Satan had been at work among this people (v. 28a). Because of this, a chasm existed between the two camps of "Israelites". The one community, described as wheat and represented by the slaves, was living under the dominion of God. The other, described as darnel, was living under the dominion of Satan (cf. 12.22–37=Mk 3.22–30).

*The Interpretation:*
*(4) "Do you want us then to go out and pick them?"*

In reaction to the master's remark that an enemy is responsible for the darnel that has appeared in his field (v. 28a), the slaves ask the master whether he wants them to go out and pick the darnel (v. 28b). The clever thing about this question is that it is at once both an inquiry and a proposal. In other words, the question calls upon Jesus Kyrios to reply to a plan of action that the Church, or at least an element within it, is already prepared to execute.

The slaves request permission to "pick" the darnel. This implies that Matthew's Church is seriously occupied with the matter of forcing a formal and irrevocable separation between itself and the rest of Judaism.[176] For example, it could be argued by some that in this way the Church could express in action the judgement that it was allegedly in duty bound to pronounce over unbelieving Israel (cf. 10.6–15). In addition, there were factors at work within the Church that would almost automatically propel it towards separation: the Church had encountered complete intransigence from the side of Pharisaic Judaism;[177] the Church had suffered persecution at the hands of the Jews;[178] and there were those in the Church who saw in separation another device for establishing the pure and holy community in analogy to the Pharisees and the covenanters of Qumran.[179] Accordingly, the topic of complete separation from Pharisaic Judaism must have been highly relevant to Matthew's Church.

The reply of the master to this proposal is negative (v. 29). The slaves are not to pick the darnel for fear that they might not only uproot darnel but wheat as well (v. 29).

The verb "uproot" ($\dot{\epsilon}\kappa\rho\iota\zeta\dot{o}\omega$) occurs only four times in the New Testament but twice in the first Gospel alone (13.29; 15.13). Because Matthew uses it in 15.13 in a sharp apology against the Pharisees (cf. 15.12b, 14) and here in 13.29 in a parable apology addressed to the Jewish crowds, we have in this term another indication that the problem occupying the centre of the stage in the parable of the Tares is indeed the Church as opposed to Pharisaic Judaism.

For the Church, the response of Jesus Kyrios obviously means that it is not to effect a final withdrawal from unbelieving Israel, thus invoking judgement upon it. However, the specific reason Jesus Kyrios gives for making this decision is striking: "lest in picking the darnel you might uproot *wheat* along with them". The thrust of this statement appears to be squarely in the direction of the mission.[180] If so, far from allowing the Church to withdraw from unbelieving Israel, Jesus Kyrios calls upon his followers to undertake further missionary endeavour. It is his will that none of those in reprobate Israel should be lost who might be brought to acknowledge him as Lord.

### The Central Thought: "Let both grow side by side until the harvest"

With v. 30, the parable of the Tares reaches its climax. The language at this point is typically Matthaean[181] and rich in eschatological imagery, alluding to the Day of Judgement (the "harvest") and the Great Assize. But despite the eschatological character of v. 30, the central thought of the parable of the Tares is not fixed on the Judgement *per se*. Rather, it is expressed in the injunction "Let both grow side by side until the harvest" (v. 30a).[182] This injunction contains several emphases. To begin with, it presupposes the passage of time; hence, it documents the delay of the Parousia as experienced by Matthew's Church.[183] Further, the words "Let both grow side by side" are a declaration to Matthew's Church to the effect that, again, it is the resolve of Jesus Kyrios that for the time being the wheat and the darnel, i.e. true Israel, which has responded to the Word, and unbelieving Israel, which has rejected the Word, are not to be irrevocably cut off from each other. Last, the phrase "until the harvest" points out that though the Church may desire separation and the immediate judgement of unbelieving Israel, it must exercise patience,[184] because the time for this is not ripe. Judgement is a matter for the Day of the Lord, and not even then will it lie within the Church's area of competence.[185] Nevertheless, continues v. 30, at the Final Judgement such separation will in fact take place, and it will be as conclusive as gathering darnel for burning and wheat for storing in the granary.

### The Church of Matthew in relation to Pharisaic Judaism

Throughout the parable of the wheat and the darnel, we have had to do with the question of the relationship between Matthew's Church and the Pharisaic-orientated Judaism of its day. In scholarly circles, there are, apart from numerous nuances, basically two poles of opinion on this topic. On the one hand, there are those who contend that a complete schism between Matthew's Church and Judaism had already taken place before Matthew ever wrote his Gospel.[186] On the other hand, there are those who contend that Matthew's Church, regardless of the large measure of internal autonomy it had attained, was at least outwardly affiliated with Judaism and perhaps even maintained some sort of relationship with its league of synagogues.[187] By itself, the parable of the Tares provides too small a basis on which to decide such a complex problem. Still, it does support the latter position, though only to the extent that it demonstrates that Matthew's Church was very much in contact with Pharisaic Judaism. However, the parable gives no indication as to whether or not the two communities were related in any organizational manner.[188]

## Summary

The parable of the Tares is the second of the five *Parables of Growth* we shall consider as we investigate chapter 13. Formally, it is a fable that is a mixed-form, an *allegorical parable*.

The *contrast* inherent in this parable is that "which exists between the time when grain and weeds grow together and the time of the harvest, when weeds and wheat are separated from each other. . .".[189] In terms of the conditions of Matthew's day, this means that the contrast is between Matthew's contemporary situation, where true Israel and unbelieving Israel are still at least involved with each other, and the time of the judgement, when the two will be unalterably separated from each other.

The *culmination* of the parable is to be found in the reply of Jesus Kyrios, which may be divided into three parts, viz. vv. 29, 30a, and 30b–d. Of these three parts, the second is the pivotal one: "Let both grow side by side until the harvest." For Matthew, these words represent a directive from Jesus Kyrios to the effect that the Church is not now to pronounce judgement on unbelieving Israel by evoking a formal withdrawal from it.

The *intention* for which Matthew employs the parable of the Tares is twofold. Spoken as it is to "them", i.e. the Jews, the parable is *apologetic*: through it Jesus, the exalted Kyrios, charges the Jews of Matthew's time with being under the dominion of Satan and threatens them with utter condemnation at the Last Judgement. Serving as it does the interests of the Church, the parable is *paraenetic*: through it Jesus Kyrios deals with the Church's ardent desire to carry out a judgement through separation between itself and unbelieving Israel both by making it clear that the Church's mandate lies in the area of the mission, not in executing judgement, and by assuring the Church that such separation, or judgement, will indeed take place at the coming of the Son of Man.

The *secret* this parable reveals about the Kingdom of Heaven is that this Kingdom, as a present reality, has confronted all Israel in the Word of proclamation. But since all Israel has not responded to the Word in faith and obedience, this people has come to be divided into two camps: true Israel, which lives under the kingly rule of God, and unbelieving Israel, which lives under the rule of Satan. Not until the End of the Age and the coming of the Son of Man is there to be any forcible change of this state of affairs.

The *function* of the parable of the Tares within its immediate context is to pick up the argument Matthew develops in the pericope on the Reason for Speaking in Parables (13.10–17). There we were told that the Jews beyond the Church do not and will not understand God's Word of proclamation; the Christians, however, do. Here we are told that these unbelieving Jews stand under the rule of Satan as opposed to the true Israelites, who stand under the rule of God, and that at the End of the Age the former will be cast into the fires of destruction while the latter will enter into God's visibly established Kingdom.

## THE PARABLE OF THE MUSTARD SEED (13.31–2)

(31) *Another parable he put before them, saying, "It is the case with the Kingdom of Heaven as with a mustard seed which a man took and sowed in his field; (32) which is the smallest of all the seeds, but when it is grown, it is the largest of the garden herbs and becomes a tree, so that the birds of the sky come and nest in its branches."*

### The Text: A Conflation of Mark and Q

Following the parables of the Sower and of the Tares, the parable of the Mustard Seed is the third Parable of Growth in Matthew's thirteenth chapter. The Matthaean version of the Mustard Seed has long been recognized by scholars as a conflation of the Marcan (4.30ff) and Q (=Lk 13.18f) sources.[190] A fresh comparison of the more important divergent readings, however, will prove instructive.

In Luke (Q), the parable of the Mustard Seed pinpoints the element of growth: a man sowed a grain of mustard seed in his garden, and it grew up and became a tree (Lk 13.19). The contrast that is so important to Mark and Matthew is present (seed–tree), but not verbally stressed.

When we look at Mark, we notice at once how prominent this contrast between the grain of mustard seed (4.31a) and the large garden herb it produces has become (4.32b; Mark does not speak of a "tree"). Mark writes that the mustard seed is "the smallest of all the seeds on earth" (4.31c) and that the grown shrub is "the greatest of all the garden herbs . . ." (4.32b). Furthermore, the Marcan tradition has taken up and even elaborated on the element of growth so distinctive of Q: the mustard seed is "sown upon the ground" (4.31b), it "grows up" (4.32b), and it "puts forth large branches" (4.32c). Hence, Mark's parable of the Mustard Seed is characterized by the two qualities of contrast and growth, the attributes that make this parable a companion pericope to the parable of the Seed Growing Secretly (Mk 4.26–9).

In turning to the first Gospel, we discover that Matthew has combined the two previous versions, but in such a manner that he strikes a neat balance between the desire to underline the element of growth and the desire for a heightened contrast. Thus, Matthew records that the mustard seed is sown "in his [the man's] field" (growth), that it is "the smallest of all the seeds" (contrast), that "when it is grown" (growth), it is "the largest of the garden herbs" (contrast), in fact, it "becomes a tree" (growth and contrast).

As we can see, Matthew develops a double trilogy with respect to the features of contrast and growth not found in either Mark or Luke (Q): on the one hand, the Marcan contrast "smallest seed—greatest herb" has become "smallest seed—greatest herb–tree"; on the other hand, the Marcan and Lucan interest in growth is neither "seed–tree" (Luke, Q) nor "seed–herb with large branches" (Mark), but "seed–herb–tree". Through such compositional technique, Matthew shows that the two features of growth and contrast are of equal importance to him, therefore calling for careful attention in any attempt to interpret this parable, and that, together with Luke, he conceives of it as a companion parable to that of the Leaven (13.33 = Lk 13.20f).[191]

*The Parable in Outline*

The text of the Mustard Seed may be divided according to the following outline: (*a*) the transitional statement, v. 31a; and (*b*) the parable proper, vv. 31b–2.

Formally, this parable is a curious admixture of narrative and explica-tion.[192] It begins as a fable, as a story narrated in past time: "The King-dom of Heaven is like a mustard seed which a man took and sowed in his field . . ." (v. 31). But the text then shifts abruptly into the present tense, a characteristic indicative of the similitude, and gives a rather detailed description of the properties of the mustard seed as it undergoes the process of growth. This coalescence of two types of speech is singularly Matthaean,[193] and, as we shall demonstrate, theologically motivated. In Mark, at any rate, the parable of the Mustard Seed has the form of a similitude; in Luke (Q), it is a fable.

## The Introduction

In the opening line of the parable, Matthew introduces his preferred idiom ὁμοία ἐστίν (lit. "it is like," v. 31b; cf. 13.33, 44, 45, 47, 52; 20.1). In addition, we encounter both the introductory dative (κόκκῳ σινάπεως, v. 31b) and incongruence, which means that the introduction should be translated according to the following formula: "It is the case with the Kingdom of Heaven as with a mustard seed . . .".[194]

With respect to the incongruence, it is erroneous to argue that this principle applies to the parable of the Mustard Seed because the point of comparison is not between the Kingdom of God (Heaven) and the grain of mustard seed, but between the Kingdom of God and the full grown mustard herb.[195] On the contrary, the Kingdom of God is indeed compared to the mustard seed,[196] but comprehensively, i.e. as a seed that is minute but grows and becomes a tree. Accordingly, the structure of the parable calls for the interpreter to concentrate both on the grain of mustard seed and on the mature mustard shrub; on this account one is justified in speaking of incongruence as an inherent feature of this parable.

## The Picture-half of the Parable

Matthew's story of the mustard seed is a lucid description of an event that was commonplace in Palestine. Yet there is one detail that stands out. In describing the planting of the mustard seed, Mark reports that it is sown "upon the ground" (Mk 4.31b), Luke that the man places it "in his garden" (Lk 13.19b), and Matthew that the man sows it "in his field" (13.31c). Textually, it seems that both Matthew and Mark have edited their sources (cf. Mt 13.31c to 13.24b, Mk 4.31b to 4.26c), a point we will want to keep in mind. Agriculturally, Matthew has the correct reading. The mustard plant was not generally known as either a garden herb (Luke) or a wild bush (Mark), but, as Matthew states, as a cultivated shrub that the farmer normally placed in his field.[197]

## The Significance of the Transitional Statement

The transitional statement "Another parable he put before them, saying . . ." (v. 31a) is, as we demonstrated above, the product of Matthew himself.[198] It derives its importance from the fact that Matthew obviously wants to stress that this parable, too, is addressed to the Jews ("them"). This informs us that the apologetic current, which has been running so strongly thus far in chapter 13, is also present here.

## The Interpretation of the Parable: (1) ". . . as with a mustard seed . . ."

Matthew begins the parable proper by comparing the Kingdom of Heaven to a "mustard seed" (v. 31b). As an object by which to illustrate the Kingdom of Heaven, the mustard seed was ideally suited for two reasons. First, although, technically speaking, the mustard seed is not in reality "the smallest of all the seeds" (v. 32a),[199] it was none the less proverbial among the Jews as the most minute of quantities (cf. 17. 20 = Lk 17.6).[200] Second, of no other small seed did the fully grown plant attain the size of the mustard herb.[201] Hence, the mustard seed could depict perfectly both the insignificant manner in which the Kingdom first appeared, namely, in the man Jesus, and the glorious form it would assume at the End of the Age.[202] In passing, however, we want to note that Jewish expectation knew nothing of the eschatological Kingdom of God coming in humility. The Jews looked to the appearance of the Kingdom of God exclusively as a manifestation in splendour.[203]

Of the mustard seed the text says, "which a man took and sowed in his field" (v. 31c). The meaning of this clause turns on the significance of the "man", the "field", and the circumstance that Matthew casts the verb "sow" in the aorist indicative (ἔσπειρεν).

What is unusual about the occurrence of the verb "sow" in the aorist indicative in v. 31c is the fact that the action in the rest of the parable is described in the present tense.[204] This use of the aorist indicative is at the basis of the phenomenon we discussed above: the curious admixture in this parable of narrative and explication, fable and similitude. Since Matthew has purposely changed Mark's text in this instance (cf. Mk 4.31b), he has apparently pointed this verb with a view towards using it to make a statement about a past event.

The significance of the "field" in v. 31c is bound up with the prepositional phrase in which it stands: "in his field" (ἐν τῷ ἀγρῷ αὐτοῦ).

A comparison with Mark and Luke reveals that only the Matthaean recension of the Mustard Seed contains this phrase. On the other hand, it can also be found in Matthew's preceding parable of the Tares (cf. 13.24b). Now it is true, as we remarked, that this phrase rightly depicts the mustard herb as a cultivated plant that the farmer in Palestine would normally place in one of his fields. Still, the possibility is strong that Matthew employs this phrase, not so much to display a superior knowledge of agricultural practice, but to assimilate the parable of the Mustard Seed to the parable of the Tares. If this is the case, Matthew makes mention of the "field" in the parable of the Mustard Seed, just as in the parable of the Tares, because it alludes to "Israel".

With respect to the significance of the man ($\check{a}\nu\theta\rho\omega\pi os$), the question is whether Matthew could conceivably have understood this figure christologically. The *a priori* postulate as well as the arguments which would deny this possibility are without solid foundation.[205] Indeed, the figure of the man may not only point laterally to the Q text (Lk 13.19b), but vertically as well, back to the parable of the Tares (cf. 13.24b). If so, the man in the parable of the Mustard Seed, like the man in the parable of the Tares, refers to Jesus.

In our analysis of the clause "which a man took and sowed in his field", we have discovered thus far that Matthew has used the aorist indicative of the verb "sow" in order that the parable might contain a statement about a past event, and that the man stands for Jesus and the field for Israel. When taken together, these facts divulge that Matthew has drafted this clause so that the parable will affirm that Jesus brought the Kingdom of Heaven to Israel.

On the basis of the preceding, we can now formulate the first part of the message we find in the parable of the Mustard Seed. We recall that the parable, which is apologetic in nature, is addressed by Jesus to the Jews, that the Kingdom of Heaven has been initially compared to a mustard seed, that the mustard seed is described as the smallest of all the seeds, that the man is a metaphor for Jesus and the field for Israel, and that the purpose for which Matthew employs the aorist indicative in v. 31c is to allow for a statement about a past event. This information, coupled with the fact that the mustard seed is said to "grow" in v. 32b,[206] may be drawn together to form the following summary statement: Matthew prepares for Jesus, the exalted Kyrios, to assert that the Kingdom of Heaven has already come to Israel, but, contrary to Jewish expectations, in an insignificant manner, in the historical person Jesus, and, through him, also in his Church.

For the Jews, such an assertion is of course threatening in tone. It contains the scarcely veiled implication, which is expressed by way of the continuity that exists between the mustard seed and the mustard "tree", that the Jews cannot reject Jesus and his Church as they have done (cf. chaps. 10–12) and still claim with any validity that they are the people of God who will inherit God's latter-day Realm.

*The Interpretation of the Parable: (2) ". . . it becomes a tree . . ."*

The second half of the parable of the Mustard Seed portrays the greatness of the mustard herb once it has reached maturity (v. 32b–d). To capture the meaning of this picture, three points must be considered.

The parable describes the mustard seed as "growing" (v. 32b). Since Matthew compares the Kingdom of Heaven to the mustard seed, he obviously envisages the growth of the Kingdom in association with the growth of the mustard seed. Furthermore, in association with the growth of the Kingdom, Matthew surely envisages also the growth of the Church, for this is but a logical consequence of his conviction that his Church stands squarely within the tradition of the Apostles and that God's kingly rule in Jesus Kyrios is a present reality in it.[207] If this is correct, the parable of the Mustard Seed shows how closely Matthew can relate the Church to the Kingdom of Heaven[208] without, however, identifying the two. Then, too, the important corollary to such reasoning is Matthew's persuasion that even as the Kingdom of Heaven confronted the Jews in Jesus, so it confronts them at a later time in the Church.

The text reads that when the mustard seed is grown, "it is the largest of the garden herbs and becomes a tree . . ." (v. 32c–d). G. E. Post claims on two counts that the mustard seed's becoming a tree is not to be thought of as an exaggeration: because the cultivated mustard shrub may well attain a height of from ten to twelve feet, and because even smaller herbs are known to have been designated in the Arab world as trees.[209] Yet the fact remains that the mustard plant cannot, by any stretch of imagination, be classified as a δένδρον (v. 32c), i.e. a tree proper. Moreover, Matthew, by forging a heightened contrast, indicates how he desires his text to be understood: in terms of the miraculous, which alone is suitable for describing God's glorious Realm. With the mention of the tree, therefore, the parable of the Mustard Seed has reached its peak, which it then maintains throughout the latter part of the verse (v. 32d).

The Old Testament quotation "the birds of the sky come and nest[210] in its branches" (v. 32d) is a Matthaean conflation of the Marcan and Q (=Lk 13.19d) renderings of this passage. The word-combinations agree perfectly with the readings we find in Daniel 4.12, 21 (Theodotion) and Psalm 103.12 (LXX), Ezekiel 31.6. The picture of a tree in which birds nest or beasts find shade is a familiar Old Testament image for a mighty empire.[211] Consequently, it is appropriate as an allusion to God's fully established Kingdom.

There is also an important connotation associated with "the birds of the sky". T. W. Manson and C. H. Dodd cogently argue that this expression represents a veiled reference to the Gentiles.[212] Jeremias concurs, adding that κατασκηνόω is an "eschatological technical term for the incorporation of the Gentiles into the people of God . . .".[213] That Matthew almost certainly understood these words in this manner is documented by all those passages in the first Gospel expressing the idea that the Kingdom of God will comprise both Jews and Gentiles.[214]

We pointed out above that the Kingdom of Heaven in this parable is compared both to the tiny mustard seed and to the tree, i.e. reference is made at once to the coming of the Kingdom in Jesus and to the splendid Realm God will establish. When, however, we relate these two "events" to the age Matthew represents, the latter falls between them. So it is that the Kingdom of Heaven is a present reality for Matthew's Church, yet the expansion the Church was undergoing and the fact that it considered itself to be the place where God openly (not in secret!) manifests his Kingdom would combine to make it impossible, from Matthew's standpoint, to say that the presence of the Kingdom in the world was as insignificant as a mustard seed. At the same time, the mustard seed had not yet become a "tree", the appearance of the Kingdom in majesty was still a hope of the future.

In view of this position "between the events", what then was Matthew's overall understanding of the parable of the Mustard Seed? The answer lies in v. 32c–d, the culmination of the parable: "it becomes a tree, so that the birds of the sky come and nest in its branches." Although Matthew's Church was certainly still awaiting the final manifestation of the Kingdom of God ("it becomes a tree"), it was none the less even now a conglomerate of both Jews and Gentiles. Hence, while the "process of growth" was by no means complete, Matthew already sees Old Testament prophecy (v. 32d) being fulfilled. Accordingly, the message we have in the latter half of the parable is the following: the process that will issue in the establishment of God's glorious Realm is under way; already God is at work gathering Jews and Gentiles together into one community.

There is very likely also an aside to this message. The parable pictures the growth of a mustard plant, i.e. the development of something that God and not man prescribes. Now we know from 24.26f (cf. vv. 23–7) that Matthew's Church was in some turmoil regarding the time when Jesus Son of Man would come again to inaugurate God's end-time Kingdom. It is at least possible, therefore, that this parable contains something of a warning to the effect that the precise time for the unveiling of the end-time Kingdom lies solely in the hands of God: just as God determines when the mustard seed becomes a tree, so God will determine when the time is ripe for the coming of his great Realm. If this is accurate, the parable of the Mustard Seed can be seen to reflect something of the delay of the Parousia as Matthew's Church experienced it.[215]

### The Parable in relation to the Time of Matthew

If we have put our finger on the message enunciated in the parable of the Mustard Seed, the situation to which Matthew relates it is presumably the following. Matthew occupies himself with the fact that the Kingdom of God has already come but is still to appear in future glory and utilizes this parable to give expression to the conviction that the Church, and not the Jews, is the eschatological community of God, because the Church is the place where God is even now gathering together Jews and Gentiles into one body in anticipation of his magnificent Kingdom; at the same time, the final revelation of this Kingdom is God's affair, and therefore not an object for speculation or concern on the part of Christians.

In order to avoid any misconceptions, the reader should observe that the interpretation of the parable of the Mustard Seed we have advanced is not the old position of liberal theology for which the Kingdom of God (Heaven) was an immanent reality that was to pervade the world as a spiritual, social, or ethical force.[216] The Kingdom of Heaven is indeed construed as a present reality in the first Gospel, but this is not to say that it is then pressed into sociological categories. The Kingdom of Heaven is the "product of God" from beginning to end.

### Summary

The parable of the Mustard Seed is the third *Parable of Growth* Matthew has incorporated into his thirteenth chapter. Essentially it is a *similitude*.

The *contrast* inherent in the parable arises quite naturally from the relationships that are compared: the very small mustard seed is for the tree that grows from it what the manifestation of the eschatological Kingdom of God in Jesus is for the future, glorious appearance of this Kingdom.

The *culmination* of the parable is found in v. 32c–d: "it becomes a tree, so that the birds of the sky come and nest in its branches". The point is that God is at work (in and through the Church) to establish his final Kingdom, since Jews and Gentiles are already being gathered into one community.

The *intention* for which Matthew employs the parable of the Mustard Seed is twofold. As a word to the Jews, the parable is *apologetic*. Through it Jesus, the exalted Kyrios, pronounces that, contrary to Jewish belief, the Kingdom of God has already come to Israel, for it was a present reality in his person, and, by extension, is now present in his Church. Moreover, just as there is continuity between the mustard seed and the tree it produces, so the Jews cannot, as they have done, reject him and his Church and still lay claim to God's latter-day Realm. As a word to the Church, the parable is *paraenetic*. Through it Jesus Kyrios fortifies the Christians of Matthew's Church in their conviction that they are in truth the eschatological community of God.

The *secret* this parable reveals about the Kingdom of Heaven is multiple: that in bringing his kingly rule in Jesus, God has chosen to manifest it in humility; that God has set in motion the process by which his kingly rule, through the agency of the Church, spreads itself out, embracing both Jews and Gentiles; and that God will one day unveil his kingly rule in majesty as a splendid Realm.

The *function* of the parable of the Mustard Seed within its immediate context is to serve as one further link in the apology against the Jews which Matthew has been steadily unfolding throughout chapter 13.

## THE PARABLE OF THE LEAVEN (13.33)

(33) *Another parable he told them, "It is the case with the Kingdom of Heaven as with leaven, which a woman took and put into three measures of wheat flour, until the whole was leavened."*

### A Companion Parable

The parable of the Leaven is the fourth Parable of Growth we shall study. It is a Q pericope (Mt 13.33 = Lk 13.20f) and also a companion parable to that of the Mustard Seed, as the structure, wording (cf. v. 33a–c to 13.31), inherent contrast (small–large), and picture of growth indicate.[217]

### The Parable in Outline

Verse 33 breaks down into the following division: (a) the transitional    v 33
statement, v. 33a; and (b) the parable proper, v. 33b–d.

From the standpoint of form, the parable of the Leaven reads as an
event narrated in past time and thus seems to be a fable. But it should
rather be classified as a similitude, because in structure it is basically a
comparison of two relationships that are of essential importance for
understanding its message: the small lump of leaven is to the mass of
leavened dough as the first appearance of the Kingdom is to its glorious
fulfilment.

### The Transition and Introduction

The transitional statement (v. 33a) is a repetition of the formula Matthew
has already employed in the two parables of the Tares and of the Mustard Seed. The one difference is that the stereotyped phraseology has
been modified to effect a smooth transition both backwards and forwards (cf. v. 33a to 13.31a and 13.34).

As for the introduction, Matthew repeats his preferred formula ὁμοία
ἐστίν, and we encounter the twin features of incongruence and the
introductory dative. Consequently, v. 33b should be translated as
follows: "it is the case with the Kingdom of Heaven as with leaven...".

But as in the case of the previous parables, the presence of incongruence does not mean that the Kingdom of Heaven is to be
compared solely with the great bulk of fully leavened bread.[218]
Instead, the interpreter is invited by Matthew to keep two quantities in
view: the small lump of yeast and the large measure of leavened bread.

### The Picture-half of the Parable

Just as it was the task of the man in Palestine to sow seed, so it was
normally the task of the woman to bake bread (cf. e.g. Gen. 18.6).
Three measures of wheat flour are the equivalent of four and one-half
pecks, or a dry measure of thirty-six quarts.[219] G. Dalman contends
that this is the largest amount of dough a single woman could knead at
one time.[220] It will produce enough bread to satisfy the needs of a
household of thirty-six members for one day,[221] or to feed more than
one hundred persons at a single meal.[222] These proportions show how
stark the contrast inherent in this parable is meant to be: on the one
hand, a fistful of yeast; on the other hand, enough bread to feed over
one hundred persons at a sitting.

Although leaven is a traditional Jewish metaphor for "bad things having great effects",[223] the stress in this parable does not lie on the "bad things" but on the "great effects".[224] This is evident from the fact that the parable reaches its climax in the characterization of these great effects, namely, in the large quantity of leavened bread ("until the whole was leavened", v. 33d).

### The Message of the Parable for the Jews

An examination of the unique traits of the parable will provide us with a clue as to its interpretation. The transition "Another parable he told them" (v. 33a) informs us that it is once again the Jews who are being chiefly addressed and that Matthew attaches also to this parable an apologetic motif. The contrast between the small lump of leaven and the great mass of bread is essentially the same as that between the tiny mustard seed and the "tree" resulting from it, an indication that Matthew is once more thinking of the insignificant manner in which the Kingdom of God manifested itself in the man Jesus and the final form that this Kingdom will assume at the End of the Age.[225] Finally, the growth Matthew attributed to the Kingdom in the parable of the Mustard Seed is likewise duplicated here in that the Kingdom is compared both to the small lump of leaven and to the great amount of bread.

In consideration of these factors, the message of this parable to the Jews is, again, that their eyes are blind to the ways of God because they have not realized in what manner God has chosen to bring his Kingdom to Israel. The Jews expect that God's Kingdom should manifest itself as "a revolution, a complete change of all conditions of life for Israel and the world".[226] Instead, the Kingdom has come in the man Jesus, and, through Jesus, in the Church, the community in which he resides as Kyrios. Furthermore, just as the fully leavened bread is dependent upon the tiny piece of yeast, so the final manifestation of God's Kingdom will issue from God's present activity, the centre of which, to repeat, is not Pharisaic Judaism, but the Church.

### The Message of the Parable for the Church

As far as Matthew's Church is concerned, the parable of the Leaven, like the parable of the Mustard Seed, confirms the Church in its consciousness of being God's eschatological community, for the Church holds that it is the place where God—to pick up the point of the parable—is operative in a special way. Specifically, the parable of the Leaven, in the eyes of Matthew's Church, embodies the thought that just as leaven brings about the massive swelling of the dough,[227] so

God, through the vehicle of the Church, is even now at work in power to spread out his kingly rule, and this will terminate only with the setting up of his latter-day Realm.

Perhaps this parable also contains a hint of caution, namely, that Christians must not be misled into false speculation as to the time when God's splendid Kingdom will arrive, when Jesus Son of Man will come in glory (cf. 24.26f). Just as leaven initiates a process that is independent of man's control, so God alone determines the course of events that will culminate in the manifestation of his splendid Kingdom.

## Summary

The parable of the Leaven is the fourth of the *Parables of Growth* with which we shall deal; basically, it is a *similitude*.

The *contrast* inherent in this parable may be expressed in terms of the relationships that are compared: the small piece of leaven is to the great mass of leavened bread as the manifestation of the Kingdom of God in Jesus (and his Church) is to the appearance of the future, magnificent Kingdom.

The *culmination* of the parable is found in the terse statement, "until the whole was leavened" (v. 33d). For Matthew, these words emphasize that God is at present active in power to bring about the advent of his end-time Kingdom.

The *intention* for which Matthew employs the parable of the Leaven is twofold. Directed as it is towards the Jews, the parable is *apologetic*. As a word of Jesus, the exalted Kyrios, it contains the argument that the Jews fail to comprehend how God has brought his Kingdom, or kingly rule, to them. Consequently, they exclude themselves from the final Kingdom of God, for this will emerge from God's present activity in the Church of Jesus in the same way as the leavened bread is the product of the fermentation effected by the little lump of leaven. As an address to the Church, the parable is *paraenetic*. Jesus Kyrios strengthens the eschatological consciousness of the Church, according to which the Church is the place where God is operative in might, manifesting and expanding his rule.

The *secret* this parable reveals about the Kingdom of Heaven is, like that of the Mustard Seed, multiple: that the Kingdom of God has already appeared, but, contrary to Jewish anticipation, in lowliness; that God is enlarging his Kingdom; and that at a time God himself will determine, this Kingdom will be revealed in splendour.

The *function* of the parable of the Leaven within its immediate context is identical with that of the parable of the Mustard Seed: it is used apologetically to develop the point that the Jews, unlike the Church, have not recognized how God has resolved to manifest his Kingdom to men.

## THE CONCLUSION: JESUS' USE OF PARABLES (13.34–5)

(34) *All these things Jesus spoke to the crowds in parables, and without a parable he tried to say nothing to them,* (35) *in order that what was spoken through the prophet might be fulfilled, who said, "I shall open my mouth in parables, I shall announce things which have been hidden from the beginning [foundation] of the world."*

With this pericope Matthew brings the first half of his parable chapter (13.1–35), which is delivered primarily to the Jewish crowds, to a close. Formally, he links vv. 34 and 35 together by means of the catchword "parable", which also provides them with an inner coherency. Otherwise, v. 34 is drawn largely from Mark 4.33f, and v. 35 is a typically Matthaean formula quotation. Because of the disparity between the two verses, we shall examine them separately.

### Verse 34

In v. 34, Matthew has made four major changes in Mark's text in order to construct a passage that will serve his theological objectives. They are the following: unlike Mark, Matthew explicitly mentions both Jesus and the crowds by name; with the simple statement "All these things Jesus spoke to the crowds in parables..." (v. 34a), Matthew eliminates any vestiges of what appears in Mark's Gospel to be a double tradition;[228] by substituting οὐδέν for Mark's οὐκ, Matthew turns Mark's matter-of-fact statement "Without a parable he did not speak to them ..." (Mk 4.34a) into the emphatic assertion: "and without a parable he tried to say [229] *nothing* to them ..." (v. 34b); and Matthew drops completely Mark's concluding remark, "but privately to his own disciples he explained everything" (Mk 4.34b).

Why has Matthew made these assorted alterations? His elimination of Mark's reference to the need of the disciples for explanation is of course motivated by his insistence that by virtue of their call the disciples are already enlightened and therefore do comprehend the person and message of Jesus. But other than this, Matthew's editorial changes on Mark 4.33f all tend exclusively in one direction: to place Jesus (and

the disciples) opposite the crowds and to accentuate the fact that inter-
course between the two groups is characterized by the speaking in
parables, i.e. what for the crowds is incomprehensible speech. Accordingly, the function of v. 34 is to recapitulate 13.1–33 by depicting the
impasse that exists between Jesus (and the Church) and the Jews (cf.
chaps. 11–12).

*Verse 35*

That v. 35 is a formula quotation is indicated by the peculiarly Matthaean statement "in order that (ὅπως) what was spoken through the
prophet might be fulfilled, who said . . .".[230] The first half of this
quotation is a literal reproduction of Psalm 77.2a (LXX), but the
second half agrees neither with the Greek nor with the Masoretic
text. Whether the blatant variation stems from Matthew's utilization
of a collection of prophecies, or from his combining particular textual
traditions, or from his quoting from memory or according to a specific
method of interpretation such as the *pesher*, is impossible to say. For
reasons that will presently become evident, we are inclined to agree
with Stendahl when he states that it is "an *ad hoc* Christian interpretation, which, moreover, is closely bound up with its context".[231]

In terms of the subject matter, one can easily get the impression that
there is a contradiction between the quotation and its context.[232]
According to 13.10–13, the parable is impenetrable without God-given
insight. Here in v. 35b, the parable is unconditionally a vehicle for
revealing mysteries. This contradiction, however, is only apparent;
the quotation merges very well with its context, as we shall now
attempt to demonstrate.

Assuming that the phrasing of v. 35b either stems from Matthew
himself or at least complies with his theological point of view,[233] it
would seem that this quotation serves several purposes. In common
with all formula quotations, it is intended to document the fulfilment
of Scripture: Jesus is acting according to the prophesied resolve of God
when he speaks in parables. Such fulfilment of Scripture is important
for Matthew, because the validity of Jesus' speech in parables is directly
dependent upon its having been authorized by God himself.

As a corollary to this stress on the fulfilment of prophecy, this
quotation further testifies to the Messiahship of Jesus. Because it is in
and through Jesus that the hidden revelation of God is disclosed, the
revelation that the prophets and righteous men of old desired in vain
to see and hear (13.16f), Jesus must necessarily be the Messiah.

There is also a recapitulation of Jesus' apology in parables. In the form in which Matthew has recorded it, this quotation describes the revelation Jesus brings as "things which have been hidden." (κεκρυμμένα). These "things which have been hidden" comprise the content of the parables of Jesus. Yet the parable, according to the context (13.10b–13), can only be understood by the person to whom God has given the necessary insight. Hence, there is a perfect correlation in the quotation between parable and revelation, between form and content.[234] Both possess the quality of "hiddenness"; in both the intent is comprehensible only to the eye of faith. Since, however, God has given the eye and ear of faith to the disciples, or Church, while withholding it from the larger body of the Jews (13.10b–13, 16f), this quotation tersely captures the hallmark of 13.1–34: the deep division between the Church and unbelieving Judaism. Therefore it does not stand at odds with its context, and it places itself fully in the service of the antithesis between Jesus and the crowds which we discovered in v. 34.

Finally, this quotation attests to the eschatological consciousness of Matthew's Church. Because the Church alone can understand the revelation of God, the question of the fulfilment of the quotation is one that pertains to the Church, not to the Jews. Yet in that Matthew's Church regards itself as the recipient of the divine revelation that has been hidden from the foundation of the world but now made known through the parables of Jesus, it gives testimony to its conviction that it is the true people of God.

*Summary*

This pericope on Jesus' Use of Parables concludes the first half of Jesus' discourse in parables (13.1–33). Thus, while we have learned, on the one hand, that the Church has heard the Word (Sower), that it is the recipient of divine revelation (Reason for Speaking in Parables), and that it lives under the dominion of God (Tares) and is the eschatological community of God (Mustard Seed and Leaven), we have learned, on the other hand, that the Jews have not responded to the Word proclaimed to them (Sower), that they are hardened towards divine revelation (Reason for Speaking in Parables), and that they stand under the dominion of Satan and at the Judgement will be cast into the fires of destruction (Tares), for they have not recognized in what manner God's kingly rule has come to them (Mustard Seed and Leaven).

As the final paragraph of this section of the discourse, the *function* of Jesus' Use of Parables is first of all to recapitulate the argument of

13.1–33 by underlining its apologetic motif: the division between Jesus (and the disciples, or Church) and the Jews. In addition, it anchors Jesus' speaking in parables within *Heilsgeschichte*, since it presents his discourse in parables as the fulfilment of prophecy. The corollary to this is that this pericope further testifies to the Messiahship of Jesus, for it ascribes to him the role of mediating divine revelation. And in that this revelation is ultimately the trust of the Church, this pericope also reflects the eschatological consciousness of Matthew's Church.

# CHAPTER 5

# Jesus' Parables to the Disciples in Private (13.36–52)

———◆◆◆———

## THE SETTING (13.36a)

(36a) *Then he dismissed the crowds and went into the house.*

Verse 36a is framework material and has been composed by Matthew. Jesus' dismissal of the crowds and his withdrawal to the house complement 13.1, where Matthew reported that Jesus "went out of the house" to address the crowds beside the sea. Accordingly, Matthew effects a major change of setting in his parable chapter. The expansive crowd scene so prominent throughout 13.1–35 now passes, and in its place Matthew pictures Jesus and his disciples in the house alone. In terms of Jesus' speech in parables, this change means that whereas the first half was directed primarily to the Jewish crowds and only secondarily to the disciples, or Church, the second half is directed exclusively to the disciples, and for this reason Matthew chooses for Jesus the privacy of the house (13.36–52).

Interestingly, Matthew's references to the house in 13.1, 36 are without counterpart in the parallel passages of Mark (cf. Mk 4.1, 35f). Why, then, should Matthew be concerned to mention the house? Does it have a special significance for him?

While Mark does not refer to the house precisely in his parable chapter, he is generally fond of it as a setting for Jesus' activity.[1] It is a place of seclusion, and as such an ideal location for staging events that have to do with the Messianic Secret. Indeed, when one catalogues the type of ministrations that occur there, one is inclined to conjecture that in the second Gospel the house not only designates a dwelling but is also a veiled reference to Mark's Church, and that Mark is grounding in the activity of Jesus the kerygmatic, didactic, cultic, and apologetic practices that took place in the assembly of the Christian community

to which he belonged.² Could the same be true of Matthew? Does
Matthew perhaps attribute a symbolical dimension to the house?

The reply is no. For Matthew, the "house" is a specific dwelling in
Capernaum³ but nothing more. In fact, Matthew is not even over-
interested in the house as a setting for the events of Jesus' ministry. A
study of οἰκία–οἶκος in the concordance shows that although Matthew
employs this combination some thirty-five times in his Gospel, only
twice does he make use of the house *as a setting* independently of Mark
or Q (9.28; 13.36).⁴

What therefore has motivated Matthew to introduce the house in
13.1 and 13.36? The answer is that in 13.1 the house is a parallel reference
to the house of Capernaum found in Mark 3.20.⁵ Now Matthew
deliberately passes over Mark 3.20.⁶ But since he takes up Mark's
outline immediately thereafter (12.22–30 = Mk 3.22–7), he faces the
later difficulty that the pericope on Jesus' True Kindred, which
immediately precedes the parable chapters of Matthew 13 and Mark 4,
clearly presupposes the house as the place of action. Matthew consequently takes account of this by citing the house in retrospect at
13.1.⁷

As regards the wider context, Matthew's reference to the house in
13.1 serves a double function. On the one hand, it binds the materials
of chapter 12 to those of the parable chapter. On the other hand, it
prepares the way for our passage, 13.36, where Matthew has Jesus
dismiss the crowds and return to the house so that he may continue the
discourse in parables with his disciples in private. When they are taken
together, Matthew's references to the house of Capernaum in 13.1
and 13.36 establish a setting that first indirectly and then directly spans
the entire parable chapter.

## AN EXCURSUS
### THE INTERPRETATION OF
### THE PARABLE OF THE TARES
#### (13.36b–43)

(36b) *And his disciples came to him and said, "Explain to us the*
*parable of the darnel of the field." (37) And he answered and said,*
*"He who sows the good seed is the Son of Man. (38) And the field*
*is the world. And the good seed, these are the sons of the Kingdom.*
*But the darnel are the sons of the Evil One, (39) and the enemy*
*who sowed them is the Devil. And the harvest is the End of the*

*Age, and the reapers are angels.* (40) *Just as therefore the darnel are gathered and burned with fire, so will it be at the End of the Age.* (41) *The Son of Man will send his angels and they will pick from his Kingdom all those who give offence and those who commit lawlessness* (42) *and will cast them into the fiery furnace. In that place there will be weeping and gnashing of teeth.* (43) *Then the righteous will shine as the sun in the Kingdom of their Father. He who has ears, let him hear.*"

We have noted that the predominant tendency among exegetes is to link the Interpretation of the Parable of the Tares to the parable itself (13.24–30), with the result that both are treated as a single subsection.[8] One can even appeal to the text in defence of this procedure, because the two units display great linguistic similarity and because v. 36 of the Interpretation pictures the disciples as asking Jesus to "explain to us the parable of the darnel of the field". But as we mentioned above, a close examination will show that the affinity between the parable of the Tares and the Interpretation is formal and accidental rather than real and essential, so that the interpreter should properly deal with each unit separately.[9]

### The Pericope in Outline

The Interpretation of the Parable of the Tares may be divided into four parts: (*a*) the introduction, vv. 36b–7a; (*b*) the catalogue of terms, vv. 37b–9; (*c*) the description of the Last Judgement, vv. 41–3a, which is introduced by the transitional statement, v. 40; and (*d*) the conclusion, v. 43b.[10]

### The Introduction

The introduction (vv. 36b–7a) stems from Matthew himself. This is evident from the vocabulary, grammar, and syntax, as Jeremias has convincingly demonstrated,[11] and from the fact that we encounter the same formula with the same sequence of action here as in 13.10–11a, which are also of Matthaean origin: in both instances, the disciples approach Jesus, ask a question, and receive his reply ("And he answered and said . . .").

Theologically, there are two points to note with respect to v. 36b-c. As we discovered in 13.10a, when Matthew invokes the idiom "And his disciples came to him and said . . .", he is attributing a divine dignity to Jesus, i.e. the disciples "approach" Jesus with the same reverent demeanour that would be due to a king or deity.[12] Hence, Matthew is once again portraying the earthly Jesus in the stature of the exalted Kyrios in order that he may speak to a situation that has become acute in the Church.

In the second place, when the disciples ask Jesus to "explain" the parable of the Tares to them, such "explaining" is not to be understood, as in Mark, as part of the ongoing efforts of Jesus to overcome the spiritual blindness of his followers, but as a token that whatever he tells the disciples they will comprehend, as 13.52 reveals. Consequently, if the disciples have not understood Jesus, it is only for the moment.[13]

Still, there is also the possibility that our text does not even suggest so much as momentary ignorance on the part of the disciples. Lohmeyer argues in view of 18.31 that the disciples make no request for an "explanation" at all; they ask instead for a "report".[14] In this case, v. 36b–c skirts the whole issue of the disciples' lack of understanding.[15]

### The Catalogue of Terms

The question as to whether the catalogue of terms, or for that matter the entire pericope, is in substance a Matthaean creation[16] or instead a piece of early tradition that Matthew inherited and reshaped[17] is not of capital importance for us. What is decisive is that the Interpretation, as we now know it, is an expression of Matthaean thought and theology to the very core.

In relation to the rest of the unit, the function of the catalogue of terms is simply to make the following description of the Last Judgement (vv. 40–3a) intelligible.[18] An investigation of the terms substantiates this, for all of the definitions given us in vv. 37b–9, with the sole exception of the mention of the Devil (v. 39a), recur in vv. 40–3a:[19] the Son of Man (vv. 37b and 41a); the world (v. 38a) as the Kingdom of the Son of Man (v. 41b); the sons of the Kingdom (v. 38b) as the righteous (v. 43a); the sons of the Evil One (v. 38c) as all those who give offence and those who commit lawlessness (v. 41b); the End of the Age (vv. 39b and 40b); and the angels (vv. 39c and 41a). Precisely because the purpose of the catalogue of terms is to prepare the hearer for what is coming, the style with which it is written is sober, almost clinical in nature, and belongs to the same literary genus as the Interpretation of the Parable of the Sower (13.18–23).[20]

### The Description of the Last Judgement

The heart of the Interpretation of the Parable of the Tares is the description of the Last Judgement (vv. 40–3a), which is followed by the

conclusion (v. 43b), an exhortation to hear aright (cf. 13.9). The difference between this section of the pericope and the preceding catalogue
of terms is striking. There the present and the future, sowing and
harvest, lie on a single plane. Here the present is totally forgotten, and
all attention is concentrated on the harvest, on the End of the Age.
There the style is matter-of-fact, didactic; here it is moving, vivid
with apocalyptic imagery, and threatening in tone. In short, while the
former material is didactic in character, the latter is homiletic.[21]

### The Dualistic Character of the Pericope

The most important feature of the Interpretation is the pronounced
dualism that governs it. The "world" forms the setting, and the actors
are the Son of Man, the angels at his command, and the sons of the
Kingdom, on the one side, and, on the other, the Devil and the sons of
the Evil One. Except perhaps for the parable of the Tares, there is in the
whole of Matthew's Gospel only one other pericope that evinces such
a developed dualism, that of the Last Judgement (25.31–46). Our
immediate objective is to examine the setting of the Interpretation as
well as the representatives of each camp against the background of
Matthew's thought.

### The Setting of the Narrative

In v. 38a, Matthew informs us that "the field is the world (κόσμος)".
This is a key statement, because our interpretation of the "world"
will necessarily circumscribe the scope of Matthew's outlook in this
pericope.

In recent years there have been principally two ways in which
scholars have preferred to interpret the "world". In the one instance
it has become conventional to understand κόσμος in terms of the
Church. G. Bornkamm has espoused this position,[22] and his pupil,
H. E. Tödt, has developed it at length.[23]

According to Tödt, the world in v. 38a is synonymous with the
Kingdom of the Son of Man mentioned in v. 41. Since this Kingdom
is described as an earthly realm (cf. v. 41 with v. 43) in which sons of
the Kingdom and sons of the Evil One coexist, and since the Son of
Man appears as the Lord of this realm as well as the one who will
execute judgement on it at the End of the Age, Tödt concludes that
Matthew has the Church in mind. He contends that Matthew is
characterizing the Church as a *corpus permixtum*, and he supports
his argument by pointing out that it is typical of Matthew to

emphasize that the Church, too, must undergo judgement at the Latter Day.[24]

Tödt is correct in his observations when he interprets the world in terms of the Kingdom of the Son of Man and defines this Kingdom as an earthly realm over which the Son of Man rules in the "present" and comes to judge in the "future". Yet to conclude from these facts that the world is therefore the Church is not compelling. As A. Vögtle has remarked, if Matthew had desired to identify the world with the Church, we should expect to find ἐκκλησία in place of "his Kingdom" in v. 41 (cf. 16.18; 18.17).[25] Or, from another point of view, when we consider the way in which Matthew otherwise uses κόσμος in his Gospel, there is nothing in this word to suggest that he might have employed it to signify the Church.[26] It would seem, then, that Tödt's deduction to the effect that the Kingdom of the Son of Man and consequently the world is to be equated with the Church is misleading.

The second manner in which scholars have recently interpreted the world is based on a suggestion made by J. Wellhausen[27] and amplified by W. Trilling.[28] According to Trilling, a form-critical analysis demonstrates that vv. 37ff constitute an independent unit almost devoid of any internal relationship with vv. 40-3. To be exact, vv. 37ff represent theological reflection upon the fact that the Church, in carrying out the command to make disciples of all nations, learns through experience that both "good" and "bad" Christians come to exist side by side in the same institution.[29] The world in v. 38, then, is to be understood as the "sphere" in which the Kingdom of God spreads itself out.[30]

Unlike Tödt, Trilling properly attributes a universal quality to the world. However, he destroys the unity of the pericope by denying that the function of vv. 37ff is to prepare for vv. 40-3, which further explains why he does not redefine the world in terms of the Kingdom of the Son of Man.[31] The question, finally, is whether Trilling's whole appeal to the literary history of the Interpretation is relevant, for this history found its termination with Matthew. Would Matthew have regarded the pericope as so loosely unified that the reader could be expected to interpret one section independently of the other?[32]

In reality, it is only by construing κόσμος at once as the Kingdom of the Son of Man and in universal dimensions that we will arrive at a satisfactory understanding of this term. Such a passage as 24.30 defines it well: "all the tribes of the earth".[33] Accordingly, the "world" is the Kingdom of the Son of Man, a Kingdom that, to use Vögtle's words, is "the globe as mankind's place of residence".[34]

*The Kingdom of the Son of Man in relation to the Kingdom of the Father*

In addition to the Kingdom of the Son of Man, Matthew also speaks in our pericope of the "Kingdom of the Father" (v. 43a). What is the relationship between the two?

As we have seen, the "Kingdom of the Son of Man" embodies the idea that in the "present age" (between Easter and the Parousia) Jesus Son of Man is Lord of the world. But the same is manifestly not true of the "Kingdom of the Father". On the contrary, the latter refers to the time after the Parousia when God will eternally establish and visibly rule over his final, glorious Realm (cf. 26.29). In the Interpretation of the Parable of the Tares, therefore, Matthew depicts the Kingdom of the Father as succeeding the Kingdom of the Son of Man.

Still, if we investigate the whole of Matthew's Gospel, we find that he can speak of the Kingdom of the Father (= Kingdom of Heaven [God]) and the Kingdom of the Son of Man coterminously. If the Kingdom of the Son of Man is a present reality (13.41), so is the Kingdom of the Father (e.g. 11.12; 12.28; 21.43).[35] And if the Kingdom of the Father can be thought of as a future reality (26.29), the same is the case with the Kingdom of the Son of Man (20.21). Hence, Matthew has incorporated into his Gospel what appear to be two lines of thought. However, they present no systematic problem, for he resolves them in harmony with the words of Jesus found in 11.27 ("all things have been delivered to me by my Father") and 28.18 ("all authority in heaven and on earth has been given to me"). In other words, because Matthew holds that God exercises his kingly rule (which is both a present and future reality) in and through Jesus, he does not hesitate to speak interchangeably of the Kingdom of the Father and the Kingdom of the Son of Man.[36]

*The Actors:* (1) *The Son of Man and his Angels*

The leader of the one regiment is the "Son of Man", who is characterized as "he who sows the good seed" (v. 37b). This stands in sharp contrast to v. 41, where the Son of Man becomes the figure who ushers in the Final Judgement. That the Son of Man in both instances is to be identified with Jesus is clear. Not so obvious is how one is to understand the relationship between the Son of Man in his "present" capacity as the sower of the good seed and his "future" capacity as the inaugurator of the Final Judgement.

In this connection, Tödt claims that Matthew alludes to two *heilsgeschichtliche* epochs: the period of the earthly activity of Jesus as preacher, and the coming time when he will return as Judge.[37] Does the text support this view?

Certainly there can be no quarrel with the latter half of Tödt's suggestion. But one has occasion to doubt whether Matthew's statement regarding the present activity of the Son of Man refers to the earthly ministry of Jesus. From Matthew's vantage point in history, this ministry was already a thing of the past. Moreover, the circumstance that Matthew has at the least edited this pericope indicates that the "present" he has in mind is the post-Easter situation of his own day.[38] For this reason we agree with Vögtle, who holds that Matthew, in his reference to the Son of Man in v. 37, is thinking of Jesus as the "exalted Christ", the enthroned Kyrios who even now exercises his lordship.[39] As the exalted Christ, Matthew can indeed ascribe to Jesus the present task of sowing the good seed, for it is he who stands behind the proclamatory activity of his Church (28.18ff).[40] Furthermore, as the exalted Christ, Jesus can also be expected to return at the End of the Age (24.42). Thus, Matthew's concept of Jesus as the exalted Christ, the ruling Kyrios, encompasses both his present work in the post-Easter era and his future return as Judge.

The crux of this interpretation, of course, is the assumption that Matthew actually does unify the present and future post-Easter activity of Jesus under the titles of both Kyrios and Son of Man, so that if the two predications are not altogether synonymous, they at least overlap in this matter. With respect to Jesus' future activity, there is ample documentation in the first Gospel by which to prove that Matthew can speak of Jesus' Parousia now as the coming of the Son of Man and now as the coming of the Kyrios (cf. 24.42 with 24.44; 25.31 with 25.37, 44). With respect to Jesus' present activity, even though Matthew favours the title of Kyrios when referring or alluding to the kingly rule that Jesus exercises between Easter and the Parousia,[41] the very fact that Matthew here in v. 41 of our pericope ascribes a Kingdom that is of this age to Jesus Son of Man demonstrates that he can also invest the term Son of Man with the connotation of "present" rulership.[42] Accordingly, through his Gospel Matthew fully authorizes us to identify the Son of Man "who sows the good seed" with Jesus Kyrios who, by means of his earthly ambassadors, establishes his kingly rule on earth in the post-Easter era of the Church and, as the Judge of all mankind, will return at the End of the Age.

Under the command of the Son of Man are angels, or "reapers" (v. 39c), who will be sent out (v. 41a) to set in motion the series of events that together constitute the Last Judgement. As we saw in the parable of the Tares (13.30), angels are a standard feature in certain apocalyptic scenes dealing with judgement.[43] In the Interpretation, they are the heavenly agents of the Son of Man.[44]

### The Actors: (2) The Sons of the Kingdom

In addition to the angels, the "good seed" who are the "sons of the Kingdom" (v. 38b), i.e. those who are of one spirit with God and consequently "akin" to God,[45] also stand under the banner of the Son of Man.[46] This group is redefined in v. 43a as the "righteous" ($\delta i \kappa \alpha \iota o \iota$).

The word "righteous" is typically Matthaean. While Matthew uses it seventeen or nineteen times (27.4, 24 are textually uncertain), in only one instance does it appear in his Gospel in conjunction with synoptic parallels (9.13 = Mk 2.17 = Lk 5.32).

In v. 43a, Matthew employs "righteous" in an absolute sense. The expression "the righteous will shine" is a Matthaean manipulation of Daniel 12.3 (Theodotion). In the original, the text reads that "those who are wise" will shine, and the righteous are mentioned only later in the verse. But in Jewish tradition the righteous generally comprised a rather broad category of people, one segment of which were also the wise.[47] Matthew has thus modified the LXX text because he intends the word righteous in v. 43a to be understood comprehensively: as all those whom the Son of Man will place "at his right hand" at the Final Judgement (25.33). This comprehensive understanding of the word rules out the notion that the righteous of v. 43 constitute any particular station or number of people within Matthew's Church.[48]

That the term righteous should occupy a prominent place specifically in the Interpretation of the Parable of the Tares and that it should allude to Daniel point to its eschatological colouring (cf. 13.49; 25.37, 46). At the same time, it is thoroughly ethical in tone. According to Matthaean thought, those who will be accounted righteous at the Latter Day will quite simply be those who have done the will of God,[49] i.e. those who have shown themselves to be obedient to the Law of God (as Jesus has handed it down) through their works of love exercised on behalf of the brother.[50] But this reveals that the Matthaean concept of the righteous is furthermore universal in outlook, for it cuts across cultic, ethnic, and institutional lines and establishes God himself as the norm for righteousness. Hence, there is an inherent protest in the word against both Pharisaic Judaism with its racial and spiritual appeal to descendency from Abraham and the patriarchs, whom Jews esteemed as the archetypes of righteousness (3.9; 8.11), and to Christians within the Church who prove themselves to be a sham. The righteous are the "few" who are chosen (ἐκλεκτοί), not the "many" who are called (22.14). They are the genuine flock of God (25.32f): the wise who know and do the will of God (7.24; 13.23), the martyrs who give testimony to their faith and are prepared to surrender their lives for it (5.10ff; 23.34f), and all Christians in general who persevere in the face of the manifold afflictions that characterize the Messianic Woes even now causing distress in Matthew's Church (24.9–13; 10.16–22). On this account, the righteous will be pronounced "blessed" by the Son of Man, and they will "inherit" the Kingdom prepared for them from the foundation of the world (25.34), thus entering into "eternal life" (25.46).

### The Actors: (3) The Devil

Opposed to the Son of Man and his forces in the Interpretation of the Parable of the Tares is, above all, the "Devil" (διάβολος, v. 39a), who is also described as the "Evil One" (τοῦ πονηροῦ, v. 38c) and the "Enemy" (ἐχθρός, v. 39a). We have already seen that when the Devil is designated in the first Gospel as the Evil One, he is viewed as the transcendent personification of all lawlessness;[51] when he is designated as the Enemy, he is seen principally as the inimical will who is bent on destroying the allegiance that is due to Jesus alone.[52] What concept, therefore, does Matthew attach to the term "devil"? To determine this, we will also want to look at its synonym, "satan".

"Devil" is a Greek word, the LXX translation of the Hebrew satan. "Satan" (σατανᾶς) is the Greek transliteration of the Aramaic satana.[53] Of the two, only "satan" is a proper noun (cf. 4.10; 16.23 = Mk 8.33).

Theologically, there is no difference in meaning between διάβολος and σατανᾶς.[54] The striking thing is that in portraying the malevolent will as the Devil, or Satan, Matthew goes into surprisingly great detail. His description is such that the Devil becomes the cosmic antagonist of Jesus, the servant, and Jesus, the Son of Man.

As the personal adversary of Jesus, the servant, whose baptism confirms his Messiahship (3.13–17), the Devil makes his début already in the Temptation Story (4.1–11).[55] In this drama, Jesus is singled out as the Son who knows and does his Father's will (4.4, 7, 10).[56] At the same time, the Devil is identified as "the Tempter" (ὁ πειράζων, 4.3); that is, according to Matthew the peculiar function, or "office",[57] of the Devil is to "tempt", whereby temptation is then understood as the endeavour to set a person, in this instance Jesus, at variance with the will of God.

In establishing the Devil as the counterpart of the Son of Man,

Matthew ascribes to him a universal field of operations. The Devil lays claim to the whole "world" ($\kappa \acute{o} \sigma \mu o s$, 4.8), even though his authority to do so is exposed as a lie (4.8ff). Moreover, he has a "kingdom" ($\beta a \sigma \iota$-$\lambda \epsilon \acute{\iota} a$), that is to say, he exercises rulership (12.26), for there are angels under his dominion (25.41), and, as our pericope indicates, his sphere of influence extends also to the human race (13.38c). In this respect, Matthew sees the Devil at work both within the Church and beyond the Church. Testimony to the Devil's influence within the Church is Jesus' rebuke to Peter, "Get behind me, Satan!" (16.23 = Mk 8.33). Testimony to the Devil's influence beyond the Church is Matthew's characterization of the leaders of the Jews as the "agents" of the Devil, for they, too, "tempt" Jesus (22.35; 16.1 = Mk 8.11; 19.3 = Mk 10.2; 22.18 = Mk 12.15).

But for all his power, the Devil is by no means a sovereign personality. He is subordinate to God (4.1) and to the Son of Man (25.31–46), and his rule is restricted to the era of the Church, since at the Latter Day he, his angels, and his "sons", i.e. those who are placed at the "left hand" of the Son of Man (25.33, 41), will be cast into the eternal fire (13.42; 25.41).

Now Matthew tells us in our pericope that it is none other than the Devil who has sown the "darnel", or "sons of the Evil One" (vv. 38c–9a). Against the background of Matthew's concept of the Devil, this statement expresses the recognition that the Devil, the arch-enemy of the Son of Man, is, like the latter, also exercising his ruling power in the world during the present age. His ambition is to raise up for himself his own followers even (and particularly) within the Church, people whose allegiance he can claim in that he leads them to live apart from the Law of God in disobedience.

### The Actors: (4) The Sons of the Evil One

The followers of the Devil, as we just mentioned, are the "sons of the Evil One", i.e. those who emulate the Evil One and therefore are "akin" to him.[58] In v. 41b, the text describes these sons as "all those who give offence ($\tau \grave{a} \ \sigma \kappa \acute{a} \nu \delta a \lambda a$) and those who commit lawlessness ($\grave{a} \nu o \mu \acute{\iota} a \nu$)".

To begin with the first member of this pair, that $\tau \grave{a} \ \sigma \kappa \acute{a} \nu \delta a \lambda a$ should be translated personally as "those who give offence" has been ably demonstrated by G. Stählin (cf. also 16.23).[59] As regards its signification, we recall that $\sigma \kappa \acute{a} \nu \delta a \lambda o \nu$, an ethico-eschatological term, basically designates a person or thing as potentially capable of causing another's spiritual ruination.[60] With this in mind, our present concern is to discover (a) who in all likelihood these people are who give (or cause) offence, (b) who their victims are, and (c) how it is that these offenders effect such spiritual ruination.

Taking up the last query first, Matthew very possibly supplies us with a direct answer to it in 16.23, a Marcan logion (8.33) into which he has interpolated the word σκάνδαλον. Here Jesus addresses Peter as "Satan", because Peter, by rejecting the idea that Jesus should suffer and die (16.21f), becomes a temptation for Jesus not to do the prescribed will of God (cf. δεῖ, 16.21).[61] By pitting his own will against the will of God (16.23d), Peter makes of himself an offence, a hindrance, a stumbling-block for Jesus. Hence, in the light of this example Matthew discloses that he conceives of those who give offence as bringing about the spiritual ruination of others by enticing them away or otherwise preventing them from doing the will of God. Moreover, whatever giving offence may involve on a practical and ethical level, it is always serious enough that it leads a believer to suffer the loss of his faith, even as Jesus, had he followed Peter's remonstrance, would have totally alienated himself from God.

As far as the victims of those who give offence are concerned, Matthew is thinking in the first place of the Christians of his Church. The pilot passage supporting this view is 18.6 (cf. Mk 9.42): "but whoever causes one of these little ones [i.e. Christians][62] who believe in me to lose his faith, it would be better for him to have a great millstone fastened round his neck and to be drowned in the depth of the sea."

Yet we must not overlook the fact that Matthew employs τὰ σκάνδαλα in 13.41 in an absolute sense. Therefore Matthew's thoughts regarding the victims of those who give offence would seem to extend even beyond the confines of the Church. Conceivably, 17.27 has relevance for us, since at the basis of the statement "in order that we might not offend them" lies the notion that people should not be hindered from coming to faith in Jesus. In other words, it appears that τὰ σκάνδαλα in 13.41 is to be construed so broadly that it encompasses not only persons who lead believers astray, but also persons who in some passive way may be hindering or preventing non-believers from ever coming to faith in Jesus. As an example of such people we would cite  the leaders of Judaism according to Matthew's invective against them in 23.13: "But woe to you, scribes and Pharisees, hypocrites! because you shut the Kingdom of Heaven against men; for you neither enter yourselves, nor allow those who would enter to go in." If this line of reasoning is correct, then the victims of those who give offence are primarily Christians who suffer the loss of their faith, yet secondarily also those who in some manner may be prevented from ever coming to faith in Jesus as the Christ.

This leads us to the final question, which has already been partially answered: can these people who give offence be identified? Matthew's reply is probably to be found in combining the statements he makes in 16.23 and 18.7.[63] With regard to 16.23, that Peter, one of the Twelve, is called a σκάνδαλον proves that among the σκάνδαλα of 13.41 we must also think of Christians in Matthew's Church, members whose behaviour is such that they become a threat to the faith of others. Nor is this thought surprising when we recall that Matthew's Church was torn by false prophets and false doctrine, by hardheartedness, lovelessness, betrayal, hatred, and members whom Matthew calls "slothful" and "worthless", i.e. people who were lax in doing the will of God as the first Gospel teaches it (cf. 7.15; 18.35; 24.10ff; 25.26, 30).

But here, too, Matthew by no means confines himself to the limits of his Church.[64] This we learn from 18.7, where Matthew pronounces a "Woe to the world because of offence [temptations by which one may lose his faith]!" The "world" in this case is mankind, and concrete representatives of this "mankind of offence" are, as we saw, leaders of the Jews (23.13), though not to be forgotten are also the Gentiles who are persecuting the Church (13.21). Accordingly, those who give offence are pseudo-Christians within the Church and Jews and Gentiles beyond the Church.

In summary, when Matthew employs τὰ σκάνδαλα in an absolute sense in 13.41, he is thinking quite universally of people both within and without the Church who make themselves responsible for the spiritual ruination of others either by preventing them from coming to faith in Jesus (e.g. the leaders of the Jews), or by causing those who already believe to lose their faith either by persecution (e.g. Jews and Gentiles) or by the advocacy of heresy or of a way of life that conflicts with the will of God (e.g. false Christians).

In addition to "all those who give offence", the "sons of the Evil One", according to our pericope, also comprise "those who commit lawlessness [ἀνομίαν]" (v. 41b). The term "lawlessness" occurs but four times in the Gospels, all of them in Matthew, and in each case it seems to owe its presence in the text to Matthaean redaction (13.41; 23.28; 24.12; cf. 7.23 with Lk 13.27).

Two closely related aspects stand out in Matthew's concept of lawlessness. The one is that he equates it with not doing the will of God (cf. 7.15, 21ff), a view that is traditionally Jewish both in thought and expression. The other is that he conceives of lawlessness as effecting lovelessness, a state of affairs he sees growing more intense with the approach of the end (24.12). Consequently, like σκάνδαλον, "lawlessness" is an ethical and eschatological term: from one standpoint, it denotes a failure to do the works of love that are at the heart of the Law of God as delivered by Jesus;[65] from another standpoint, it denotes prodigious offences against the Law of God which suggest a prevalence of moral chaos (e.g. apostasy, betrayal, hatred, leading others astray, etc.). In short, "lawlessness", in Matthaean categories, is the contrary of "righteousness" (δικαιοσύνη).

Matthew predicates lawlessness of two groups in particular. The one is the "false prophets" (7.15). From what the first Gospel tells us, the false prophets apparently reside within the Church, since they acknowledge Jesus as "Lord" (7.21) and validate their activities as having been done in his name (7.22). Such activities find their focal point in the act of prophecy, the casting out of demons, and the doing of miracles (7.22). In other words, these prophets are enthusiasts.[66]

But in spite of their appeal to Jesus, Matthew, through the words of Jesus, charges these prophets with fraudulence and leading many astray, i.e. into perdition (24.11). He has them compared to a bad tree that bears evil fruit and will therefore be cut down and thrown into the fire (7.17, 19). Indeed, on the Day of Judgement Jesus will reject them outright: "I never knew you; depart from me, you workers of lawlessness" (7.23).

In view of all this, the nature of the lawlessness of these prophets seems to be that their preoccupation with charismatic gifts leads them to repudiate (in some undetermined measure) the doing of the good works that Matthew believes to be an essential part of the disciple's obedience towards the Law. Conceivably, G. Barth is correct when he argues that the error of the false prophets consists in their belief that a principal reason for the coming of Jesus was to abrogate the Law.[67]

The second group exemplifying lawlessness for Matthew are the leaders of the Jews, the scribes and Pharisees. The accusation is that although outwardly they appear righteous, inwardly they are full of hypocrisy and lawlessness (23.28). This is tantamount to saying that while they ostensibly obey the Law, in reality they annul it. Throughout his Gospel Matthew lends substance to this accusation. In 15.6, he declares that for the sake of their Tradition of the Elders, the scribes and Pharisees "make void the law (word) of God" (cf. 15.3). In 23.23, he assails them for tithing "mint and dill and cummin", but neglecting the "weightier matters of the Law, justice and mercy and faithfulness".

In 9.13 and 12.7, he holds it up to the Pharisees that the heart of God's Law is "mercy", not "sacrifice". Therefore according to Matthew, the leaders of the Jews practise lawlessness because they are found wanting in the works of love.

In our passage, the expression "those who commit lawlessness" is in no way qualified; like τὰ σκάνδαλα, it is used in an absolute sense. This fact and the manner in which Matthew understands and applies the term lawlessness indicate that when Matthew in 13.41 identifies the sons of the Evil One as those who commit lawlessness, he is thinking of all those both within and without the Church, above all the false prophets and the leaders of the Jews, who strike at the heart of God's Law because they neither advocate nor keep the commandments as he understands Jesus to have promulgated them.

Finally, with respect to the relationship between "those who give offence" and "those who commit lawlessness", the two phrases are related and complementary but not identical. Both refer to groups that reside within the Church and beyond the Church, and therefore both have a universal slant. Both are also ethically determined and pass judgement on a man's deeds or way of life in the light of the Law as interpreted by Jesus. And both are eschatologically oriented, assuming their place within the broad confines of the Messianic Woes.

Yet each has its own character. In "those who give offence" the stress is on offence against one's neighbour: on preventing another from coming to faith in Jesus or on leading believers astray so that they lose their faith. In "those who commit lawlessness" the stress is on the individual's own offence, on his own disobedience towards the Law of God with its centre in the works of love demanded by Jesus. That under certain circumstances the same person or group of persons may fall under the heading of both expressions is self-evident. Taken together, they reveal that Matthew places the "sons of the Evil One" in the same broad category as those who will be placed "at the left" of the Son of Man in the Final Judgement (25.33).

### The Message of the Pericope and its Apocalyptic Imagery

In our attempt to obtain a relatively reliable picture of the two hostile groups confronting each other in the Interpretation of the Parable of the Tares, that of the Son of Man and that of the Devil, we have been compelled to range over the whole of Matthew's Gospel. By contrast, the elemental message of the Interpretation is easily recognizable. It focuses on the "harvest", defined as the "End of the Age" (v. 39b), and what is to take place at this time. We are told that the Son of Man will send out his angels to inaugurate the Great Assize and therefore the Final Judgement, and that as the outcome of this the sons of the Evil One will experience the condemnation of fire but the righteous the splendour of the Father's Kingdom (vv. 40–3).

While this message of itself stands out, it is set forth in language rich in apocalyptic imagery. Reference is made to the "fiery furnace" (v. 42a), where there is "weeping and gnashing of teeth" (v. 42b), and to the Kingdom of the Father, where the "righteous will shine as the sun" (v. 43a). In the interest of gaining a better understanding both of the purpose for which Matthew intended this pericope and of the way in which he would have it achieve this purpose, we shall briefly explore the meaning of these metaphorical images for the Christians of Matthew's Church.

The key concept is the "End of the Age" ($\sigma\upsilon\nu\tau\acute{\epsilon}\lambda\epsilon\iota\alpha$ [$\tau o\hat{\upsilon}$] $\alpha i\hat{\omega}\nu os$), a formula found in no other Gospel than the first.[68] It denotes the termination of the existing world order when present history has run its course (24.3; 28.20), after which there will be a transformation of all things, and God will reign supreme (13.43; 25.34, 41; 26.29).[69] The immediate arrival of the End of the Age will be signalled by the return of Jesus Son of Man[70] and the beginning of the Last Judgement[71] centring in the Great Assize. Because of these temporal and eschatological connotations, this formula inherently bears the character of promise and threat. Hence, it assumes ethical overtones as well, since the mention of the End of the Age should motivate the Christian to re-examine his life in view of the coming Judgement of God. The full complement of these temporal, eschatological, and ethical nuances are incorporated in Matthew's use of this formula in vv. 39b, 40b.

The "fiery furnace" ($\tau\grave{\eta}\nu$ $\kappa\acute{\alpha}\mu\iota\nu o\nu$ $\tau o\hat{\upsilon}$ $\pi\upsilon\rho\acute{os}$, v. 42a; cf. 13.50) symbolizes eternal damnation.[72] It is the place reserved for those who will be forever condemned at the Final Judgement because of their godlessness (13.41; 25.41).[73] Since these godless include Gentiles as well as Jews (25.32),[74] the symbol of the fiery furnace has a universal bent; and since the individual is consigned to it on the basis of his works,[75] it also has ethical implications. In short, the fiery furnace is the stark alternative to the bliss of God's end-time Kingdom (13.43; 25.34), to "eternal life" (25.46).

In the fiery furnace there will be "weeping and gnashing of teeth" (v. 42b). "Weeping" most likely alludes to the intense distress ("strong pain") that the godless must endure in the hell of fire,[76] and the "gnashing of teeth" to the despondency and rage that reputedly engulf the godless when, after death, they realize that they are impotent to alter their plight in Gehenna.[77] The whole expression, then, is one of anguish and remorse.[78]

In v. 43a, we read that "the righteous will shine as the sun in the Kingdom of their Father".[79] This thought is one variation of a theme that is typical of Jewish apocalyptic. God himself is conceived as the source of all light (2 Baruch 54.13).[80] Therefore to shine like the sun,[81] or to be made like the light of the stars,[82] or to become like angels[83] is to partake of (or, according to the Rabbis, "behold") God's glory,[84] to exist in the state of eternal and absolute bliss that is indicative of being in God's presence. P. Volz has succinctly captured the essence of the concept in the following statement:

> When the Blessed are designated as heavenly bodies, they are thereby intended to be portrayed as cleansed from all imperfection and endowed with all divine perfection, as invested with divine $\delta\acute{o}\xi\alpha$, with physical impeccability, with moral purity, and with a religious kinship to God. Thus, "Light" is a comprehensive concept for the external and internal aspect of salvation and for the corporeal as well as the spiritual blessings of the Blissful Age.[85]

## The Purpose of the Pericope

For what reason does Matthew narrate a pericope that is so dire with threat yet so elevated in promise? Four factors within the Interpretation of the Parable of the Tares indicate how he desires it to be understood. The function of v. 40, a transitional passage, is to direct the reader's attention to the "End of the Age". In vv. 41–3a, the eternal consequences of the Great Assize, by which the Final Judgement will be inaugurated, are elaborately dramatized in the vivid imagery of Jewish apocalyptic: the lawless are to be surrendered to the tortures and despair of the hell of fire, while the righteous are to participate in God's glory and live in eternal bliss. According to vv. 36–7a, the Interpretation is addressed by Jesus to the disciples, or Church. Last, at the end of the Interpretation Matthew has appended the exhortation to hear aright (v. 43b).

In combination, these four factors reveal that by raising the spectre of the End of the Age, by allowing for the graphic portrayal of the destiny of the righteous and the damned, and by stipulating that Jesus addresses the Interpretation to the Church and calls it to hear aright, Matthew endows the Interpretation of the Parable of the Tares with a markedly paraenetic (ethico-eschatological) character.[86] The purpose Matthew gives it, then, is that of exhorting the Christians of his Church to be sons of the Kingdom (those who do the will of God) in a dual manner: positively, by depicting the reward of the sons of

the Kingdom; negatively, by depicting the fate of those who in this
age do not do the will of God but prove themselves to be sons of the
Evil One.

Yet to say that the purpose of the Interpretation of the Parable of the
Tares is to exhort the Christians of Matthew's Church to do the will of
God is not to mitigate the fact that the outlook of the pericope is
thoroughly universal. Principally, we encounter the same situation
here as in the parable of the Last Judgement (25.31–46), for on the Last
Day there will, finally, be nothing other than the two "existential"
alternatives of salvation and damnation, and they will apply equally to
the members of the Church and to all of mankind.[87] Consequently,
there is no contradiction in maintaining that the Interpretation of the
Parable of the Tares at once assumes universal dimensions and still is
envisaged in the first instance for the members of Matthew's Church.

## Summary

The *intention* for which Matthew employs the Interpretation of the
Parable of the Tares is *paraenetic*: Jesus, the exalted Kyrios, exhorts the
Christians of Matthew's Church to be sons of the Kingdom who do the
will of God. Accordingly, this pericope reflects a strong ethical concern that comes to expression in a message put across with the aid of
apocalyptic imagery. Because of this, it provides us with a further
demonstration of how closely Matthew conceives eschatology to be
bound up with ethics, i.e. he sees the coming End of the Age as exerting
a pressure that works itself out in the practical life of the Christian.[88]

In point of fact, it is asserted in the Interpretation that the End of the
Age is determinative, not only for Christians, but for all of mankind,
for there is chiefly, though not absolutely, a dual alignment of power
in the world. On the one hand, there is Jesus, the Son of Man, who is
Lord of the entire inhabited world. In the present age between the
Resurrection and the Parousia, the Son of Man raises up sons of the
Kingdom, people who know and do the will of God as Jesus has
revealed it. At the End of the Age, the Son of Man will return with his
heavenly accompaniment, his angels, and inaugurate the Great Assize
which no nation or people can escape. When this takes place, the
obedience of the sons of the Kingdom towards the heavenly Father,
particularly in the face of the Messianic Woes, will be acknowledged,
and, as the righteous, they will enter into the eternal bliss of the Kingdom which the Father has prepared for them, that is to say, they will
participate in the glory of the Father and sing his praises.

At the same time, there is the Devil, the arch-enemy of the Son of

Man, who also, even though fraudulently, lays claim to the world. He, too, is at work in the present age. It is his design to raise up sons of the Evil One. The mark of the sons of the Evil One is that they live apart from the Law of God, whether within the Church or beyond the Church. They are, for example, false Christians who lead the brother astray, or who do not concern themselves with the works of love that form the heart of God's Law, or who are morally lax. They are the leaders of the Jews, who likewise bring Christians to fall, or who prevent men from coming to faith in Christ, or who annul the Law of God in the erroneous belief that they are keeping it. And they are the Gentiles, who testify to their disobedience towards God by persecuting the Church. At the End of the Age, the lot of the sons of the Evil One will be the fiery furnace, i.e. eternal damnation, where they will experience the pain, the wrath, and the despair of those who are for ever cut off from God. Because Matthew sees these opposing forces locked in combat in the world, before which ethnic, cultic, and institutional barriers break down, he meets the situation with Jesus' admonition to the Christians of his Church to be sons of the Kingdom who do the will of God.

The *function* of the Interpretation of the Parable of the Tares within its immediate context is to pave the way for the parables of the Hidden Treasure (13.44) and of the Pearl (13.45f). The Interpretation exhorts Christians to be sons of the Kingdom who do the will of God, and these two parables tell of the exclusive claim God's kingly rule lays upon the Christian.


## THE PARABLES OF THE HIDDEN TREASURE (13.44)
## AND OF THE PEARL (13.45–6)

(44) *"It is the case with the Kingdom of Heaven as with a treasure which has remained hidden in a field, which a man found and concealed; and because of his joy he goes and sells all he possesses and buys that field. (45) Again, it is the case with the Kingdom of Heaven as with a merchant who was on the lookout for fine pearls. (46) And when he had found a very valuable pearl, he went away and sold everything that he possessed and bought it."*


*Companion Parables*

The parables of the Hidden Treasure and of the Pearl can be treated together since they are perhaps a perfect example of companion parables, even though some scholars believe that at an earlier stage in the tradition the two circulated independently.[89] The relatedness of these units to each other may be seen in the following characteristics: in both the introductory formula is the same (cf. v. 44a to v. 45), the structure of both is that of the fable, i.e. in both we have to do with a single event narrated in past time,[90] and the major thought of both is, as we shall presently see, the same. In addition, $\pi\acute{a}\lambda\iota\nu$ ("again", v. 45) is a connective which, among other things, can indicate that what follows (the parable of the Pearl) is intimately related to what has preceded (the parable of the Hidden Treasure).[91]

### Incongruence and the Introductory Dative

As in the case of the other parables in chapter 13, the opening lines of the parables of the Hidden Treasure and of the Pearl bear the twin traits of incongruence and the introductory dative. Admittedly, it is not readily apparent that incongruence is a feature of the parable of the Hidden Treasure, because the Kingdom of Heaven is indeed like a "treasure", exactly as the text reads (v. 44a). Yet to say this does not mean that one has therefore captured the major thought of the parable, for which reason the Hidden Treasure does in fact display incongruence. With respect to the parable of the Pearl, the incongruence is obvious, for the purpose of the narrative is manifestly not to promulgate the idea that the Kingdom of Heaven is like a "merchant" (cf. v. 45). Accordingly, the introduction of both parables should be translated as follows: "It is the case with the Kingdom of Heaven as with a treasure (merchant) . . .".

### The Setting and the People Addressed

Both the setting and the principals governing the Interpretation of the parable of the Tares remain the same for the parables of the Hidden Treasure and of the Pearl (cf. v. 36a). The disciples, or Church, are the recipients of these two pericopes, and we can expect that the same paraenetic interest Matthew evinces in the Interpretation will be present here also.

### The Picture-half of the Parable of the Hidden Treasure

In the picture-half of the parable of the Hidden Treasure there is one feature that has proved to be rather disturbing to exegetes: a man discovers a treasure in a field not his own and purchases the field without divulging his find to the owner, with the result that the man seems to

come into possession of the treasure by fraudulent means. To resolve
this matter, the standard explanation has come to be that this feature of
the parable, since it is of little interest to the interpreter who must be
concerned with the main point of the narrative, should properly be
relegated to the trappings of the story.[92] Some scholars even attempt to
rescue this seemingly bad situation by arguing that the man in question
at least remained within the bounds of the law.[93] Unfortunately, this
position only begs the question concerning the morality of the man's act.

In a very enlightening article, J. D. M. Derrett specifically takes up
this question, and, rejecting the aforementioned solutions, concludes
that "the finder was perfectly entitled in morals and in law to do what
he did. His behaviour was proper, and indeed inevitable."[94]

Derrett analyses the parable and points out that the principle of
"lifting" would come into play in this story, i.e. to get possession of a
movable object, one would have to take hold of the object physically
and move it, "shifting [it] from its position with the intention of
acquiring".[95] Now the treasure, reasons Derrett, was buried in "open
country" and "almost certainly in an earthenware jar".[96] Therefore
under consideration of the text of the parable and of Rabbinic law, the
owner of the field had never in fact acquired the treasure, "and so he
did not own it".[97]

Derrett next concentrates his attention on the person of the man who
discovers the treasure. By an elaborate process of elimination, he
deduces that the man in all probability was a "day-labourer"[98] who,
according to the legal codes of the Rabbis, could indeed acquire a
treasure he might find in the course of his work, if he were able "to
drop his work, obtain his discharge from employment, and then, if he
could, return and lift the find".[99] This was a distinct possibility, since,
claims Derrett, "it was recognized that no workman could be compelled to work out his day".[100]

But to evaluate the case properly, continues Derrett, it is of the
utmost importance to note that the text does not say that the man
found the treasure and then "buried it again".[101] On the contrary,
the situation depicted in the parable of the Hidden Treasure is the
following:

> [the man] took care only that he should not be anticipated by the owner or
> any other person who might pass that way. He would cover it [the treasure]
> well, since his behaviour in leaving his work suddenly would arouse suspi-
> cion. He would say nothing about the treasure until he had it. Anyone who
> went to the spot could lift it and acquire it, and would owe him nothing.
> Since the owner of the field had no rights in the treasure there was no reason

whatever why he should be told of it: indeed if he were told the whole plan
would fail. So the finder manages to buy the field and goes in his own proper
person as owner of the field, and not as any man's servant or agent, and lifts
it and acquires it for himself.[102]

## The Picture-half of the Parable of the Pearl

While the central figure in the parable of the Hidden Treasure is a
relatively poor day-labourer, the leading character in the parable of
the Pearl is a wealthy "merchant" who was accustomed to conducting
business on a large scale.[103]

This merchant is described as a man "on the lookout for fine pearls"
(v. 45). In the Near East, the pearl was esteemed as a precious stone,[104]
and consequently was a very cherished and valuable object. It was used
primarily in the making of jewellery.[105] For the most part, pearls of
greatest quality came from fisheries that worked the Indian Ocean,
but the intermediaries between the sources of supply and demand
were Jewish, Syrian, and Arab traders.[106]

The situation portrayed in our parable is that of one of these mer-
chants who deals in precious stones suddenly coming upon an especially valuable pearl.[107] The merchant's immediate reaction is to
realize all of his assets so that he will be in a position to purchase this
one rare jewel. He obviously intends to take advantage of a highly
infrequent opportunity to gain even greater wealth. As Dodd puts it,
the successful financier knows when to make the plunge.[108]

## The Central Thought of the Parables

The situations depicted in the parables of the Hidden Treasure and of
the Pearl are relatively uncomplicated: in each we have to do with a
man who unexpectedly finds a very precious object and sells all so that
he might obtain that object. On the other hand, to locate the main point
of these parables is somewhat more problematic. Commentators argue
that the major emphasis is to be placed variously on the "value" of the
discovered articles,[109] on the "sacrifice",[110] or, in variation of this
term, on the "total investment" (der ganze Einsatz)[111] the men made to
realize their ambitions, or on the "joy" that motivated them to take
such calculated risks.[112] In addition, with a side glance towards the
topic "Kingdom of Heaven", several scholars accentuate such features
as the "hiddenness" of the precious goods, or the "searching" ($\zeta\eta\tau\acute{\epsilon}\omega$,
v. 45) and the "finding" ($\epsilon\acute{\nu}\rho\acute{\iota}\sigma\kappa\omega$, vv. 44b, 46) that characterize,
respectively, the action of the merchant and of the day-labourer.[113]

In the face of this panoply of opinion, how does Matthew understand these parables? First of all, it does not seem likely that he attaches

great significance to the factors of "hiddenness", "searching", and "finding". From Matthew's standpoint, the Kingdom of Heaven is not hidden *per se*. It is a present reality: present in Jesus as a historical personage and present in Jesus as the exalted Kyrios who calls "all nations" into God's kingly rule through the Kerygma of his earthly ambassadors (24.14; 26.13; 28.18ff). In brief, Matthew sees God's kingly rule as making itself manifest in and through the Church (5.13–16; chap. 10; 16.18; 18.20; 28.18ff.). That the Jews, for example, have rejected God's rule is not due to the fact that it is a hidden reality, but to the fact that because of their obduracy God has made them blind to it (cf. chaps. 11–13; 13.11ff; 23.13).

As far as the searching is concerned, the parable of the Pearl does not say that the merchant set out to find exclusively one particularly valuable pearl. He was looking for all types of fine pearls as a mere matter of course (v. 45). Consequently, there is no real analogy between the random searching of the merchant and the resolute pursuance of a specific goal as expressed in a passage like 6.33 (cf. also 18.12; 28.5): "But seek first his Kingdom and his righteous-ness . . .".

With regard to the finding, in both of these parables the man in question stumbles upon the fortune unawares. But "finding" of this nature has precious little in common with Matthew's description of how God makes his Kingdom available to men. Matthew speaks of deliberate action on God's part in and through Jesus in fulfilment of Old Testament prophecy, and, by extension, through the Church (cf. chap. 10; 24.14; 26.13; 28.18ff). The counterpart of this is a special response on the part of men (cf. 4.20, 22; 8.22; 9.9; chap. 10; 19.21, 27ff). Hence, Matthew's use of $εὑρίσκω$ in the parables of the Hidden Treasure and of the Pearl is not to be treated as though it were a commentary on finding the way to the Kingdom, or "life" (cf. 7.14). In point of fact, the three moments of hiddenness, searching, and finding in these parables belong strictly to the scenic framework of the narrative.

In other respects, we must also reject the position that Matthew may have placed the accent in these parables on the element of joy. Strictly speaking, "joy" is explicitly mentioned only in the parable of the Hidden Treasure (v. 44c).[114] This alone should caution one against making it the central feature of both pericopes. Then, too, the purpose for recording the joy of the labourer is to underline the great value of the treasure he has found, a treasure so rich that it opens up undreamed-of possibilities for him if only he can obtain it.

When we thus narrow down the alternatives, it becomes evident that there are only two features that seriously come into question as possible points of stress in the parables of the Hidden Treasure and of the Pearl: the "value" of the discovered objects, and the "sacrifice", or "total investment",[115] the men made. Both features are prominent in both narratives. In the parable of the Hidden Treasure, value is emphasized in that the story designates the find of the labourer as a "treasure" (v. 44a), mentions the labourer's "joy" over his find (v. 44c), and depicts his preparedness to "sell all" in order to obtain the field in which he knows the treasure is buried (v. 44c). In the parable of the Pearl, value is emphasized in that the text characterizes the pearl as a "particularly valuable" one (v. 46a), and describes the merchant's willingness to "sell everything" in order to purchase it (v. 46b). In both parables, sacrifice, or total investment, is emphasized by the almost identical statements standing out so markedly at the end of the pericopes: the labourer "goes and sells all he possesses and buys that field"; the merchant "went away and sold everything that he possessed and bought it [the pearl]".

Since there are ostensibly two points of stress in these parables, how are they to be related to each other? In both instances, the pattern is that the "find" (value) of each man induces him to "sell all" (total investment) in order to obtain the desired object. Hence, there is an established cause-and-effect relationship between the finding of the costly goods and the resulting behaviour of the two men.

Yet to avoid misunderstanding these parables we must once again call to mind that Matthew is addressing them to the disciples, or Church, and that he has designated both as parables of the Kingdom. If, therefore, we ask what significance, from Matthew's standpoint, the valuables mentioned in these parables would have for the disciples of his community, the answer would have to be that they allude to the Kingdom itself. Still, in saying this, we must not lose sight of the fact that in Matthew's eyes the disciple is one who has, to remain within the language of the parables, "found" the Kingdom already. But this in no way detracts from the further fact that throughout his Gospel Matthew also asserts that even the disciple who has "found" the Kingdom is in need of the constant admonition to stand by his "find", that is, under no circumstances to flag in doing the will of God as stipulated by Jesus. For Matthew, then, the culmination of the parables of the Hidden Treasure and of the Pearl would lie in the sphere of sacrifice, or total investment,[116] which we prefer to designate as "total commitment" (cf. 5.29f; 8.22; 10.34–9; 18.8f; 19.12, 21, 29).

Moreover, from a formal viewpoint the parables themselves support this conclusion, for the idea of total commitment is described in both in considerable breadth, comes in both at the end of the story, which is the position of stress, and receives particular emphasis in the parable of the Hidden Treasure through the sudden shift from past to present tenses (cf. v. 44a–b with v. 44c).

On the basis of this discussion, we may formulate the major thought of the two parables as follows: even as the labourer who found a treasure in a field and the merchant who found an especially valuable pearl responded by selling all they possessed in order to obtain, respectively, the field with its treasure and the pearl, so the disciple responds to God's kingly rule by committing himself without reserve to the doing of God's will.

### The Parables in relation to the Time of Matthew

This call to radical obedience can by no means be classified as a mere truism in the case of Matthew's Church. As we have seen, this Church was threatened from within and without by moral laxity, false doctrine, and persecution, just to single out broad areas of pressing problems. In such a situation of doctrinal, ethical, and even physical peril, Matthew was concerned that the members of his Church should in fact be sons of the Kingdom, not sons of the Evil One (13.38). To this end, Matthew includes in his Gospel the parables of the Hidden Treasure and of the Pearl, for in them Jesus Kyrios points out to the Christian disciple that he is in truth a son of the Kingdom when he commits himself without reserve to the doing of God's will.

### Summary

The parables of the Hidden Treasure and of the Pearl are companion parables. Formally, they are fables, and since they contain metaphors, they can be seen to be *allegorical parables*.

The *culmination* of these parables is to be found, respectively, in v. 44c, where the labourer "goes and sells all he possesses . . .", and in v. 46b, where the merchant "went away and sold everything that he possessed . . .". For Matthew, these statements are meant to convey the picture of total commitment.

The *intention* with which Matthew employs the two parables is *paraenetic*: through them Jesus Kyrios calls the members of a Church that was suffering from the turmoil of internal and external conflict to be disciples who are unremittingly dedicated to the doing of God's will.

The *secret* these parables reveal regarding the Kingdom of Heaven is ethical in nature, though implicitly also eschatological by virtue of the context and the fact that ethics and eschatology are interrelated in the first Gospel: that the response of the disciple to God's kingly rule is to be one of radical obedience to the will of God. The corollary to this "secret" is that the Kingdom of Heaven in these pericopes is viewed as a present reality.

The *function* of the parables of the Hidden Treasure and of the Pearl within their immediate context is to complement the line of thought begun in the Interpretation of the Parable of the Tares. In the Interpretation, the Christians of Matthew's community are exhorted to be sons of the Kingdom who do the will of God. In these twin parables, they are told that this implies total commitment on the part of each of them.

## THE PARABLE OF THE NET (13.47–50)

(47) *"Again, it is the case with the Kingdom of Heaven as with a drag-net which was thrown into the sea and gathered up [fish] of every kind; (48) which, when it was full, they pulled up on the shore and sat down and gathered the good ones into containers, but threw the bad ones away. (49) So will it be at the End of the Age. The angels will go out and will separate the evil from among the righteous (50) and will throw them into the fiery furnace. In that place there will be weeping and gnashing of teeth."*

### This Parable in relation to that of the Tares

Widespread opinion among scholars holds that the parable of the Net is formally and/or materially a companion parable to that of the Tares (13.24–30).[117] The nub of this contention is that in both parables we find a contrast as well as a reference to separation, and it is further pointed out that vv. 49f, which contain an explanation to the parable of the Net, are a mere repetition of the ending of the Interpretation of the Parable of the Tares (vv. 40b and 42 with traces of v. 41).

There are a number of factors, however, which do not favour this position. Unlike other instances where we find companion parables (e.g. Mustard Seed–Leaven, Hidden Treasure–Pearl), the parable of the Net does not stand in juxtaposition to the parable of the Tares. Moreover, as we have already remarked, even the parable of the Tares

(13.24-30) and the pericope known as its Interpretation (13.36b-43) do not in themselves form a single unit.[118] What is more, the situation depicted in the parable of the Tares is different from that of the Net: while the coexistence of "bad and good" is simply assumed in the Net (vv. 47ff), this same feature is the major topic of discussion in the Tares (13.27-30a). Again, the parable of the Tares reaches its climax in the admonition to "let both grow side by side until the harvest" (13.30a), but the parable of the Net does so in the declaration that the "evil ones" will be separated "from among the righteous" (v. 49b). Further, the parable of the Tares deals essentially with the problem of "believing Israel" (Church) as opposed to "unbelieving Israel" (Pharisaic Judaism),[119] whereas the parable of the Net, as we shall see, deals with the problem of "bad and good" in the same institution, the Church. And although the similarity in speech between the explanation of the parable of the Net (vv. 49f) and the Interpretation of the Parable of the Tares (13.40b, 42) demonstrates that both pericopes are oriented towards the Great Assize, this does not abrogate the central fact that the Interpretation is universal in outlook while the explanation of the parable of the Net is particular, i.e. restricted to the Church.[120]

Our conclusion, then, is that the parable of the Net is a companion pericope neither to the parable of the Tares nor to the Interpretation of the Parable of the Tares. The relationship between the three is not one of identity, but of progression: in the parable of the Tares the major issue is believing Israel as opposed to unbelieving Israel within a regional framework; in the Interpretation of the Parable of the Tares it is the sons of the Kingdom as opposed to the sons of the Evil One within a universal framework; and in the parable of the Net it is the righteous as opposed to the evil within the framework of the Church. In oversimplified terms, the dominant theme in all three pericopes may well be described as "good v. evil"; nevertheless, the aspect under which this theme is treated in each case varies greatly.

C. H. Dodd lists the parable of the Net with the Parables of Growth even though it has nothing to do with the world of agriculture.[121] His reason for doing so is based on the assertion, which we have just dismissed, that the parables of the Net and of the Tares are double parables. Still, Dodd's classification is valid, for the parable of the Net, like the other Parables of Growth, contains a contrast (present-future), and the motif of the "harvest" (harvest of the sea)[122] is also present.

## The Parable in Outline

The lines of division are so clearly drawn in the parable of the Net

that the following outline is easily discernible: (*a*) the parable proper
(vv. 47f); (*b*) the transitional statement (v. 49a); and (*c*) the interpretation of the parable (vv. 49b–50).

From the standpoint of form, the parable of the Net has traits that are
characteristic both of the similitude and of the fable. On the one hand
the story has to do with a typical event; on the other hand, the action
in the story is described in the past tense. But since, as we shall discover,
Matthew operates with metaphors in this unit, we would do best to
catalogue it as a fable that is a mixed-form, i.e. an allegorical parable.

### The Introduction

True to Matthaean custom, the opening line of the parable of the Net
(v. 47a) exhibits the twin features of incongruence and the introductory
dative (σαγήνη, "drag-net", v. 47). The incongruence, however, does
not arise from the fact that the Kingdom of Heaven is not at all compared to a "drag-net",[123] but because the parable focuses attention on
the separation of the fish (vv. 48, 49b) as well as on the net that catches
them (v. 47).[124] The introduction, then, should be translated as
follows: "Again, it is the case with the Kingdom of Heaven as with a
drag-net . . .".

### The Picture-half of the Parable

The picture-half of the parable (vv. 47f) portrays a very commonplace
scene in Palestine: fishermen in pursuit of a catch with a drag-net.
A. E. Ross, who describes the drag-net as of "immense size", relates
how it is used as follows:

> A common way of working the seine [drag-net] is to have one end of it
> attached to the shore, while the other is taken seawards by a boat in a wide
> circuit, and at length brought to land again. The upper side of the net is
> sustained by corks, while the lower, being weighted, sweeps along the sea-
> bottom. The ends are gradually drawn in till the whole net is brought up on
> the beach, carrying with it all the fish in the area through which it has
> passed.[125]

Once the fish are on the shore, they are sorted, just as depicted in the
parable. The "good" ones are gathered into containers, or basins made
of stone and clay, while the undesirable ones (fish that are inedible or
without scales or fins) are thrown away, that is to say, they are left on
the shore or dumped back into the sea.[126]

### The Development of the Story

To understand how Matthew interpreted the parable of the Net, it is instructive to observe the development of the story and some of the detail. Thus, the parable unfolds in two scenes: the net gathers fish of every kind (v. 47); and the gathered fish are sorted according to "good" and "bad" (v. 48). Furthermore, in the first scene only the net is explicitly mentioned; the fish and the fishermen are merely inferred. In the second scene, only the fish are mentioned ("the good ones", "the bad ones"); the net and the fishermen receive only pronominal reference ("which", "they"). Third, both scenes are introduced, respectively, by a participle (v. 47) and a finite verb (v. 48) in the passive voice. Fourth, the sea, which is the scene of action in v. 47, may, among its many connotations in Old Testament and Jewish literature,[127] symbolize also the "world" or the "nations of the world".[128] Last, fish were a metaphor that the Jews could apply to the members of their community[129] and that Christians adopted at a very early date,[130] employing it variously, but quite notably to signify the mission (cf. 4.19).[131]

When we take these factors into account, they indicate at least the direction our interpretation is to take. The clear division within the parable between the gathering of the fish (v. 47) and the sorting of the fish (v. 48) is analogous to what we found in the Interpretation of the Parable of the Tares (13.36b–43): Matthew differentiates between a "present" and a "future".[132]

### The Interpretation of the Parables: (1) The Present Age

In the present age, the drag-net, thrown into the sea, gathers fish of every kind (v. 47). This activity of gathering fish is introduced by a participle in the passive voice ($\beta\lambda\eta\theta\epsilon i\sigma\eta$). Now the significance of the passive is its capability of signalling divine action, examples of which we have already encountered (cf. 13.11f). Add to this use of the passive the fact that the sea is a Jewish metaphor for the nations and that the catching of fish prefigures the Christian mission, and the first part of the message of the parable becomes apparent: in the present age, Jesus Kyrios calls men of all nations ("of every kind", v. 47) into God's kingly rule through the medium of his earthly ambassadors.

Pragmatically speaking, this of course means that the Church preaches its Kerygma and that those who respond to it join the ranks of the believers. For all practical purposes, then, the net becomes a picture for the Church, and the Church factually becomes the empirical representative of God's kingly rule on earth.[133] This, in turn, explains how Matthew can therefore closely associate (not identify! cf. vv. 49f) the Kingdom of Heaven with the Church, reveals why it is that the net occupies such a central position in v. 47, and demonstrates that Matthew is once again thinking of the Kingdom of Heaven in v. 47 as a present reality. In addition, the reference to the net's gathering up fish "of every kind" is one further indication that Matthew's Church was universally oriented and that the theological problem raised by the Gentile mission was no longer acute.

### The Interpretation of the Parable: (2) The Future Age

The gathering of the fish in the present age is followed by the sorting of the fish in the future age. A glance at vv. 49f, the explanation of the parable, shows that this "separation" is the point in the narrative which Matthew proposes to accentuate.[134]

In harmony with this, a series of redefinitions takes place. The verb ἐπληρώθη ("it was full", v. 48a) is interpreted eschatologically as the "End of the Age" (v. 49a). The act of sitting down and gathering the good ones into containers and throwing the bad ones away (v. 48b–c) becomes "separating the evil from among the righteous" (v. 49b). The "good" fish (καλά, v. 48b) are redefined as the "righteous" (δικαίων, v. 49b), the "bad" fish (σαπρά, v. 48c) as the "evil" (πονηρούς, v. 49b), and the throwing away of the bad fish (v. 48c) is made to mean the "throwing" of the evil into the "fiery furnace" (v. 50).

We observed that the first scene in the parable of the Net is introduced with a participle in the passive voice (βληθείσῃ, v. 47). This use of the passive is repeated in the second scene with the verb ἐπληρώθη (v. 48). Moreover, if βληθείσῃ alludes to the present activity of Jesus who, as the exalted Kyrios, even now sends out his earthly ambassadors to call men into God's kingly rule, it follows that ἐπληρώθη alludes to the fact that this same Jesus, whom the Interpretation of the Parable of the Tares identified as the Son of Man (13.37), will return at the End of the Age, sending out his agents, the angels, to carry out the Great Assize and thus begin the Final Judgement (vv. 49f).

Yet the stress in this parable, to say it once again, is not that of the Judgement, or Great Assize, as related to the broad spectrum of the nations (cf. 13.36b–43; 25.31–46). It is the Great Assize as related solely to the Church. Matthew indicates this already in v. 47 both by equating the net with the Church and by employing a picture that is itself selective: while the net can gather fish "of every kind", it certainly cannot gather all the fish in the entire sea.[135] In v. 49, Matthew further indicates that the focal point is the Church and not the nations, for his text reads that the angels will separate the evil "from among" (ἐκ μέσου) the righteous. Hence, throughout the parable of the Net

Matthew consistently presses the thought that the Church, too, will experience the Great Assize.

The fish are divided into the "good" (v. 48b) and the "bad" (v. 48c), which correspond, respectively, to the "righteous" (v. 49b) and the "evil" (v. 49b). The terms "righteous" and "evil" in the first Gospel are ethically as well as eschatologically coloured. Together they embody the doctrine of the "Two Ways", a theme that is deeply rooted in biblical and biblically related documents. It is found, for instance, in the literature from Qumran,[136] and is especially prominent in the Testament of the Twelve Patriarchs[137] and the Didache. As Matthew puts it, there are only two, mutually exclusive, ways open to man; the way of "life", and the way of "destruction" (7.13f). Consequently, no Christian can pretend to serve "two masters" (6.24), for he cannot serve "God and mammon" (6.24).

In this scheme, the righteous go the way of life. As we have seen, Matthew holds that those people will be accounted "righteous" at the Latter Day who have done the will of God, i.e. who will have shown themselves to be obedient to the Law of God as revealed by Jesus through works of love exercised on behalf of the brother.[138]

The evil, on the other hand, go the way of destruction. Matthew construes "evil" as the contrary of righteousness, of God's demand that the individual should be wholly dedicated to him in obedience to his will (cf. chaps. 5–7). Accordingly, Matthew's understanding of "evil" (πονηρός)[139] is fundamentally that of double-mindedness, or duplicity, towards God. In the case of a Christian, double-mindedness is indicative of a conflict of allegiance (6.23).[140]

In view of this, if we are to get some idea of the kind of people Matthew has in mind when he speaks in this parable of the "evil ones", the best procedure is to review the examples of evil, or double-mindedness, which Matthew has set down for us in his Gospel.

As one example of double-mindedness, Matthew directs us to the third slave in the parable of the Talents (25.14–30). This slave, who hid the one talent with which his master had entrusted him, is castigated as being "evil", "slothful", and "worthless" (25.26, 30), because he was more concerned about his own welfare than about engaging himself in his master's business (25.18, 24–30). Hence, this slave becomes the archetype of a brand of lukewarm Christianity which may have been prevalent in Matthew's Church: a laxity in religious life and practice justifying the charge against particular persons that they were lacking in single-hearted devotion to God and therefore guilty of lawlessness (cf. 22.37f).

Perhaps the prime example in the first Gospel of double-mindedness is lovelessness. Lovelessness in the sense of "evil" encompasses offences against the second table of the Law (15.19; cf. 19.18f; 22.39). Cases in point are the merciless servant who refused to forgive the paltry debt of a fellow slave (18.33), and the selfish labourers who objected to the owner's generosity in paying a full day's wage to men who had worked less than the normal number of allotted hours (20.15).

A further type of double-mindedness is the heresy of the false prophets (7.15).[141] To Matthew's way of thinking, the false prophets are "workers of lawlessness" (7.23) because their deeds are like "evil fruit" (7.17f) and thus they "lead many astray" (24.11).

Finally, since Matthew uses the term πονηρός in an absolute sense in our text, the distresses he cites in registering the Messianic Woes should probably also be considered under the category of "evil". In addition to heresy and lovelessness, Matthew mentions apostasy, hatred among Christians, and the betrayal of one another as sins to be deplored (24.10ff).

To recapitulate, when Matthew speaks in v. 49 of "the evil" as those who will be separated from among the righteous at the End of the Age, it appears that he refers to persons in his Church who were guilty of moral and religious laxity, or heresy, or acute lovelessness in all of its varied forms. According to Matthew, such persons are "evil" because they overturn the Law of God and withhold from him the single-hearted devotion he demands.

Unlike the Interpretation of the Parable of the Tares, Matthew says nothing concerning the bliss of the righteous in his explanation to the parable of the Net. In point of fact, he concentrates his attention in vv. 49f almost exclusively on the evil. It is the evil who will be separated from among the righteous, and it is the evil who will be thrown into the "fiery furnace", where there will be "weeping and gnashing of teeth". This preoccupation with the evil ones is not inconsistent with the intention Matthew has set for this parable: by depicting the fate of the wicked, the parable of the Net contains *e contrario* the exhortation to do the will of God.

Since we have already discussed in detail such apocalyptic images as the "fiery furnace" and the "weeping and gnashing of teeth",[142] we need only repeat in summary fashion that the "fiery furnace" is regarded as the eternal residence of those who, at the Final Judgement, are condemned for their godless works, while the "weeping and gnashing of teeth" denote the suffering and remorse that is expressive of the anguish the condemned experience when they recognize that they have been eternally rejected and cut off from God.[143]

### The Message of the Parable

We can now attempt to delineate the message which the parable of the Net is meant to convey. We recall that it is spoken by Jesus to the disciples, or Church, that within it the present age (v. 47) is differentiated from the future age (v. 48), and that the passive voice is used to indicate that both present and future stand under divine ordinance. These facts signify the following: Jesus, the exalted Kyrios, tells the members of Matthew's Church that the gathering together into one community of both "bad" and "good" is quite in harmony with the resolve of God.[144]

This is the preliminary message of the parable. Its importance is that it dispenses with any notion that may have been circulating within the body of Matthew's Church to the effect that the Church should attempt to establish a pure community of the "holy".

As for the further, the principal, message of the parable, Jesus Kyrios informs the members of Matthew's Church that this situation in which bad and good, the evil and the righteous, are gathered together into one body is only temporary. At the End of the Age, the evil will indeed be separated from the righteous and, what is more, consigned to the eternal torments of damnation. Because of this, each Christian must examine himself to make certain that he is not one of the "bad" who will be declared "evil" and separated from the righteous at the Latter Day. To put it positively, each Christian is to do the will of God.

### Summary

The parable of the Net is the fifth and last of the *Parables of Growth* found in Matthew's Gospel. Formally, it is a mixed-form, or *allegorical* parable.

The *contrast* inherent in the parable is between the present age, in which both bad and good elements are gathered together in the Church, and the age to come, when the evil will be separated from the righteous and condemned to eternal damnation.

The *culmination* of the parable is found in v. 49b: "The angels will go out and will separate the evil from among the righteous . . .". For Matthew, this statement denotes that the present inclusion of the evil in the community of the Church will be superseded by their future exclusion at the time of the Great Assize.

The *intention* for which Matthew employs the parable of the Net is *paraenetic*: with it Jesus Kyrios depicts the separation of the evil from the righteous and the bitter end awaiting the evil in order to exhort the Christians of Matthew's Church to do the will of God.

The *secret* this parable reveals regarding the Kingdom of Heaven is the following: that while it is the resolve of God that the Church, the empirical representative of the Kingdom of Heaven on earth, is in the present age a *corpus mixtum*, it is likewise the resolve of God to terminate this state of affairs in the Great Assize at the End of the Age.

The *function* of the parable of the Net within its immediate context is to complete the extended argument initiated with the Interpretation of the Parable of the Tares (13.36b–43) by reminding the members of the Church that they have good reason to be attentive to the exhortation to do the will of God, since the Church, too, will be subjected to the Great Assize.

## THE CONCLUSION:
## TREASURES NEW AND OLD (13.51–2)

(51) *"Did you understand all these things?" They said to him, "Yes." (52) And he said to them, "Therefore it is the case with every scribe who has been instructed about the Kingdom of Heaven as with a man, a master of a house, who brings out of his treasure things new and old."*

The pericope on Treasures New and Old forms the conclusion to the second half of Matthew's parable chapter (13.36–50). The setting has been the house (v. 36a), and Jesus has delivered his discourse solely to the disciples.

### The Pericope in Outline

Verses 51f do not constitute a particularly well integrated unit. They divide themselves into the following three parts, the first two of which stem from the hand of Matthew: (*a*) Jesus' question and the disciples' reply, v. 51; (*b*) a transitional statement, v. 52a; and (*c*) the parable of Treasures New and Old, v. 52b–c.

### Verse 51

That v. 51 is a Matthaean literary construction is evident from the fact that it is directly related to v. 36c, which is likewise Matthaean.[145] In this verse, the disciples are depicted as requesting Jesus to "explain" to them the parable of the darnel of the field, whereupon Jesus begins with the second half of his parable discourse. With the discourse at an end, Matthew now has Jesus ask the disciples if they were able to "understand" all these things, and to this question the disciples reply in the affirmative (v. 51). Thus, vv. 36–52 are bound together by a framework that moulds them into a single section.

The focal point of v. 51 is συνήκατε ("did you understand"), and the function of this verse is to reinforce Matthew's picture of the disciples as the enlightened followers of Jesus. According to Matthew, the disciples, i.e. the Church, are indeed capable of understanding the message of Jesus.[146]

### The Introduction to the Parable of Treasures New and Old

In the opening line of the parable of Treasures New and Old (v. 52b), each term presents a problem in interpretation. First of all, the logical force of "therefore" (διὰ τοῦτο) is not immediately discernible.[147] As the text stands, "therefore" can only refer back to v. 51,[148] so that the argument would appear to be the following: because the disciples have understood the secrets delivered to them in parables, they *therefore* qualify as scribes in the sense that they have been instructed (and are thus informed) about God's kingly rule.

With this we have already broached the second problem: the difficulty of ascertaining the antecedent of πᾶς γραμματεύς ("every scribe"). The prevailing view among scholars is that this expression is an explicit reference to the circle of learned men within Matthew's Church corresponding to the Jewish (Pharisaic) scribes.[149] That such a group of Christian scribes existed seems certain (cf. 23.34). Yet the fact remains that it is the disciples, i.e. the entire Church, who are being addressed in our pericope (v. 51). To interpret "every scribe" in terms of a particular group within Matthew's Church is to destroy the logical cohesion between v. 52 and its immediate context, including v. 51, with the result that v. 52 is reduced to less than an adequate conclusion to 13.36–50. The only reasonable alternative is to suppose that Matthew identified "every scribe" with those members of his Church who have, in the words of v. 51, understood all these things.

A further question concerns μαθητευθείς, namely, is it to be derived from the deponent μαθητεύομαι (to "be [become] a disciple") or from the transitive μαθητεύω (to "make a disciple of", to "teach" or "instruct")?[150] Without repeating the many facets of a rather long and complex argument,[151] it seems that in this instance the aorist passive μαθητευθείς stems from the transitive μαθητεύω[152] and means "is instructed", "has been instructed".[153] Two considerations stand behind this conclusion. The one is that the matter of "being [becoming] a disciple", as we shall demonstrate, does not get to the heart of the issue under discussion in this pericope. The other is that such key words as "explain" (v. 36c) and "understand" (v. 51a), which largely determine the character of 13.36-52, do not at all favour the definition "be a disciple", but readily suggest the meaning "instruct".

The final difficulty involves the dative ($\tau \hat{\eta} \, \beta \alpha \sigma \iota \lambda \epsilon \acute{\iota} \alpha \, \tau \hat{\omega} \nu \, o \mathring{v} \rho \alpha \nu \hat{\omega} \nu$) which is governed by $\mu \alpha \theta \eta \tau \epsilon \upsilon \theta \epsilon \acute{\iota} s$. In view of the previous paragraph, this dative may either be construed as that of advantage ("*for* the Kingdom of Heaven")[154] or as that of respect ("*concerning* the Kingdom of Heaven").[155] The latter alternative is preferable, for in this case the Kingdom of Heaven becomes the object about which the scribe in question has been instructed, a concept that complies with Matthew's position that the parables of Jesus reveal truths, or secrets, concerning God's kingly rule to those to whom God has given the eyes of faith (13.11). However, there is no denying that the idea that the scribe is instructed to the end that he might come to possess the Kingdom (dative of advantage) is thoroughly Matthaean in tone and content. Hence, the choice is not to be pressed unduly.

### The Interpretation of the Parable of Treasures New and Old

To turn to the parable proper (v. 52b–c), incongruence and the introductory dative require that the opening line be translated as follows: "Therefore it is the case with every scribe . . . as with a man . . .". From the standpoint of form, the parable of Treasures New and Old most closely resembles the similitude. At the same time, we hope to demonstrate that the word "treasure" and the phrase "things new and old" have a significance for Matthew that extends beyond their literal sense. The parable, then, is a similitude which is a mixed-form.

In treating the term "master of the house" ($o \mathring{\iota} \kappa o \delta \epsilon \sigma \pi \acute{o} \tau \eta s$) in the parable of the Tares, we observed that Matthew employs it variously to refer to God, Jesus, or even Christians.[156] In this unit, it is plainly the Christian who is the master of the house.

The master of the house is described as having a "treasure" ($\theta \eta \sigma \alpha \upsilon \rho \acute{o} s$, v. 52c), which is a "storehouse", or "storeroom", in the literal sense of the word: a place where the master would keep provisions of every kind in order to meet the assorted needs of his household. At the same time, Matthew's use of this word in other instances shows that he often invests it with a second dimension. To state it somewhat abstractly, Matthew holds that a man's treasure—that to which he gives his undivided allegiance—exercises such a controlling influence over his life that a man may be identified by his treasure: "for where your treasure

is, there will your heart be also" (6.21=Lk 12.34; cf. 6.19f). Now the
Christian who is a true disciple of Jesus has his treasure "in heaven"
(19.21; 6.20), which is another way of saying that his heart, i.e. he
himself, is devoted to God alone (19.16-21; 6.19ff; cf. 6.22f, 24). If this
is correct, the initial thought of the parable is that as the householder
draws from his storeroom, so the Christian lives out of a heart that is
devoted to God. This is the very thought Matthew echoes elsewhere:
"For out of the abundance of the heart the mouth speaks; the good man
out of his good treasure brings forth good . . ." (12.34b-5a; cf. Lk
6.45).

The text goes on to say that the householder brings out of his
treasure "things new and old" (καινὰ καὶ παλαιά, v. 52c). In view of
the context, i.e. Jesus' question to the disciples, "Did you understand
*all these things*?" (v. 51a), the expression "things new and old" should
probably be construed as a circumlocution for the totality of the
revelation that God has imparted to the disciples, or Church, through
Jesus. Moreover, since in Matthew's view the centre of God's revelation in Jesus may well be described in terms of knowing and doing
God's will, we may draft the major idea of the parable of Treasures
New and Old as follows: as the householder brings out of his treasure
things new and old, so the disciple, in that he knows and does God's
will, draws from his heart the revelation God has imparted to him
through Jesus.

### The Message of the Pericope

On the basis of the discussion thus far, we can now attempt to formulate
in the following manner the whole of the message Matthew brings in
this concluding pericope on Treasures New and Old: the Christian
disciple, in that he has been instructed about the Kingdom of Heaven,
is like a scribe, for he both knows and does God's will as revealed in and
through Jesus in the same way as a master of a house will dispose of all
the necessary provisions to meet the needs of his household.

From this central thought it is evident that v. 52 is somewhat of a
commentary on v. 51. In v. 51, the disciples declare that they have
understood all of the things Jesus has told them regarding the Kingdom
of Heaven (13.36-50). By countering with the parable of Treasures
New and Old, Jesus reiterates that true understanding involves knowing the will of God and doing it with single-hearted devotion. And
because Matthew forges vv. 51 and 52 into a single unit, he discloses
once more how closely he conceives ethics to be related to eschatology:
the eschatological message is seen as evoking the ethical imperative.

*The Pericope in relation to its Context*

As a conclusion to 13.36–50, Treasures New and Old nicely sums up the argument we have traced through this section. The manner in which this argument develops has largely been determined by Matthew, since he has edited the materials and played a role in defining the concepts. From Matthew's standpoint, however, this does not mean that we then have to do with a "Matthaean argument", for Matthew, we will remember, construes 13.36–50 as an address of Jesus to the Church; to the Church, namely, to which also he belongs.

With this in mind, we may briefly review the pattern of thought in 13.36–50 as well as in Treasures New and Old. To begin with, Jesus Kyrios enjoins the members of Matthew's Church to be sons of the Kingdom who do the will of God (13.36b–43). Yet, he impresses upon them, this is no easy matter, because it demands of them nothing less than total commitment (13.44–6). Their situation, however, is one marked by urgency: since not even the Church will be spared from the Great Assize, Christians must do the will of God now if they are to escape the eternal fire awaiting the godless (13.47–50). The question, then, is whether the members of Matthew's Church understand this (13.51). If so, they will show it by devoting themselves to the very thing to which they have been exhorted: the doing of the will of God as he, Jesus, has revealed it to them (13.52).

# CHAPTER 6

# Observations and Conclusions

———◆◆◆———

## CHAPTER THIRTEEN WITHIN
## THE GROUND PLAN OF MATTHEW'S GOSPEL

The function of chapter 13 within the ground plan of Matthew's Gospel
is to signal the great "turning-point". By definition, the great turning
point has to do with the flow of events in the ministry of Jesus as
recorded by Matthew in general dependence on Mark. Thus, Matthew
depicts Jesus as coming to the Jews with a ministry of teaching, preaching, and healing (4.17, 23; 9.35; 11.1). In addition, Jesus empowers and
dispatches his twelve disciples to undertake an identical mission (10.1–
8). But in spite of such activity, the Jews on all sides reject Jesus as the
Messiah and inaugurator of God's eschatological Kingdom (chaps.
11–12). In reaction to this, Jesus himself turns against the Jews. He
charges them with being a people that is blind, deaf, and without understanding in regard to God's revelation to them (13.13), and he lends
substance to this charge by speaking to them, not openly as before, but
in parables, which are enigmatic forms of speech (13.10f, 13). The
reverse of this is that Jesus addresses his disciples as the true people of
God (13.10–17). This phenomenon, namely, Jesus' turning away from
the Jews and towards his disciples, is what is meant by the great
"turning point".

For Matthew, the great turning-point is not a mere matter of
past history. It has immediate relevance for the Church to which he
belongs. This Church stands in the tradition of the twelve Apostles and
considers itself to be the agent through which Jesus continues his
mission in the time after the Resurrection. Now the Church, too, has
carried on a mission to the Jews, and it, too, has for the most part experienced failure in converting them. Indeed, the relationship between
the Church and contemporary Pharisaic Judaism is marked by virulent
animosity. Each side denounces the other and claims that it exclusively
is the true people of God, the heir to God's end-time Kingdom.

Because, ultimately, the great turning point as portrayed by Matthew puts forward this very claim on behalf of the Church, we see how relevant the issue it denotes was to the Christians of Matthew's Church.

In chapter 13, Matthew calls attention to the great turning-point both formally and materially. Formally, he does so in several ways. For example, he studiously avoids designating Jesus' speech in parables to the Jews as teaching ($\delta\iota\delta\acute{a}\sigma\kappa\epsilon\iota\nu$) or preaching ($\kappa\eta\rho\acute{\upsilon}\sigma\sigma\epsilon\iota\nu$); instead, he describes it as $\lambda\alpha\lambda\epsilon\hat{\iota}\nu$, i.e. a "speaking" which, following the pattern of 23.1, is apologetic in nature. Furthermore, Matthew consistently refers to the Jewish crowds in 13.1–35 as "them" ($\alpha\mathring{\upsilon}\tau o\hat{\iota}s$); hereby he depicts the Jews as a people that stands outside the circle of those to whom God imparts his revelation and promises his end-time Kingdom. Again, Matthew introduces the term $\pi\alpha\rho\alpha\beta o\lambda\acute{\eta}$ into his Gospel for the first time at chapter 13, and thus differentiates with respect to the Jews between a time when Jesus speaks to them openly and a time when he speaks to them enigmatically. What is more, Matthew employs $\pi\alpha\rho\alpha\beta o\lambda\acute{\eta}$ no less than twelve times in this one chapter, in this way underlining the fact that the parable is a form of speech that is incomprehensible to the Jews but comprehensible to the disciples. Finally, Matthew gathers together eight parabolic units and two so-called parable explanations, embeds them in a framework, and consequently drafts a grand "parable speech" in two parts. This is the compositional counterpart to his use of the terms $\lambda\alpha\lambda\acute{\epsilon}\omega$, $\alpha\mathring{\upsilon}\tau o\hat{\iota}s$, and $\pi\alpha\rho\alpha\beta o\lambda\acute{\eta}$.

The most succinct expression of the material side of the great turning-point is the unifying thought that lies at the basis of chapter 13. The following facts indicate how we are to define it: all of the parables in chapter 13, except for that of the Sower, which is only an apparent exception, are explicitly designated as parables about the Kingdom of Heaven; and the closing pericope of the parable chapter (13.51f) tells us, first, that through Jesus' speech in parables the disciples have been instructed about the Kingdom of Heaven (13.52; cf. 13.35), second, that this instruction has met with (God-given) understanding on the part of the disciples (13.51; cf. 13.11), and third, that such understanding has for its object the doing of God's will (13.52; cf. 13.23). When they are taken together, these facts reveal that Matthew views the whole of his parable chapter concerning the Kingdom of Heaven, in which he treats such matters as the nature of the Kingdom, how God brings it to men, and what the response of the individual who is called into the Kingdom is to be, as teaching that is related to the knowing and doing of God's will. Therefore "knowing and doing God's will" is the unifying thought behind chapter 13.

Matthew develops this thought in both a positive and a negative manner. Negatively, he depicts the Jews as those who do not know and do God's will; positively, he depicts the disciples, who represent the Church of his day, as those who do know and do God's will. Technically, this contrasting attitude comes to expression as apology and paraenesis, which characterize, respectively, the two main sections of chapter 13 (vv. 1–35, 36–52). We will recall, of course, that the apology against the Jews is not without paraenetic significance for the disciples, or Church.

## MATTHEW'S PORTRAIT OF JESUS

Matthew's portrait of Jesus in chapter 13 is unusually variegated. Jesus is presented in his historical role and as Kyrios and Son of Man.

To begin with, Matthew touches on the historical role of Jesus. In this connection, one must differentiate between the framework and traditional materials. In the framework, Matthew depicts Jesus as the Messiah, for Jesus' speaking in parables is divinely authorized and is an imparting of God's revelation to men and the bringing of Old Testament prophecy to fulfilment (13.34f). Moreover, even though the Jews do not comprehend Jesus' speech, it does not therefore forfeit its revelatory character; the disciples, for example, understand it.

In other respects, Matthew's picture of the historical Jesus in the framework of chapter 13 is one which attributes to him a regal, in fact, even divine, dignity. Already the setting beside the sea (13.2) alludes to this status, for Jesus' taking his seat in the boat while great crowds stand before him is reminiscent of God's sitting upon his throne in the heavens while on every side great throngs stand in praise of him. Further, when the disciples approach Jesus to engage him in conversation (13.10, 36), Matthew has them do so in a demeanour that reflects awareness that he is of exalted station.

In the traditional materials, or parables, Matthew calls attention to the historical role of Jesus by portraying him, under the guise of the farmer or sower, as the inaugurator of God's eschatological Kingdom on earth. For Matthew, this simultaneously implies that Jesus is the founder of the Church, because, properly understood, the Church is the empirical representative of the Kingdom of God in the human realm.

Yet for all this, Matthew does not really dwell upon the historical theme in chapter 13. For the most part, we encounter Jesus as Kyrios and Son of Man, two concepts which, though not coterminous, nevertheless overlap in that they both can denote the "present" activity of Jesus between the Resurrection and the Parousia and his "future" activity of coming as Judge.

Because the present activity of Jesus between the Resurrection and the Parousia primarily falls under the concept of Jesus Kyrios, and because Matthew looks upon the materials of chapter 13 as being relevant to his own age, it is principally as the exalted Kyrios (Lord) that Jesus delivers his speech in parables. Rejected as Lord by the Jews, Jesus Kyrios pronounces against this people the apology we find in 13.1–35. As the Lord of the Church, Jesus Kyrios addresses himself to the needs of the community over which he presides: he instructs, exhorts, warns, and comforts his followers. As the Lord of the world, Jesus Kyrios also speaks through his missionary ambassadors: in this way he reaches out to men of all nations, Jews and Gentiles, in order to gather them into his Church and make of them disciples who know and do the will of God. To a large extent, then, chapter 13 brings us face to face with Jesus Kyrios.

But Jesus is likewise the Son of Man, and he exercises this office, too, between the Resurrection and the Parousia, as is evident from Matthew's statement that Jesus Son of Man rules over the inhabited world and is at work raising up sons of the Kingdom (13.38). Still, the chief tendency in chapter 13 is to cast Jesus Son of Man into the future role of Judge. In this capacity Jesus will visibly come again in great power at the End of the Age, he will dispatch his heavenly agents, the angels, to separate the righteous from the wicked, and thus the Great Assize, with its eternal consequences of bliss or pain for all mankind, will take place.

There is yet another element that forms an integral part of Matthew's portrait of Jesus, namely, Satan. In chapter 13, Matthew describes Satan by a rich variety of names. He is, for example, the "Evil One", the transcendent fountainhead of all lawlessness. He is also the "Enemy", the inimical will who would destroy the allegiance that men are to render to Jesus alone. And he is the "Devil", the personal adversary of Jesus, the servant, and of Jesus, the Son of Man. In the present age, Satan enjoys an apparent freedom and power. He is not, however, a fully sovereign personality; at the End of the Age, he, his angels, and the sons of the Evil One, i.e. those persons who have given him their fealty, will be consigned by the Son of Man to eternal fire, so that Jesus will reign supreme.

## MATTHEW'S PORTRAIT OF THE CHURCH

In chapter 3, we dealt at length with Matthew's conception of the relationship between the Church and the Kingdom of Heaven. Our interest here is to review the external and internal situation of the Church, or community, to which Matthew belongs. Its composition, we will recall, is mixed: it incorporates both Jews and Gentiles.

Externally, the contact of Matthew's Church with its environment is marked by missionary endeavour and persecution. With reference to the mission, Matthew's Church possesses a universal perspective, so that the "world" is its field of operations and the struggle once evoked in early Christian circles over Jewish particularism is no longer actual. This universal orientation, however, does not mitigate the fact that Matthew's Church pursues Jewish converts. Though Matthew considers the leaders of Pharisaic Judaism to be incorrigible as far as the matters of salvation are concerned, the same does not hold true for the Jewish people as such. Accordingly, the missionary efforts of Matthew's Church are directed at once towards Jew and Gentile.

At the same time, Matthew's Church also experiences persecution from the side of both Jew and Gentile. This persecution is religiously motivated and seems variously to involve legal proceedings, verbal and physical assault that may not even exclude martyrdom, as well as other less severe forms of harassment. Those who engage in such persecution pose a grave threat to the faith of Christians. The reaction of the members of Matthew's Church to persecution is to construe it as divinely ordained affliction, indeed, as a hallmark of discipleship, and therefore as something to be joyfully endured, if they are finally to be saved.

Internally, Matthew's Church does not at all present a monolithic front in matters of doctrine and practice. According to Matthaean theology, the essence of being a Christian is knowing and doing the will (Law) of God as revealed and enjoined by Jesus. With this as norm, we can follow the struggle in Matthew's Church against the false prophets on the one hand and moral laxity on the other.

Concerning the false prophets, Matthew does not so specify their error as to preclude any necessity on our part for calculated guessing. It appears certain, however, that the false prophets are enthusiasts, and it may be that their emphasis on exercising the charismatic gifts of the Spirit has led them to assert that one of the main purposes of the coming of Jesus was the abrogation of the Law (in some undetermined measure). If this is the case, the false prophets are so designated because they assume a position that is diametrically opposed to Matthew's contention that Jesus did not come to repudiate the Law but to establish it and reveal its true intention.

With respect to moral laxity, here is a very broad area of difficulty with which Matthew's Church has to contend. As a relatively wealthy congregation in a heathen environment, materialism and secularism are immediate problems cropping up in the ranks of the faithful. In addition, there is spiritual slothfulness in regard to participating in the work of the Church; there is hatred among Christians; there is love-lessness, as exemplified, for example, by a lack of generosity or an un-willingness to forgive the brother; there are cases of apostasy, an evil compounded by the fact that even Christians, and not merely non-believers, make themselves guilty of effecting the spiritual ruination of other Christians; and there is a certain prevalence of lawlessness in general, which may be defined as disobedience of all kinds towards the Law of God. In scanning such a catalogue of religious aberration, it is not surprising that Matthew sternly warns the Christians of his Church about the Judgement that is to come and exhorts them at almost every turn to do the will of God, which is the mark of those who will be pronounced "righteous" at the Latter Day.

## MATTHEW'S USE OF PARABOLIC SPEECH

There is no support in the first Gospel for the thesis that Matthew establishes a theory of parables in the formal sense of the term. Strictly speaking, Matthew has incorporated a double tradition into his Gospel regarding the nature of parabolic speech (cf. chap. 13 with chap. 21). The presence of this double tradition reveals that the guiding factor in Matthew's use of such speech is not something like his abstract reflec-tion upon the character of the parable as such, but rather the immediate theological objective he desires any given parable or series of parables to serve.

Chapter 13 illustrates this well. To begin with, Matthew appropriates the Marcan tradition according to which parables are enigmatic forms of speech, i.e. riddles. Next, he attributes to the disciples, or Church, the ability to comprehend such "revelatory riddles", but denies this ability to the Jews on the grounds that they have proved themselves to be obdurate in the face of God's revelation. The result is that Matthew is able to depict the disciples, or Church, as the true people of God, but the Jews as hardened and standing under God's judgement (13.10–13, 16f). Hence, through the medium of the parable and the

Marcan concept associated with it, Matthew has achieved a theological objective. Yet exactly because Matthew does work with parabolic speech in this manner, "pragmatically" rather than "theoretically", the interpreter errs if he attempts to derive from Matthew's pericope on the Reason for Speaking in Parables (13.10–17) either Matthew's concept of parabolic speech *per se* or that of Jesus.

From the standpoint of form, the seven major parabolic units of chapter 13 possess characteristics that are common to many, but particularly to Rabbinic, traditions. The basic schema of these units is one commonly found among Rabbinic *meshalim*: a transitional statement, an introductory formula, the parable proper culminating at the end, and, in at least one case (the Net), an application. In addition, the parabolic units of chapter 13, with perhaps the exception of the Leaven, which is a pure parable, are mixed-forms, or allegorical parables. Again, like Rabbinic *meshalim* they are also designed for paraenetic use: for instruction, assurance, exhortation, and debate. And they reflect the techniques for storytelling which the Rabbis employed.

On the other hand, there are a number of formal elements in chapter 13 in relation both to the parabolic units and to their framework which are typically, if not always uniquely, Matthaean. Some of these are the following: the presence of incongruence and the introductory dative; the occurrence of direct speech; the tendency to single out one particular element in a parable and enlarge upon it at length; the practice of attaching an application in order to inform the reader of the manner in which any given parable is to be interpreted; the liberal application of stereotyped phraseology; and the use of editorial methods to interpret past traditions.

To turn to the theological sphere, one of the most important principles we have established is that Matthew employs parables of Jesus in order that Jesus Kyrios, who lives in the midst of his Church, can address himself to the situation of the Church's own day. This reveals that Matthew conceives of Jesus' parabolic tradition as a living tradition, for through it Jesus directs, teaches, and exhorts Christians of a later age. This, in turn, explains why the parables in chapter 13 have assumed a paraenetic character and why they are strongly oriented towards the Kingdom of Heaven as a present reality. Then, too, the phenomenon that Jesus might speak through his parables to a new and later generation would necessarily activate the principles of change we outlined in the preceding paragraphs on form. It is for this same reason that Matthew has "allegorized" the parables of Jesus, thus adapting their features to the time and situation in which they are to "speak".

In conclusion, Matthew's use of parabolic speech may be summarized with the sweeping principle that even as Jesus utilized parables to meet the demands of his own situation, so Matthew has adopted the parables of Jesus and utilized them in such a fashion that they should be able to meet the demands of Matthew's own age of the Church.

This process of appropriating and applying the parables of Jesus did not, of course, terminate with Matthew. On the contrary, it has been carried out in every generation throughout the history of the Church. Today, too, it is being carried out: by the preacher who would find in the parables of Jesus a message for the present-day people of God. Like Matthew, the preacher adapts these parables to meet the needs of a new and vastly changed situation. Like Matthew, the preacher proclaims them in the sure confidence that through his exposition of them Jesus Kyrios, residing in the midst of the Christian assembly, will once again speak to his followers, instructing, exhorting, and admonishing them. Thus, for the preacher and his congregation as for Matthew and his congregation, the parables of Jesus are a living tradition, for through them Jesus Kyrios brings men face to face with that total grace and that total demand that are part and parcel of the Kingdom of Heaven. Consequently, today, too, even as at the time of Matthew, the parables of Jesus can be seen to be an instrument of God for raising up "sons of the Kingdom": people who, as Matthew would put it, discover the joy of knowing and doing the will of God.

# NOTES

## CHAPTER 1

1. *Gleichnisreden*, 1–11. Publication details of those works listed in the Selected Bibliography will be found there.
2. Cf. e.g. Jeremias, *Gleichnisse*, p. 16 (ET, *Parables*, p. 20).
3. Jülicher, *Gleichnisreden*, I, p. 52.
4. Ibid.
5. Ibid., pp. 52–8.
6. Ibid., pp. 58–80.
7. Ibid., pp. 69–80.
8. Ibid., pp. 92–111.
9. Ibid., p. 101.
10. Ibid., pp. 112–15.
11. Ibid., chap. 6.
12. *Parabeln*.
13. *Altjüdische Gleichnisse; idem, Gleichnisreden Jesu.*
14. In addition to Bugge and Fiebig, other scholars who have examined Jülicher's parable theory in depth and have called for some revision of it are: M. J. Lagrange, "La parabole en dehors de l'Évangile", *RB*, 6 (1909), pp. 198–212, 342–67; D. Buzy, *Introduction aux paraboles évangéliques* (Paris, J. Gabalda, 1912); L. E. Browne, *The Parables of the Gospels in the Light of Modern Criticism* (Cambridge, University Press, 1913); O. Eissfeldt, *Der Maschal im Alten Testament* (Giessen, Alfred Töpelmann, 1913); Hermaniuk, *Parabole*; Dahl, "Parables", pp. 133–40; F. Hauck, *ThW*, V, pp. 741–50; M. Black, "The Parables as Allegory", *BJRL*, 42 (1960), pp. 273–87.
15. Fiebig, *Altjüdische Gleichnisse*, pp. 25f (my translation).
16. Ibid., pp. 34f (my translation).
17. Ibid., pp. 31ff (my translation).
18. *Der Rahmen der Geschichte Jesu* (Berlin, Trowitsch & Sohn).
19. *Die Formgeschichte des Evangeliums* (3. Aufl.; Tübingen, J. C. B. Mohr, 1959) [ET by B. L. Woolf, *From Tradition to Gospel* (New York, Charles Scribner's Sons, 1935)].
20. *Tradition*.
21. *Die synoptischen Streitgespräche* (Berlin, Trowitzsch & Sohn).
22. Cf. Dibelius, op. cit., pp. 247–58 (ET, pp. 246–58); Bultmann, *Tradition*, pp. 179–222 (ET, pp. 166–205).
23. These comments of Bultmann which we reproduce represent our translation or paraphrase of selected statements taken from *Tradition*, pp. 194–208 (ET, pp. 179–92).

24. *Parables.*

25. *Parables.*

26. *Gleichnisse* (ET, *Parables*).

27. Cadoux, *Parables*, p. 50; Dodd, *Parables*, pp. vii, 1–12; Jeremias, *Gleichnisse*, pp. 14f (ET, *Parables*, pp. 18f).

28. Cadoux, *Parables*, chap. 4; Dodd, *Parables*, chaps. 4–6; Jeremias, *Gleichnisse*, p. 9, chap. 2 (ET, *Parables*, pp. 12f, chap. 2).

29. Cadoux, *Parables*, chap. 2; Dodd, *Parables*, chaps. 4–6; Jeremias, *Gleichnisse*, chap. 2 (ET, *Parables*, chap. 2).

30. Cadoux differs from Dodd and Jeremias at this point, since his book has no particular eschatological accent. Then, too, it is commonly known that Dodd's view of "realized eschatology" (*Parables*, p. 35) is not the same as Jeremias' "eschatology in process of realization" (*sich realisierende Eschatologie*) [*Gleichnisse*, p. 227 (ET, *Parables*, p. 230)].

31. Cadoux, *Parables*, pp. 54ff; Dodd, *Parables*, pp. 13f; Jeremias, *Gleichnisse*, p. 18 (ET, *Parables*, p. 22). In this connection, the reader should also observe that these scholars in effect redefine the form-critical term *Sitz im Leben*, with the result that it no longer refers to a situation in the early Church but to one in the ministry of Jesus (cf. Dodd, *Parables*, p. 85; Jeremias, *Gleichnisse*, p. 19) [ET, *Parables*, p. 23].

32. *Hermeneutik* (2. Aufl.; Bad Cannstatt, R. Müllerschön Verlag, 1958), pp. 211–30.

33. Cf. e.g. Fuchs' article, "Die Frage nach dem historischen Jesus", [*Zur Frage nach dem historischen Jesus*] (Tübingen, J. C. B. Mohr, 1960), pp. 143–67.

34. *Gleichnisse* (ET, *Parables*).

35. *Paulus und Jesus* (Tübingen, J. C. B. Mohr, 1962). Fuchs' influence on recent developments in the field of parable exegesis can also be clearly seen in the work of the following men: G. Eichholz, *Einführung in die Gleichnisse* (Neukirchen-Vluyn, Neukirchener Verlag, 1963); G. V. Jones, *The Art and Truth of the Parables* (London, S.P.C.K., 1964); E. Biser, *Die Gleichnisse Jesu* (München, Kösel Verlag, 1965); R. W. Funk, *Language, Hermeneutic, and Word of God* (New York, Harper & Row, 1966); D. O. Via, Jr, *The Parables* (Philadelphia, Fortress Press, 1967).

36. Jüngel, op. cit., pp. 135f.

37. Hamburg, Furche Verlag, 1966, pp. 7–43. ET, *Rediscovering the Teaching of the Evangelists* (London, S.C.M. Press; Philadelphia, Westminster Press, 1969).

38. Baumbach, *Verständnis des Bösen*, pp. 53–121.

39. Cf. e.g. K. W. Clark, "The Gentile Bias in Matthew", *JBL*, 66 (1947), pp. 165–72; Strecker, *Weg*, pp. 15–49; Nepper-Christensen, *Matthäusevangelium*, chaps. 7–8.

This is also the position of Walker (*Heilsgeschichte*, pp. 114–27), whose book did not appear until after this manuscript had been completed. In a sentence, Walker's thesis is that Matthew intended with his Gospel to write a history of the life of Jesus Messiah (p. 114), doing so in such a way as to depict the blindness of Israel towards the Gospel of the Kingdom (as it was delivered to it by John the Baptist, Jesus, and the "disciples" of Jesus, respectively), which, in turn, resulted in Israel's own rejection (the concrete expression of which was the destruction of Jerusalem in A.D. 70) and the subsequent mission to the Gentiles (who then assumed Israel's place in the History of Salvation). The strength of Walker's study is that he succeeds in demonstrating that the chief opponents of Jesus in Matthew's Gospel (the so-called "representatives of Israel": scribes, Pharisees, Sadducees, etc.) comprise a uniform front against him (pp. 11–33). What we cannot accept as having been proved is, first of all, Walker's insistence that Matthew, at his time, had nothing to do with Judaism and, indeed, was ignorant of it from a historical point of view (cf. pp. 20, 23, 32, 44, etc.). For Walker arrives at this conclusion after examining only the names of the "representatives of Israel" and the phrase "their synagogues" (pp. 11–35). But this is too small a basis on which to decide a thesis of such consequence. Moreover, throughout the rest of his study, Walker simply makes Matthew's text corroborate his thesis; hence, his methodology, too, is subject to question. These same criticisms, secondly, also apply to Walker's concept of "Israel". Thus he establishes his concept of Israel solely on the basis of an interpretation of the phrase "this generation", and promptly makes it normative, operating with it in an absolute manner. The result is that Walker imposes a particular understanding of Israel on terms such as $\ddot{o}\chi\lambda os$, $\lambda a\acute{o}s$, $'I\sigma\rho a\acute{\eta}\lambda$, and $'I ov\delta a\hat{i}os$ (cf. the original Greek words Walker renders in his book as "Volk" or "Israel" [passim]), even though he does not first investigate them systematically to determine whether in their own right and in relation to one another, they comply with his initial understanding of "Israel". Had Walker investigated Matthew's treatment of $\ddot{o}\chi\lambda os$, for example, he would have discovered that the "Jewish crowds" and the "Jewish leaders" do not form a monolithic front in the first Gospel (cf. e.g. 23.1, a passage Walker does not discuss, and contrast it with 23.13, 23, etc.; also see below, pp. 25–8). In the third place, Walker further establishes on the basis of "this generation" the period of Heilsgeschichte he believes Matthew to have been principally concerned with (the "time of Israel", which began with John the Baptist and ended with the destruction of Jerusalem in A.D. 70 [pp. 37f]), and attempts to understand the text of Matthew's Gospel in relation to this period. So it is that Walker maintains that chapters 24–5 alone are directed primarily to the "time of Matthew" (the years after A.D. 70), whereas the rest of the Gospel has to do essentially with past history (pp. 114–27; esp. pp. 118ff). On the contrary, the "time of Matthew" plays a much greater role in the first Gospel than Walker grants. As proof of this we need only point to chapter 18, with which, significantly, Walker does not deal. Moreover, it would seem that in practice Walker himself modifies his position on this matter, for he describes numerous passages within chapters 1–23, passages that clearly refer to the time of Matthew, as "anticipating" the situation of the later Church (p. 99), or as "bursting" their context (p. 120), or as being "timelessly valid" (p. 118) or "binding to the end" (p. 25). Are not such statements as these tantamount to a concession that the various parts of Matthew's Gospel do, in fact, provide us with a primary witness to the time of Matthew? Last, Walker's view that Matthew was chiefly concerned with the time of Isarel leads him to declare that the Jesus of Matthew's Gospel is above all the "earthly Jesus"; indeed, Matthew so "absolutizes" the earthly Jesus, says Walker, that there "remains for the exalted Lord only a modest role" (p. 116). By reason of the fact that the predominate christological predication in Matthew's Gospel is precisely that of "Kyrios" (=Lord), Walker's assertion is remarkable. He could make it only because he determines Matthew's presentation of Heilsgeschichte without taking this term into account (hence, he does not, except in a footnote, even mention it in discussing the christological titles Matthew employs [pp. 128–32], even though he does touch on that of "Son of Man"). But until Walker delineates the place of Jesus Kyrios in Matthew's presentation of Heilsgeschichte, his study must remain less than authoritative.

40. Cf. Trilling, *Israel*, pp. 90–6, 221f. Hare (*Jewish Persecution*, p. 127) approaches this position when he asserts that although the process of the formal separation of Christianity from Judaism had not yet been completed at the writing of the first Gospel, nevertheless Matthew's Church by this time already stood totally outside the synagogue community.

41. Cf. Bornkamm, "Enderwartung", pp. 17ff, 36, 46, n. 4 (ET, "End-Expectation", pp. 20ff, 39, 50, n. 3); Hummel, *Auseinandersetzung*, pp. 28–33.

42. Cf. Blair's highly informative, though no longer fully current, review of scholarly opinion on this question (*Matthew*, pp. 26–34). Cf. also J. Gnilka, "Die Kirche des Matthäus und die Gemeinde von Qumran", *BZ*, 7 (1963), pp. 43, 62f.

# CHAPTER 2

1. Cf. e.g. Allen, *Matthew*, pp. 149f; J. W. Doeve, *Jewish Hermeneutics in the Synoptic Gospels and Acts* (Assen, Van Gorcum, 1953), pp. 100–3; W. L. Knox, *The Sources of the Synoptic Gospels* (Cambridge University Press, 1957), II, pp. 129–32.

2. See below, pp. 30f.

3. On the theological significance of αὐτοῖς, see below, p. 47.

4. Cf. Mk 4.2, 12, 33, 34 with Mk 4.11, 13, 21, 24.

5. Cf. Jeremias, *Gleichnisse*, p. 81, n. 8 (ET, *Parables*, p. 83, n. 59).

6. For an analysis of 13.1, see below, pp. 22f, 92f.

7. For an analysis of 13.10a, see below, pp. 40f.

8. See below, pp. 19f.

9. Ibid., pp. 117f.

# CHAPTER 3

1. *Worte*, pp. 75–119.

2. "Eingehen".

3. *Israel*, pp. 143–51.

4. *Weg*, pp. 166–72.

5. Dalman, *Worte*, p. 76.

6. Ibid., pp. 77f.

7. Ibid., pp. 79–83

8. Ibid., p. 80.

9. Ibid., pp. 80–3. Cf. also T. F. Glasson, "The Kingdom as Cosmic Catastrophe", *StEv*, III, pp. 190f.

10. Mt 5.20; 7.21; 18.3; 19.23f; 23.13. But in 23.13, an adapted Q logion (cf. Lk 11.52), it appears that Matthew is speaking of entering the Kingdom as a "present" possibility.

11. Mt 18.8f; 19.17; cf. also 7.14; 25.46.

12. Mt 25.21, 23.

13. Cf. Windisch, "Eingehen", pp. 163–7.

14. Mt 5.20; 23.13.
15. Mt 8.12; cf. 13.42, 50; 22.13; 25.30.
16. Cf. P. Volz, *Eschatologie*, pp. 367f; Dalman, *Worte*, pp. 90f.
17. Cf. 10.8 to 11.5; 12.28; 4.23; 9.35.
18. Trilling (*Israel*, pp. 61ff) and Strecker (*Weg*, p. 169) argue that the future tense in 21.43 (lit. "will be given") is "future" in so far as Jesus spoke of a coming event, but "past" in so far as Matthew, from his vantage point in history, was looking back on this event. R. J. Dillon ("Towards a Tradition-History of the Parables of the True Israel [Mt 21.33—22.14]", *Bib*, 47 [1966], pp. 15, 20f) supports this position, but Bornkamm ("Enderwartung", p. 40 [ET, "End-Expectation", pp. 43f]) and Hummel (*Auseinandersetzung*, pp. 149f) contend that the future tense in question is "future" also for Matthew. What Bornkamm and Hummel want to guard against is the danger of understanding Matthew's statement regarding God's taking his Kingdom away from the Jews and giving it to the Church in terms of an identification of the Church with the Kingdom of God, especially since this error is often coupled with the false notion that to become a member of the Church is to be guaranteed a place in the final, magnificent Kingdom of God. But the aforementioned view of Trilling and Strecker does not at all necessitate identifying the Church with the Kingdom of God (cf. Trilling, *Israel*, pp. 151, 162) and, in fact, seems to capture the intention of 21.43.
19. With respect to the role of Jesus Kyrios in Matthew's theology, cf. Trilling, *Israel*, pp. 21–51; O. Michel, "Der Abschluss des Matthäusevangeliums", *EvTh*, 10 (1950/51), pp. 16–26; E. Lohmeyer, "Mir ist gegeben alle Gewalt", *In Memoriam Ernst Lohmeyer*, edited by W. Schmauch (Stuttgart, Evangelisches Verlagswerk, 1951), pp. 22–49; Vögtle, "Mt 28, 18–20"; G. Bornkamm, "Der Auferstandene und der Irdische: Mt 28, 16–20," *Zeit und Geschichte* (Festschrift Rudolf Bultmann), edited by E. Dinkler (Tübingen, J. C. B. Mohr, 1964), pp. 171–91.
20. Cf. 10.32f, 40; 21.42f; 25.31–46.
21. As the reader may already have observed, we have incorporated into the body of this study a system of capitalization that is designed to alert him to our use of technical terms (Word, Kingdom, Kyrios, Son of Man, Devil, End of the Age, Great Assize, Last Judgement, etc.).
22. Cf. Trilling, *Israel*, p. 144; Strecker, *Weg*, pp. 129f; Hahn, *Mission*, p. 105 (ET, pp. 121f).
23. The two "parables of the Kingdom" in Mark are the Seed Growing Secretly (4.26–9) and the Mustard Seed (4.30–2); in Luke they are the Mustard Seed (13.18f) and the Leaven (13.20f).
24. Trilling, *Israel*, p. 151.
25. Ibid.

# CHAPTER 4

1. Allen (*Matthew*, p. 142), Klostermann (*Matthäus*, p. 118), and M'Neile (*Matthew*, pp. 186f) hold that the words τῆς οἰκίας are probably a gloss meant to explain ἐξελθών. But although it is correct that certain texts, primarily of the Western tradition, omit these words, the great majority contain them. Indeed, the actual textual disagreements do not centre around

"the house", but around the authenticity of the prepositions ἐκ and ἀπό. Therefore from a purely textual standpoint and because of the balance Matthew strikes between 13.1 and 13.36, the Nestle text, which retains τῆς οἰκίας, most likely has the original reading.

2. This word occurs 19 times in Matthew, 11 times in Mark, and 13 times in Luke. As a rule, wherever we call attention to the number of times that any particular Greek word appears in books of the New Testament, we rely upon the statistics given in R. Morgenthaler, *Statistik des neutestamentlichen Wortschatzes* (Zürich, Gotthelf Verlag, 1958).

3. That the purpose of v. 1 is strictly preparatory in nature is evident both from the fact that the reference to the "house" remains virtually meaningless until 13.36 and from the fact that Jesus' sitting "by the sea" is a feature Matthew has taken from the Marcan text (cf. Mk 4.1a). Mark has a penchant for having Jesus meet the crowds in the vicinity of the lake to teach them (Mk 2.13; 4.1f) and heal them (Mk 3.7–10; 5.1 [cf. 5.14–17]; 5.21 [cf. 5.27—6.1]). Not so Matthew. According to him, if there is any one place where Jesus teaches and heals the crowds, it is on the mountain (5.1; 7.28; 15.29b–31). Consequently, there can be no question of ascribing a typological significance to the seashore in the first Gospel. "By the sea" has meaning for Matthew only because it represents an open area that is ideally suited for the crowd scene he is about to stage.

4. C. Schneider, *ThW*, III, pp. 444ff.

5. Ibid., p. 444.

6. Cf. E. Hilgert (*The Ship and Related Symbols in the New Testament* [Assen, Van Gorcum, 1962], pp. 84ff, 97ff [cf. also J. Mánek, "Fishers of Men", *NovTest*, 2 (1957), pp. 140f]) who shows that the boat has clearly become a symbol for the Church in the pericopes of the Stilling of the Storm (8.23–7 = Mk 4.35–41) and the Walking on the Water (14.22–33 = Mk 6.45–52).

7. See below, pp. 40f, 42f, 89f, 94f, 132f. But see also above, pp. 18f.

8. Cf. Hummel, *Auseinandersetzung*, pp. 136f, 144ff.

9. Cf. M'Neile, *Matthew*, pp. 47f, 232f; J. Jeremias, *Jesu Verheissung für die Völker* (Stuttgart, W. Kohlhammer Verlag, 1956), p. 29 (ET by S. H. Hooke, *Jesus' Promise to the Nations* [London, S.C.M. Press, 1958], pp. 34f); Lohmeyer *Matthäus*, pp. 257f; Davies, *Sermon on the Mount*, pp. 327f.

10. Trilling, *Israel*, pp. 130–8.

11. Mt 26.3f, 14, 47, 57, 59, 62f, 65; 27.1, 3, 6, 12, 20, 41, 62; 28.11f.

12. This is in contrast to 26.5 (= Mk 14.2), where λαός denotes the Jewish crowds as distinct from their leaders, and 27.64, where it simply means "populace" (cf. Arndt—Gingrich, p. 467).

13. Mt 8.1; 14.13; 19.2; 20.29.

14. Mt 8.1–4; 9.1–8, 32ff; 12.22ff; 17.14–18; 20.29–34.

15. Mt 9.1–8; 12.22–30; 15.1–20; 21.10–17, 23–7; 22.23–33.

16. Mt 9.8, 33.

17. Mt 21.11; cf. 21.46.

18. Mt 15.31.

19. Mt 12.23; 21.9. That 12.23 is a question with μήτι does not mitigate the fact that Matthew understands these words as a tribute to Jesus. The function of μήτι is merely to inform the reader that this is not a confession of faith

such as that of the disciples (14.33; 16.16 = Mk 8.29) or the centurion (27.54 = Mk 15.39).

20. So e.g. Strecker, *Weg*, pp. 107ff.

21. This is the main thrust of Trilling's argument (*Israel*, pp. 102, 105).

22. Cf. Barth, "Gesetzesverständnis", p. 94, n. 2 (ET, "Law", p. 100, n. 4); Hahn, *Mission*, pp. 108-11 (ET, pp. 125-8). This interest of Matthew's Church in the Jews does not compromise the universal commission of 28.19f, but is a distinct facet of the same.

23. This word occurs 49 times in Matthew, 38 times in Mark, and 41 times in Luke.

24. Bornkamm, "Enderwartung", p. 35, n. 1 (ET, "End-Expectation", p. 38, n. 1).

25. Wilkens, "Redaktion", p. 309.

26. Cf. Hahn, *Mission*, pp. 104ff (ET, pp. 120ff); G. Friedrich, *ThW*, III, pp. 701-14.

27. Freidrich, op. cit., p. 713; Bornkamm, "Enderwartung", p. 35, n. 1 (ET, "End-Expectation", p. 38, n. 1); Strecker, *Weg*, pp. 127f.

28. Thus Matthew refers to the entire Sermon on the Mount as "teaching" (cf. 5.2; 7.28f).

29. K. H. Rengstorf, *ThW*, II, pp. 143ff.

30. Note the tension between Mk 4.11f and 33.

31. In Mk 4.11, 13, 21, 24, "them" ($\alpha\vec{v}\tau o\hat{i}\varsigma$) refers solely to the disciples; this contrasts sharply with Matthew's use of this pronoun (see above, p. 13). In Mk 4.26, 30, the indefinite transition "And he said" introduces parables addressed both the the disciples and the crowd.

32. Cf. e.g. 5.25f; 6.19ff, 22ff; 7.24-7; 9.16f; 11.16-19; 12.43ff; 18.12ff, 23-35; 20.1-16; 21.28-32; 24.43f, 45-51; 25.1-13, 14-30.

33. See below, pp. 48f.

34. Cf. Gnilka, *Verstockung*, pp. 66 (esp. n. 114), 82f.

35. In referring to Gospel units by name, we have adopted the section headings found in *Synopsis Quattuor Evangeliorum*, edited by K. Aland (Stuttgart, Württembergische Bibelanstalt, 1964).

36. C. W. F. Smith, *Parables*, p. 60; Michaelis, *Gleichnisse*, p. 24; Dahl, "Parables", p. 154; Jeremias, *Gleichnisse*, pp. 149f (ET, *Parables*, pp. 149ff).

37. B. Weiss, *Kritisch exegetisches Handbuch über das Evangelium des Matthäus* (7. Aufl.; Göttingen, Vandenhoeck & Ruprecht's Verlag, 1883), p. 289; Jülicher, *Gleichnisreden*, II, p. 514; Plummer, *Matthew*, p. 187; G. Dalman, "Viererlei Acker", *PJ*, 22 (1926), p. 120; G. E. Ladd, "The Sitz im Leben of the Parables of Matthew 13: the Soils", *StEv*, II, pp. 203-10.

38. Zahn, *Matthäus*, p. 487; Cadoux, *Parables*, pp. 155f; B. T. D. Smith, *Parables*, p. 126; Schniewind, *Matthäus*, pp. 165f; C. Masson, *Les Paraboles de Marc IV* (Neuchatel, Delachaux & Niestlé, 1945), p. 39; K. D. White, "The Parable of the Sower", *JThS*, 15 (1964), p. 307.

39. See below, p. 148, n. 80.

40. To the best of our knowledge, Dodd (*Parables*, p. 140) was the first scholar to attach this superscription to the parables of the Sower, Tares, Seed Growing Secretly, Mustard Seed, Leaven, and Drag-net, because he held that the

constituent feature common to all of them was the "idea of growth" or a variation of the same.

41. See below, p. 53.

42. Lohmeyer, *Matthäus*, p. 195.

43. D. Haugg, "Das Ackergleichnis", *ThQ*, 127 (1947), p. 190; Dahl, "Parables", p. 152; Jeremias, *Gleichnisse*, p. 149 (ET, *Parables*, p. 150).

44. Dalman (op. cit., p. 131) relates his experience with yields of wheat in Palestine and states that on one occasion the average increase of each seed was 151-fold and that on another it was 46-fold. Sprenger ("Jesu Säe- und Erntegleichnisse", *PJ*, 9 [1913], pp. 85f), Haugg (op. cit., pp. 199f), and White (op. cit., pp. 301f) support Dalman, affirming that the yield of grain cited by the parable is credible. Many scholars, e.g. Jeremias (*Gleichnisse*, p. 150 [ET, *Parables*, p. 150]; *idem*, "Palästinakundliches zum Gleichnis vom Säemann", *NTS*, 13 [1966/67], p. 53), argue that the parable is hyperbolic in this respect, but on the whole they do so for theological reasons.

45. In telling of the grain that fell on good soil ("a hundredfold . . . sixty . . . thirty"), Matthew inverts the order of Mark's text (cf. v. 8b with Mk 4.8c). This inversion may be explained in one of two ways. If it were not intended to alter the meaning of Mark's text, it may be understood as another example of Matthew's predilection for *chiasmus* (cf. J. C. Fenton, "Inclusio and Chiasmus in Matthew", *StEv*, I, pp. 174–9). But if it is not of a purely literary nature and springs from theological reflection, it may allude to the circumstance that even in the case of Jesus' followers the response to the Word is such that it does not achieve the same increase in each person (cf. Haugg, op. cit., pp. 200f).

46. So Dodd, *Parables*, pp. 146f; cf. also Dahl, "Parables", p. 154. *Contra*: C. W. F. Smith, *Parables*, p. 65.

47. Jeremias, *Gleichnisse*, pp. 149f (ET, *Parables*, pp. 150f); cf. also Dahl,, "Parables", pp. 153f.

48. As long as one adheres to the parable of the Sower in a form that agrees substantially with the text as we find it in the first and second Gospels, this criticism holds true regardless of whether the interpreter attempts to understand this parable from the viewpoint of Jesus or that of Matthew.

49. See above, pp. 18f.

50. In Mark's Gospel, the exhortation "Whoever has ears to hear, let him hear !" (Mk 4.9b) properly stands outside the body of the parable. Indeed, the transition "And he said" (Mk 4.9a) shows that this logion was most likely first attached to the parable of the Sower by an unknown editor somewhat prior to the time of Mark (cf. Mk 4.26a, 30a [Jeremias, *Gleichnisse*, p. 10, n. 2 (ET, *Parables*, p. 14, n. 8)]). In this instance Matthew makes two changes: he eliminates the transition, thus making of the call to hear aright an integral part of the parable itself, and he edits the saying, thus assimilating it to the formula he employs elsewhere in his Gospel independently of Mark (cf. 11.15; 13.43).

51. In enumerating the several points, we have borrowed extensively from Stendahl, *School*, pp. 129–32. Cf. also Oesterley, *Parables*, pp. 53f; S. E. Johnson, "The Biblical Quotations in Matthew", *HThR*, 36 (1943), pp. 137f; Gnilka, *Verstockung*, pp. 103ff. On the other hand, L. Cerfaux ("La connaissance des secrets du Royaume d'après Matt. XIII. 11 et parallèles", *NTS*, 2 [1955/56], pp. 248f) argues that both the verbal identity of Mt 13.14f with the LXX version of Isa. 6.9f and the peculiar reading of the

introduction to this quotation (13.14a) indicate that Matthew's text goes back to an earlier source to which both Matthew and Mark had access. On the contrary, these two factors suggest the opposite, not that 13.14f point back to a stratum of tradition lying behind Matthew and Mark, but that these verses are a later interpolation into Matthew's Gospel. Cf. the body of the study.

52. Cf. Stendahl, *School*, pp. 97–127; Strecker, *Weg*, pp. 49–76.

53. Stendahl, *School*, p. 131.

54. Cf. Gnilka, *Verstockung*, p. 104.

55. Ibid., p. 105.

56. So Michaelis (*Matthäus*, II, pp. 197f) as well as any number of scholars who propose such an interpretation also for Mark's text: Manson, *Teaching*, p. 78; Jeremias, *Gleichnisse*, pp. 13f (ET, *Parables*, pp. 17f); Marxsen, "Parabeltheorie", p. 269; C. E. B. Cranfield, *The Gospel according to Saint Mark* (Reprinted edn; Cambridge University Press, 1963), p. 156.

57. Trilling, *Israel*, pp. 131f.

58. Cf. H. J. Held, "Matthäus als Interpret der Wundergeschichten", *Ueberlieferung und Auslegung im Matthäusevangelium* (2. Aufl.; Neukirchen, Neukirchener Verlag, 1961), pp. 214ff (ET by P. Scott, "Matthew as Interpreter of the Miracle Stories", *Tradition and Interpretation in Matthew* [London, S.C.M. Press, 1963], pp. 226ff).

59. This word occurs 52 times in Matthew, 6 (6) times in Mark, and 10 times in Luke.

60. This is not to deny that προσέρχομαι can also have a Rabbinic colouring. Thus the phrase προσέρχομαι πρός is the Greek equivalent of the Rabbinic technical term for "going to a rabbi for instruction" (Davies, *Sermon on the Mount*, p. 422). But while it is true that the disciples receive instruction from Jesus in 13.10–23, the question is whether Matthew does not use προσέρχομαι to attribute an honour to Jesus which is still greater than that which is Rabbinic in nature (cf. the body of the study).

61. J. Schneider, *ThW*, II, p. 681.

62. Ibid.

63. Ibid.

64. In only three instances is Jesus himself the subject of this verb, viz. 17.7; 26.39; 28.18, and in 26.39 the scene is Gethsemane, where Jesus approaches his heavenly Father in prayer.

65. Cf. Bornkamm, "Enderwartung", pp. 38f (ET, "End-Expectation", pp. 41ff).

66. Cf. 10.1; 11.1; 20.17 (critical apparatus); 26.20.

67. Cf. 9.37 and 10.1f, 5; 28.7f and 16. Cf. also Strecker, *Weg*, p. 191. E. R. Martinez ("The Interpretation of *hoi mathetai* in Matthew 18", *CBQ*, 23 [1961], pp. 285–92) advances the thesis that Matthew distinguishes in his Gospel between "*his* disciples" (=an indefinite group of Jesus' followers) and "*the* disciples" (=the Twelve). However, Matthew's text at 10.1 and 11.1 alone makes such a differentiation untenable.

68. Cf. J. C. Hawkins, *Horae Synopticae* (2nd edn; Oxford, Clarendon Press, 1909), pp. 121f; Allen, *Matthew*, pp. xxxiii–xxxiv; Lagrange, *Matthieu*, pp. LXVII–LXIX; Strecker, *Weg*, pp. 193f.

69. Allen, *Matthew*, pp. xxxiii–xxxiv; Lagrange, *Matthieu*, pp. LXVII–LXVIII; Blair, *Matthew*, pp. 102–8; Barth, "Gesetzesverständnis", pp. 99–104 (ET, "Law", pp. 105–10); Gnilka, *Verstockung*, pp. 95f.

70. The presence of ἀκμήν ("still") in 15.16, however, shows that the lack of understanding is only temporary.

71. The failure of the disciples to comprehend the person and teaching of Jesus right up to the time of the Resurrection is one of the most pronounced themes in Mark (cf. 4.13; 6.52; 7.18; 8.17–21; 9.6, 10, 32; cf. also W. Wrede, *Das Messiasgeheimnis in den Evangelien* [3. Aufl., Göttingen, Vandenhoeck & Ruprecht, 1963], pp. 67, 114). In Luke, such ignorance on the part of the disciples is depicted by their inability to grasp the significance of Jesus' repeated predictions concerning his suffering, death, and resurrection (cf. 9.45; 18.34). The extent of their perplexity, however, is not fully disclosed until after the Passion. Thus, the third evangelist devotes the whole of chapter 24 to relate how the disciples' lack of faith and understanding was finally overcome (cf. 24.6ff, 10f, 25ff, 37f, 44ff). In John, the situation is likewise clearly defined. The reader is pointedly told that the disciples did not comprehend the meaning of the mission and message of Jesus until after the Resurrection (cf. 2.22; 12.16; 16.4). In Matthew, on the other hand, there is none of this. Indeed, the first evangelist even attributes a certain awareness to the disciples as they accompany Jesus into his suffering and death (cf. 26.2).

72. Cf. P. Bonnard, *Matthieu*, p. 193; Barth, "Gesetzesverständnis", pp. 93, n. 2, 103f (ET, "Law", pp. 100, n. 2, 110f); Trilling, *Israel*, pp. 159, 213. *Contra*: Strecker, *Weg*, p. 194.

73. H. Schlier, *ThW*, I, pp. 341f.

74. F. Hauck, *ThW*, IV, pp. 369f.

75. Matthew's reference to "righteous men" in place of "kings" (Lk 10.24) is probably a mark of his editorial activity, for only in his Gospel are "prophets" and "righteous men" mentioned in conjunction with one another (cf. 23.29; 10.41). Cf. also Manson, *Sayings*, p. 80; D. Hill, "Δίκαιοι as a Quasi-Technical Term", *NTS*, 11 (1964/65), p. 298. Then, too, the term δίκαιος occurs 17 times in Matthew, but only twice in Mark and 11 times in Luke. On the other hand, E. Käsemann ("Die Anfänge christlicher Theologie", *Exegetische Versuche und Besinnungen* [Göttingen, Vandenhoeck & Ruprecht, 1964], II, pp. 90f) and Bonnard (*Matthieu*, p. 196) hold that it was not Matthew but Luke who has emended the logion we find in 13.17, because Luke no longer understood its Palestinian colour.

Strictly speaking, the term "prophets" designates those who have proclaimed and interpreted the will of God to men, i.e. the people of the Old Testament, while the term "righteous" designates those who have obeyed the Torah, living in accordance with the will of God (23.28, 29–36; 25.37–40). Hill (loc. cit.) suggests that the word "righteous" applies to the Jewish post-exilic "teachers of the law". But in view of the inclusive nature of 13.17, this interpretation is too narrow.

76. Cf. 7.7, 11; 10.19; 13.12; 19.11; 25.29; 28.18.

77. Statistics show that Matthew employs the word "God" no fewer than 51 times, which is more even than Mark (48 times).

78. Concerning the origin and background of this term, cf. J. A. Robinson, *St Paul's Epistle to the Ephesians* (2nd edn; London, Macmillan, 1928), pp. 234–40, and the following articles by R. E. Brown: "The Pre-Christian Semitic Concept of 'Mystery' ", *CBQ*, 20 (1958), pp. 417–43; "The Semitic

Background of the New Testament *mysterion*", *Bib*, 39 (1958), pp. 426-48; 40 (1959), pp. 70-87.

79. Here in v. 11 (=Lk 8.10) we encounter one of those rare instances where Matthew and Luke agree against Mark within a manifestly Marcan pericope. This harmony between the first and third Gospels covers the following four points: in both, the word order of the passage is precisely the same; Mark's καὶ ἔλεγεν αὐτοῖς appears as ὁ δὲ εἶπεν; the verb to "know" occurs, which is not present in Mark's text; and Mark's "secret" has become "secrets". In spite of such far-reaching correspondence between Matthew and Luke, one must warn against making v. 11a-b the basis for source-critical conjecture, for there is no way of telling whether this logion has been taken from Q (cf. Jülicher, *Gleichnisreden*, I, p. 129, n. 1; Cerfaux, op. cit., pp. 240f) or whether it represents the form of a Marcan passage that is older than our present version of Mk 4.11 (cf. J. P. Brown, "An Early Revision of the Gospel of Mark", *JBL*, 78 [1959], pp. 221f; J. Weiss, *Das älteste Evangelium* [Göttingen, Vandenhoeck & Ruprecht, 1903], p. 172). Wrede (op. cit., p. 62) suggests even a third possibility, namely, that Mt 13.11a-b=Lk. 8.10a-b is the result of the assimilation of either Gospel passage to the other.

80. Cf. e.g. 4.3 ("stones . . . bread(s)") with Lk 4.3; 8.26 ("winds") with Mk 4.39; 26.15 ("silver pieces") with Mk 14.11; 13.5 ("rocky ground(s)") with Mk 4.5; 13.4, 5, 7 ("some . . . others") with Mk 4.4, 5, 7; and 12.46; 13.2; 14.22; 15.36; 21.46; 23.1; 27.20, where Matthew changes Mark's "crowd" to "crowds".

81. Wrede, op. cit., p. 80; G. Bornkamm, *ThW*, IV, pp. 823f; Gnilka, *Verstockung*, pp. 26, 96.

82. O. Michel, "Der Abschluss des Matthäusevangeliums", *EvTh*, 10 (1950/51), p. 24.

83. Ibid.

84. Cranfield, *The Gospel according to Saint Mark*, p. 153; cf. also Gnilka, *Verstockung*, pp. 34-44.

85. That Matthew should apply the "secrets of the Kingdom of Heaven" at once to the spheres of ethics and eschatology is more striking than first appearances admit. To be sure, R. E. Brown ("The Pre-Christian Semitic Concept of 'Mystery' ", pp. 427-43) provides material from which one can easily see that there is in both Jewish apocalyptic and the literature from Qumran at least something of a precedent for such an application (cf. also Gnilka, *Verstockung*, p. 177). Yet the fact remains that when the latter refer to the secrets of God, it is predominantly with respect to those events that will take place as history moves towards its consummation (cf. O. Betz, *Offenbarung und Schriftforschung in der Qumransekte* [Tübingen, J. C. B. Mohr, 1960], pp. 82-7; G. Bornkamm, *ThW*, IV, pp. 821ff). As we point out in the body of the study, that Matthew can accentuate the ethical aspect of revealed knowledge to a degree that the above mentioned could not, stems from his completely dissimilar view of God's eschatological Kingdom, namely, as a reality that is already of the present and not exclusively of the future.

86. B. Weiss (*Kritisch exegetisches Handbuch über das Evangelium des Matthäus* [7. Aufl.; Göttingen, Vandenhoeck & Ruprecht's Verlag, 1883], p. 290) refers to v. 12 as a "maxim", while Zahn (*Matthäus*, p. 475) and Schlatter (*Matthäus*, p. 430) view it as a "rule". Lohmeyer (*Matthäus*, p. 202) terms it an "eschatological statute".

87. Cf. e.g. Allen, *Matthew*, p. 145; Zahn, *Matthäus*, pp. 475f; Plummer, *Matthew*, p. 189; Schlatter, *Matthäus*, pp. 430f; Michaelis, *Matthäus*, II, p. 193.

88. See above, p. 148, n. 86.

89. Ibid., p. 38.

90. Ibid., p. 13.

91. Israel's tradition attributed all things, both good and evil, to God. Concerning the principle that God could somehow be responsible for evil, cf. Amos 3.6b; Exod. 4.21; 7.3; 9.12; 10.1, 20, 27; 11.10; Isa. 6.10.

92. Cf. 21.43, and note the combination ἀρθήσεται–δοθήσεται.

93. Both Matthew (13.10) and Mark (4.10) speak of "parables", although, strictly speaking, only one parable, that of the Sower, has thus far been narrated. The importance of this plural most probably lies in the fact that Matthew and Mark intend Jesus' statements regarding his use of parables to assume programmatic significance as far as those units recorded in Mt 13 and Mk 4 are concerned (cf. G. Bornkamm, *ThW*, IV, pp. 823f; Michaelis, *Matthäus*, II, p. 191; Marxsen, "Parabeltheorie", pp. 260f, 267; G. H. Boobyer, "The Redaction of Mark 4.1–34", *NTS*, 8 [1961/62], p. 64). Moreover, Matthew, if not Mark (Marxsen, "Parabeltheorie", pp. 260f; Jeremias, *Gleichnisse*, p. 10, n. 1 [ET, *Parables*, p. 14, n. 1]) is certainly using this plural in echo of an earlier verse, as the parallel phraseology suggests (cf. v. 10b to 13.3a).

94. Jülicher, *Gleichnisreden*, I, pp. 122f; H. Windisch, "Die Verstockungsidee in Mc 4.12 und das kausale ἵνα der späteren Koine", *ZNW*, 26 (1927), pp. 203–9; C. E. B. Cranfield, "St Mark 4.1–34, Part II", *SJTh*, 5 (1952), pp. 57ff; T. A. Burkill, "The Cryptology of Parables in St Mark's Gospel", *NovTest*, 1 (1956), pp. 246, 249; Gnilka, *Verstockung*, pp. 80–3, 187.

95. See above, pp. 41f.

96. Ibid., pp. 15f, 34f.

97. Marxsen ("Parabeltheorie", p. 271) remarks that it is also a misnomer to refer to Mark's statements on parables (Mk 4.11f) as a "parable theory".

98. So, e.g. Jülicher, *Gleichnisreden*, I, pp. 142–8.

99. C. E. B. Cranfield, "St Mark 4.1–34, Part I", *SJTh*, 4 (1951), pp. 405–12. Cf. also R. E. Brown, "Parable and Allegory Reconsidered", *NovTest*, 5 (1962), pp. 40–5.
    Unfortunately, the debate over the authenticity of both the Interpretation of the Parable of the Sower and the Interpretation of the Parable of the Tares (13.36b–43) has not been resolved by the discovery of the Gospel of Thomas. For even if one grants the disputed thesis that the Gospel of Thomas contains a tradition of Jesus' parables which is independent of that of the synoptic Gospels, the fact that there are no parable interpretations in the Gospel of Thomas such as those of the Sower and of the Tares does not authorize the conclusions (*a*) that Jesus therefore provided no parable interpretations and (*b*) that the parable interpretations found in the synoptics must necessarily be secondary. The reason these conclusions are apt to be faulty is that Thomas, since he was a Gnostic, may have deliberately suppressed parable interpretations because of a predilection for secrecy. Consider the following statement by H. Montefiore (*Thomas and the Evangelists* [London, S.C.M. Press, 1962], p. 64): "Probably the reason why no allegorical details are included in Thomas's text, and no allegorical explanations

are appended to Thomas's parables is to be found in the desire to keep the 'true' spiritual interpretation of the sayings hidden from all except gnostic initiates." So again, the question of whether the Interpretations of the Sower and of the Tares in some form go back to Jesus must be decided primarily on the basis of factors other than those which can be determined from the Gospel of Thomas.

100. Jeremias, *Gleichnisse*, pp. 75ff (ET, *Parables*, pp. 77ff).

101. Contrary to W. E. Bundy, *Jesus and the First Three Gospels* (Cambridge, Harvard University Press, 1955), p. 227. On the other hand, cf. Allen, *Matthew*, p. 147; Gnilka, *Verstockung*, p. 109.

102. Wellhausen, *Matthaei*, p. 68.

103. So e.g. B. T. D. Smith, *Parables*, p. 128; Jeremias, *Gleichnisse*, pp. 75ff (ET, *Parables*, pp. 77ff).

104. Contrary to B. T. D. Smith, *Parables*, pp. 59, 128; Jeremias, *Gleichnisse*, p. 77 (ET, *Parables*, p. 79).

105. "Lawlessness" is a *terminus technicus* that denotes disobedience to the Law of God as revealed in and through Jesus (cf. esp. chaps. 5–7).

106. Grammatically, the antecedent of the object "what has been sown" ($\tau\grave{o}$ $\dot{\epsilon}\sigma\pi\alpha\rho\mu\acute{e}\nu o\nu$) is the "Word". That the gender is neuter results from the fact that the Word in the parable of the Sower is depicted as grains of seed ($\ddot{\alpha}$, 13.4), and Matthew has taken this into account.

107. Cf. Baumbach's comprehensive study of the word "evil" (*Verständnis des Bösen*, pp. 56–93). Though this investigation into the milieu and theology of Matthew's Gospel is helpful in many respects, it suffers from the fundamental error that every passage in which the term "evil" occurs is interpreted against the background of an intra-congregational controversy. This, in turn, leads to a second error: the "false prophets" (7.15; 24.11) and the "Pharisees" are simply identified as a single party *within* the Church. It seems, however, that Matthew's Church was not apparently but really in debate with contemporary Judaism.

108. G. Harder, *ThW*, VI, p. 554.

109. Ibid., pp. 550f. Cf. Baumbach, *Verständnis des Bösen*, p. 93.

110. Cf. B. Noack, *Satanás und Sotería* (Kobenhavn, G. E. C. Gads Forlag, 1948), pp. 46–9. Baumbach (*Verständnis des Bösen*, p. 58) designates Satan as the "representative of lawlessness".

111. Cf. Barth, "Gesetzesverständnis", pp. 149–54 (ET, "Law", pp. 159–64); Hummel, *Auseinandersetzung*, pp. 66–75; Baumbach, *Verständnis des Bösen*, pp. 53–121.

112. Contrary to Baumbach (*Verständnis des Bösen*, p. 57), "receiving" the Word cannot be equated with "understanding" it, since the proof of genuine comprehension, namely, the bearing of fruit, fails.

113. Arndt—Gingrich, p. 362.

114. Contrary to Strecker (*Weg*, p. 44), who views "affliction" as a future, not present, calamity that Matthew's Church must still endure.

114a. Cf. Lohmeyer, *Matthäus*, p. 95. Hare (*Jewish Persecution*, pp. 119ff., 126) argues that the verb "persecute" is restricted in its meaning and denotes only such kinds of ill-treatment as blows, insults, and threats.

115. Cf. Kilpatrick, *Origins*, pp. 109–23; Bonnard, *Matthieu*, p. 197; Davies, *Sermon on the Mount*, pp. 278f, 289f, 297; Hare, *Jewish Persecution*, chap. 3.

115a. Hare(*Jewish Persecution*, p. 163) holds that Matthew has "de-eschatologized the persecution-situation". To arrive at this position, he interprets chapter 10 and therefore vv. 16–23 apart from chapter 24 (cf. ibid., pp. 163f), and does not stress the eschatological element which is intrinsic to the Beatitudes (cf. ibid., pp. 114–21).

116. G. Stählin, *ThW*, VII, p. 345.

117. Cf. 5.29f; 24.10; 11.6=Lk 7.23; 18.6, 8f=Mk 9.42f., 45, 47.

118. G. Stählin, *Skandalon* (Gütersloh, G. Bertelsmann, 1930), pp. 223–34.

119. Kilpatrick, *Origins*, chap. 7.

120. Ibid., pp. 124ff.

121. Cf. Schniewind, *Matthäus*, p. 168.

122. Cf. Strecker, *Weg*, p. 229; Baumbach, *Verständnis des Bösen*, p. 57.

123. Cf. Barth, "Gesetzesverständnis", pp. 99–104 (ET, "Law", pp. 105–12); Gnilka, *Verstockung*, pp. 95f.

124. Cf. J. Behm, *ThW*, III, pp. 614ff.

125. Concerning the relationship in the first Gospel between "understanding" and "believing", or "faith", cf. Barth, "Gesetzesverständnis", pp. 105–8 (ET, "Law", pp. 112–16).

126. Two other proposals, however, deserve mention. W. C. Allen (*Matthew*, pp. 149ff) arrives at what seems to be the correct solution to the problem (see below, pp. 64f) with his Logia hypothesis, but for the wrong reasons, since it is improbable that Matthew followed the outline of any source in compiling the middle section of chapter 13 (see above, pp. 12–15). Recently, Wilkens ("Redaktion", pp. 315ff) has argued that Matthew could not incorporate the parable of the Seed Growing Secretly into his Gospel, because v. 28 contains the idea of growth, which in Matthew's Gospel would appear very much like a foreign body. But Wilkens' argument is overruled by the fact that in the parable of the Tares Matthew mentions no less than three stages of growth as it is: seedtime (v. 24), the budding of the stalks (v. 26), and the producing of fruit (v. 26). Then, too, if the idea of growth were disturbing to Matthew, he still could have appropriated Mark's parable and made it acceptable merely by excising v. 28.

127. *Studies in Matthew* (London, Constable, 1930), pp. 85, 97, 216f.

128. *Teaching*, pp. 222f; *idem*, *Sayings*, pp. 192f.

129. "Mixed State", pp. 150–3.

130. Manson, *Teaching*, p. 222; *idem*, *Sayings*, pp. 192f; C. W. F. Smith, "Mixed State", pp. 150f.

131. R. Liechtenhan ("Das Gleichnis vom Unkraut unter dem Weizen", *KRS*, 99 [1943], p. 146) compares the parable of the Tares with that of the Seed Growing Secretly precisely on this matter of similarity and concludes that the two are not to be construed as a "doublet".

132. So J. W. Doeve, *Jewish Hermeneutics in the Synoptic Gospels and Acts* (Assen, Van Gorcum, 1953), p. 101.

133. Marxsen, "Parabeltheorie", pp. 258ff.

134. Manson, *Sayings*, p. 192; B. T. D. Smith, *Parables*, p. 131.

135. Jülicher, *Gleichnisreden*, II, pp. 555, 558f, 563; Manson, *Sayings*, p. 193; W. E. Bundy, *Jesus and the First Three Gospels* (Cambridge, Harvard University Press, 1955), pp. 232, 236; C. W. F. Smith, "Mixed State", pp. 150f.

Regretfully, the Gospel of Thomas sheds no new light on the problem of origin, for scholars are increasingly in agreement, both that Thomas's version of the parable of the Tares is later than its Matthaean counterpart, and that it is a compression of the same (cf., e.g. R. Kasser, *L'Évangile selon Thomas* [Neuchatel, Delachaux & Niestlé, 1961], pp. 83f; B. Gärtner, *The Theology of the Gospel of Thomas*, translated from the Swedish by E. J. Sharpe [London, Collins, 1961], pp. 45f; W. Schrage, *Das Verhältnis des Thomas-Evangeliums zur synoptischen Tradition und zu den koptischen Evangelienübersetzungen* [Berlin, Verlag Alfred Töpelmann, 1964], pp. 124f). Even H. Montefiore (*Thomas and the Evangelists* [London, S.C.M. Press, 1962], p. 51), who stoutly defends the thesis that traditions in Thomas are often to be regarded as primary to parallels found in the synoptics, refers to Thomas's recension of the Tares as "a striking instance of compression to the point of absurdity . . .".

136. See above, pp. 12f; see below, p. 74.

137. A liberal use of direct discourse is indicative of Matthew's style: cf. 12.10 with Mk 3.2; 12.38 with Mk 8.11; 14.26 with Mk 6.49; 14.33 with Mk 6.51; 15.22 with Mk 7.25; 17.9 with Mk 9.9; 19.3 with Mk 10.2; 26.2 with Mk 14.1; 26.15 with Mk 14.10b; 26.27 with Mk 14.23.

138. Allen, *Matthew*, pp. 149ff; Doeve, op. cit., pp. 100–3.

139. See above, pp. 12–15.

140. Cf. Jülicher, *Gleichnisreden*, II, pp. 546–63; Zahn, *Matthäus*, pp. 491–6; Schlatter, *Matthäus*, pp. 445f; I. K. Madsen, *Die Parabeln der Evangelien und die heutige Psychologie* (Kopenhagen, Munksgaard, 1936), pp. 41–7; Manson, *Sayings*, pp. 192–6; Oesterley, *Parables*, pp. 57–70; Michaelis, *Gleichnisse*, pp. 42–53; Schmid, *Matthäus*, pp. 224ff; Bornkamm, "Enderwartung", p. 17 (ET, "End-Expectation", p. 19); E. Grässer, *Das Problem der Parusieverzögerung in den synoptischen Evangelien und in der Apostelgeschichte* (2. Aufl.; Berlin, Verlag Alfred Töpelmann, 1960), pp. 145f; Gnilka, *Verstockung*, pp. 96, 109; C. W. F. Smith, "Mixed State", pp. 150–3; Baumbach, *Verständnis des Bösen*, pp. 58–64.

141. Cf. e.g. Lohmeyer, *Matthäus*, p. 214.

142. Matthew regularly prefers the dative to the nominative in parable introductions (cf. Jeremias, *Gleichnisse*, p. 101 [ET, *Parables*, p. 102]).

143. Ibid., pp. 100, 222 (ET, pp. 101, 224).

144. Cf. Bugge, *Parabeln*, p. 128; Strecker, *Weg*, pp. 214f.

145. Fiebig, *Gleichnisreden Jesu*, p. 255.

146. This is an altered version of the translation proposed by Jeremias, *Gleichnisse*, pp. 100, 222 (ET, *Parables*, pp. 101, 224).

147. Cf. Wilkens, "Redaktion", pp. 318f.

148. Matthew employs this word seven times: once in a Q pericope (24.43 = Lk 12.39), and six times independently of both Mark, who uses it once, and Luke, who uses it four times.

149. See below, pp. 68f.

150. Mt 25.31; 16.27 = Mk 8.38.

151. Mt 13.39, 41a; 16.27 = Mk 8.38; 24.31a = Mk 13.27.

152. Mt 13.41; 24.31 = Mk 13.27.

153. Mt 25.31–46; 16.27 = Mk 8.38.

154. Mt 13.41f, 49f; 24.31 = Mk 13.27. Cf. G. Kittel, *ThW*, I, pp. 83f.

155. K. H. Rengstorf, *ThW*, II, p. 273.

156. Plummer, *Matthew*, pp. 296f; M'Neile, *Matthew*, p. 309; Schniewind, *Matthäus*, p. 218; P. Gaechter, *Das Matthäusevangelium* (Innsbruck, Tyrolia Verlag, 1963), p. 686.

157. Klostermann, *Matthäus*, p. 173; Lohmeyer, *Matthäus*, p. 313; Schmid, *Matthäus*, p. 305; Jeremias, *Gleichnisse*, p. 70 (ET, *Parables*, p. 72).

158. Jeremias, *Gleichnisse*, p. 66 (ET, *Parables*, pp. 68f); cf. also V. Hasler, "Die königliche Hochzeit, Matth. 22, 1–14", *ThZ*, 18 (1962), pp. 31ff. Other scholars content themselves with a simpler twofold division of the slaves into the prophets of old (22.3, 4, 6) and the Apostles or the early Christian missionaries (22.8, 10): Plummer, *Matthew*, pp. 301f; T. H. Robinson, *Matthew*, p. 179; Schniewind, *Matthäus*, p. 221; Schmid, *Matthäus*, p. 311. W. Trilling ("Zur Ueberlieferungsgeschichte des Gleichnisses vom Hochzeitsmahl Mt 22, 1–14", *BZ*, 4 [1960], pp. 264f) identifies the first two groups of slaves with the Old Testament prophets, but rejects any set interpretation for the slaves who appear in vv. 6, 8, 10.

159. Zahn, *Matthäus*, p. 677; Wellhausen, *Matthaei*, p. 127; Plummer, *Matthew*, p. 341; Klostermann, *Matthäus*, p. 198; M'Neile, *Matthew*, p. 358.

160. Jeremias, *Gleichnisse*, p. 55 (ET, *Parables*, p. 58); Manson, *Sayings*, pp. 117f; Schmid, *Matthäus*, p. 342.

161. This is most notably the case with the parables of the Wicked Husbandmen (21.33–46 = Mk 12.1–12 = Lk 20.9–19) and of the Great Supper (22.1–14 = Lk 14.15–24), but cf. also the opening lines of the parable of the Good Servant and the Wicked Servant (24.45 as opposed to Lk 12.41f).

162. W. Foerster, *ThW*, II, p. 814; cf. also Schniewind, *Matthäus*, p. 169; Michaelis, *Matthäus*, II, p. 224.

163. A study of ἐχθρός reveals that Matthew follows his sources in using this term. He employs it seven times. It occurs once in the Interpretation of the Parable of the Tares (13.39), but here it is dependent upon 13.25, 28, i.e. upon the parable of the Tares itself. Ἐχθρός further appears in 5.43f; v. 43, however, is a Q logion (= Lk 6.27), and v. 44 is merely antithetically parallel to it. In the final two instances, ἐχθρός is embedded in quotations taken from the Old Testament (10.36 = Mic. 7.6; 22.44 = Ps. 110.1).

164. Cf. W. Foerster, *ThW*, II, pp. 811ff.

165. See above, pp. 56f; see below, pp. 101f; and cf. Baumbach, *Verständnis des Bösen*, p. 64.

166. Cf. Arndt—Gingrich, p. 769.

167. Cf. D. Buzy, *Les paraboles traduites et commentées* (8e edd.; Paris, Gabriel Beauchesne, 1932), p. 427; Schniewind, *Matthäus*, p. 169. W. Grundmann (*ThW*, III, p. 547) speaks of the seed as the "Word about the dominion of God", i.e. the Kerygma.

168. In this connection, cf. the instructive remarks of P. Carrington in his exposition of the Interpretation of the Parable of the Sower (*According to Mark* [Cambridge, University Press, 1960], pp. 108f).

169. This is discernible in statements where persons are addressed under the guise of pictorial speech: "Thus you will know them by their fruits" (7.20); "for the tree is known by its fruit" (12.33c); and "As for the [seed] which was sown on the good soil, this is the person who . . . indeed bears fruit . . ." (13.23).

170. G. Dalman, *Arbeit und Sitte in Palästina* (Gütersloh, C. Bertelsmann, 1932), II, pp. 248f.

171. Billerbeck, I, p. 667.

172. Ibid. Cf. also F. Brown, S. R. Driver, and C. A. Briggs, eds., *A Hebrew and English Lexicon of the Old Testament* (reprinted edn; Oxford, Clarendon Press, 1959), pp. 266, 275.

173. Cf. F. Hauck, *ThW*, IV, pp. 738f.

174. Matthew's Church can very appropriately be described as a body of "Israelites", even though the members were of both Jewish and Gentile origin (cf. Hahn, *Mission*, pp. 107–11 [ET, pp. 124–8]), for, as Trilling (*Israel*, *passim*) has demonstrated, Matthew looked upon the Church to which he belonged as the "true Israel". Cf. also K. W. Clark, "The Gentile Bias in Matthew", *JBL*, 66 (1947), p. 166.

175. Cf. 8.10–13; 11.20–4; 13.11ff; 13.58; 15.7ff; 21.42f; 23.13ff, 29–36, 37f.

176. Cf. Wilkens, "Redaktion", p. 318.

177. Cf. 3.7–12; 5.20; 9.3, 11, 34; chap. 12; 15.1–20; 16.1–12; 19.3–9; 20.18; 21.23–46; chaps. 22–3.

178. Cf. 5.10ff, 44; 10.16f, 22f, 28; 13.21; 16.25; 21.35–9; 22.6f; 23.32–6. Cf. also Hare, *Jewish Persecution*, *passim*.

179. Cf. e.g. 3.7–10, 12; 15.13; 16.6, 12; 23.13, 15. Cf. also C. W. F. Smith, "Mixed State", pp. 160–8.

180. Cf. also M. Kiddle, "The Conflict between the Disciples, the Jews, and the Gentiles in St Matthew's Gospel", *JThS*, 36 (1935), pp. 42f.

181. The verbs συλλέγω, κατακαίω, and συνάγω are thoroughly Matthaean, as are such traits as the way in which the "reapers" symbolize angels and the "harvest", the Day of Judgement.

182. B. T. D. Smith, *Parables*, p. 198; Schmid, *Matthäus*, p. 221; Wilkens, "Redaktion", p. 317.

183. Cf. Jülicher, *Gleichnisreden*, II, p. 550; Grässer, op. cit., pp. 145–8.

184. Cf. Jeremias, *Gleichnisse*, p. 224 (ET, *Parables*, p. 226); Grässer, op. cit., p. 147.

185. Note again that Matthew distinguishes between the reapers and the slaves in v. 30.

186. Nepper-Christensen, *Matthäusevangelium*, *passim*; Trilling, *Israel*, pp. 79, 90–6; Strecker, *Weg*, pp. 30–5; Baumbach, *Verständnis des Bösen*, pp. 82–91; Hare, *Jewish Persecution*, p. 127.

187. A. Schlatter, *Die Kirche des Matthäus* (Gütersloh, C. Bertelsmann, 1930), pp. 17ff; Kilpatrick, *Origins*, chap. 6; L. Goppelt, *Christentum und Judentum im ersten und zweiten Jahrhundert* (Gütersloh, C. Bertelsmann, 1954), pp. 178–85; Bornkamm, "Enderwartung", *passim* (ET, "End-Expectation", *passim*); Hummel, *Auseinandersetzung*, pp. 28–33; Davies, *Sermon on the Mount*, pp. 290, 332.

188. Cf. C. F. D. Moule, "St. Matthew's Gospel: Some Neglected Features", *StEv*, II, pp. 92ff.

189. Dahl, "Parables", p. 151.

190. Cf. e.g. B. H. Streeter, *The Four Gospels: A Study of Origins* (10th impression; London, Macmillan, 1961), pp. 246ff.

191. See below, p. 84.

192. Cf. Lohmeyer, *Matthäus*, p. 216.

193. It is interesting to observe that the recension of the parable of the Mustard Seed found in the Gospel of Thomas (Logion 20) should also diverge from Matthew at this point; it has the present tense throughout.

194. Jeremias, *Gleichnisse*, pp. 101, 146 (ET, *Parables*, pp. 101f, 147).

195. Ibid., p. 146 (ET, p. 147).

196. Cf. E. Percy, *Die Botschaft Jesu* (Lund, C. W. K. Gleerup, 1953), pp. 210f.

197. Billerbeck, I, p. 669.

198. See above, pp. 12f.

199. Cf. R. C. Trench, *Notes on the Parables of Our Lord* (reprinted edn; London, Pickering & Inglis, 1953), p. 113.

200. Billerbeck, I, p. 669; G. E. Post, "Mustard", *DB*, III, p. 463.

201. G. Dalman, *Arbeit und Sitte in Palästina* (Gütersloh, C. Bertelsmann, 1935), II, pp. 293f.

202. Cf. Dahl, "Parables", p. 148; Jeremias, *Gleichnisse*, p. 148 (ET, *Parables*, p. 149).

203. See above, pp. 15f.

204. The aorist verb in v. 32b ("is grown") is no real exception to this statement, because both the tense and the mood is governed by ὅταν. On the other hand, cf. Lk 13.19c.

205. In the main, there are three points advanced by those who would oppose a christological interpretation of the "man" (cf., e.g. Michaelis, *Matthäus*, II, p. 226; R. Schnackenburg, *Gottes Herrschaft und Reich* [3. Aufl.; Freiburg, Herder, 1963], p. 107): that the reference to the man need be no more than an element Matthew has taken from Q (cf. Lk 13.19b); that the man in the parable of the Mustard Seed corresponds to the woman in the parable of the Leaven (13.33c) and no religious community with a semi-Jewish constituency would have recognized in the woman a metaphor for Jesus; and that the man does not occupy a position of prominence within the narrative. In refutation of these arguments, one may counter (*a*) that there is nothing to prevent Matthew from using a Q element as a transparent symbol for Jesus, (*b*) that the appeal to the man and the woman as parallel figures says nothing, in reality, as to whether Matthew did or did not attribute an extended meaning to the man, but only proves that he could not allegorize his parabolic materials beyond the extent to which they themselves permit, and (*c*) that the importance or insignificance of the role of the man in the parable of the Mustard Seed is totally dependent upon the message conveyed by the clause that tells of him (13.31c).

206. See below, p. 81.

207. See above, pp. 18f.

208. That Matthew could indeed associate the Church with the Kingdom of Heaven and see in the growth of the one a growth of the other is evident from an illustration we find in the literature of the Qumran community. This community referred to itself as a "twig", or "rootstock", that "shall put forth thick leaves, become an evergreen, give shade to all things; [the branches shall tower] to hea[ven], the roots sink down to the abyss. All the rivers of Eden [shall water] its boughs; it shall thrive beyond [all bounds, burgeon beyond all] measure" (1 QH 6.15f): T. H. Gaster, *Scriptures of the Dead Sea Sect* (London, Secker and Warburg, 1957; Garden City, Double-

day & Co., 1956), pp. 155f. Cf. 1 QH 8.4–14; also F. Mussner, "1 Q Hoda-joth und das Gleichnis vom Senfkorn (Mk 4, 30–32 Par.)", *BZ*, 4 (1960), pp. 128f; O. Betz, *Was wissen wir von Jesus?* (Stuttgart, Kreuz-Verlag, 1965), pp. 35f.

209. Post, op. cit., p. 463.

210. That the verb in question denotes "nesting", and not a temporary "perch-ing", has been established by W. Michaelis, "Zelt und Hütte im biblischen Denken", *EvTh*, 14 (1954), pp. 34f.

211. Dan. 4.11f, 20ff; Ezek. 31.3–9; Judg. 9.15; 1 Baruch 1.12. Cf. Dahl, "Par-ables", p. 147; C. H. Cave, "The Parables and the Scriptures", *NTS*, 11 (1964/65), pp. 385f.

212. Manson, *Teaching*, p. 133, n. 1; *idem*, *Sayings*, p. 123; Dodd, *Parables*, pp. 153f.

213. Jeremias, *Gleichnisse*, p. 146 (ET, *Parables*, p. 147).

214. Cf. 8.11; 10.6; 12.21; 15.24; 21.43; 24.14; 25.32; 26.13; 28.19.

215. Cf. e.g. E. Grässer, *Das Problem der Parusieverzögerung in den synoptischen Evangelien und in der Apostelgeschichte* (2. Aufl.; Berlin, Verlag Alfred Töpelmann, 1960), pp. 148f. Contra: Trilling, *Israel*, pp. 43ff, 150.

216. Cf. G. Lundström, *The Kingdom of God in the Teaching of Jesus*, translated from the Swedish by J. Bulman (Edinburgh, Oliver and Boyd, 1963), chaps. 1–3; N. Perrin, *The Kingdom of God in the Teaching of Jesus* (London, S.C.M. Press, 1963), chaps. 1–3.

217. Cf. Manson, *Sayings*, p. 123; Michaelis, *Matthäus*, II, pp. 225f; Dahl, "Parables", pp. 148f; E. Lohse, "Die Gottesherrschaft in den Gleichnissen Jesu", *EvTh*, 18 (1958), p. 149. Lohmeyer (*Matthäus*, p. 219) and W. E. Bundy (*Jesus and the First Three Gospels* [Cambridge, Harvard University Press, 1955], p. 233) wrongly contend that Matthew himself did not con-strue the Mustard Seed and the Leaven as companion parables. In other respects, a number of scholars hold that in the early stages of the Gospel tradition these two parables circulated independently of each other (cf. e.g. Bultmann, *Tradition*, p. 186 [ET, p. 172]; Klostermann, *Matthäus*, pp. 121f; Dodd, *Parables*, pp. 154f). This latter view finds support in the fact that the Mustard Seed and the Leaven are found as companion parables neither in Mark nor in the Gospel of Thomas (Logia 20, 96).

218. So Jeremias, *Gleichnisse*, p. 146 (ET, *Parables*, pp. 146f). On the other hand, cf. E. Percy, *Die Botschaft Jesu* (Lund, C. W. K. Gleerup, 1953), pp. 210f.

219. Arndt—Gingrich, p. 752.

220. *Arbeit und Sitte in Palästina* (Gütersloh, C. Bertelsmann, 1935), IV, p. 56.

221. Lohmeyer, *Matthäus*, p. 219, n. 3.

222. Jeremias, *Gleichnisse*, p. 146 (ET, *Parables*, p. 147).

223. Dahl, "Parables", p. 148.

224. Cf. 16.6=Mk 8.15=Lk 12.1b; 16.11f; 1 Cor. 5.6ff; Gal. 5.9. Cf. also Lohse, op. cit., p. 149.

225. The fact that Matthew conceives of the parable of the Leaven as a companion parable to that of the Mustard Seed greatly increases the plausibility of understanding the contrast in this manner.

226. Dahl, "Parables", p. 149.

227. With regard to the process of leavening, cf. T. H. Robinson, *Matthew*, p. 122; Dodd, *Parables*, p. 155.

228. In 4.11f, Mark states that Jesus spoke to the crowds in parables "in order that" they may not see, hear, or understand. In 4.33, Mark states that Jesus "spoke the word to them [the crowd], as they were able to hear it . . .". Since the latter remark seems to presuppose that the crowd was, after all, able to understand something of Jesus' speech in parables, it tends, at least on the surface of things, to compromise the former remark.

229. The words "tried to" represent a translator's attempt to capture the meaning of the imperfect in the light of Matthew's line of reasoning (cf. e.g. E. G. Jay, *New Testament Greek*, pp. 24, 250).

230. According to Jewish terminology, this introductory formula should read "Scriptures" in place of the "prophet", since the quotation is taken from Ps 78.2 (LXX 77.2). Strecker (*Weg*, p. 71) holds that the discrepancy is merely due to the fact that Matthew used a collection of prophecies. Stendahl (*School*, p. 118) is perhaps closer to the truth when he suggests that this inaccuracy may be attributed to two factors acting reciprocally: Asaph, to whom Ps 78 (77) is ascribed, is mentioned as one of several prophets in 1 Chron. 25.2, and the very nature of the saying could easily give rise to the understanding that it was prophecy. Then, too, Stendahl's suggestion is further supported by a number of old manuscripts in which the name "Asaph" has actually been interpolated into v. 35 of Matthew's text, apparently in response to the textual difficulty. That other notable manuscripts interpolate the name "Isaiah" most likely stems from an attempt to assimilate v. 35 to the several Matthaean formula quotations where "Isaiah" does legitimately occur. However, of two things regarding this introductory formula we may be certain: the word "prophet" is a standard component in all of the Matthaean formula quotations, and Matthew obviously wants to document Jesus' speaking in parables as a fulfilment of Old Testament promise.

231. Stendahl, *School*, p. 117.

232. Strecker, *Weg*, p. 71; Bonnard, *Matthieu*, p. 203; Wilkens, "Redaktion", p. 320.

233. Cf. the linguistic analysis of this quotation by Stendahl, *School*, pp. 116f; Gnilka, *Verstockung*, pp. 106f; Davies, *Sermon on the Mount*, p. 234. For a contrary viewpoint, cf. Strecker, *Weg*, pp. 70ff.

234. Cf. Lohmeyer, *Matthäus*, p. 221.


## CHAPTER 5

1. Mark explicitly mentions the house as the scene for Jesus' activity on eleven occasions: 1.29; 2.1, 15; 3.20; 5.38; 7.17, 24; 9.28, 33; 10.10; 14.3. In five of these instances, namely, 1.29; 2.15; 3.20; 9.28; 10.10, the house serves as a setting for more than one pericope, so that Mark links no fewer than nineteen such subsections either directly or indirectly to the environs of the house.

2. It is in a house that Jesus preaches, teaches, hears petitions for those in need, offers forgiveness of sins, confounds his critics, graciously dispenses his blessings in the laying on of hands, heals and restores life, participates in table fellowship with his disciples and followers, reveals himself as the Hidden Messiah, and permits himself to be reverenced as the anointed Lord whose Messiahship carries him even into death (for the exact references, cf. a concordance).

3. Strecker (*Weg*, pp. 95f) argues that Matthew's use of the word "house" is basically governed by his tendency to "historicize", which in this instance means that Matthew consistently views the house as a specific dwelling in Capernaum.

4. An exception to this is that the house once appears inconsequentially in the infancy narratives (2.11). On the other hand, even Matthew's mentioning the house in 9.28 may have been dictated to a large extent by the point of the story in which this verse is located, for the house represents an obstacle to faith which is successfully overcome.

5. Allen (*Matthew*, p. 142) states that Matthew's reference to the house in 13.1 is a "reminiscence" of Mk 3.20. That Mk 3.20 reads οἶκος, whereas Matt. 13.1 reads οἰκία, is of no great import, since Matthew has elsewhere made an identical substitution (9.23 = Mk 5.38).

6. Matthew purposely omits any reference to Mk 3.20f, and consequently to the house, because the idea that Jesus is thought to be beside himself does not at all harmonize with Matthew's concept of the royal dignity of Jesus. Nor does Matthew introduce the house at the next logical place, 12.22, for unlike Mark, he is reluctant to stage crowd scenes in a house (cf. 8.16f with Mk 1.32ff; 9.1–8 with Mk 2.1–12; cf. also Mk 3.20–35).

7. That such a transposition of a Marcan datum is not uncharacteristic of Matthew's editorial technique is demonstrated by 17.24f. Here Matthew relocates the setting Mark has established for the pericope on True Greatness (Mk 9.33), with the result that Mark's setting is found in the first Gospel attached to the narrative concerning the Payment of the Temple Tax.

8. See above, p. 65f.

9. Ibid.

10. Cf. Jeremias, "Deutung", p. 59.

11. Ibid.; *idem, Gleichnisse*, pp. 81f (ET, *Parables*, pp. 82f).

12. See above, pp. 40f.

13. Ibid., p. 41.

14. Lohmeyer, *Matthäus*, p. 223.

15. Whether the interpreter finally decides that v. 36b–c does or does not deal with the question of the disciples' lack of comprehension hinges on a textual problem: should the text read διασάφησον with Nestle and be interpreted in line with 18.31, or read φράσον with the critical apparatus and be interpreted in line with 15.15? Jeremias (*Gleichnisse*, p. 81, n. 9 [ET, *Parables*, p. 83, n. 60]) argues for the latter choice. The Nestle reading, however, is well attested, and, beyond this, the situation is such that Matthew uses the two verbs in question so seldom that there is no real basis for choosing between them. Hence, the Nestle text should be retained. But in either case the fact remains: according to Matthew the disciples do understand Jesus. Cf. also Gnilka, *Verstockung*, pp. 109f.

16. Jeremias, "Deutung", pp. 60–3; *idem, Gleichnisse*, pp. 79–83 (ET, *Parables*, pp. 81–5).

17. M. de Goedt, "L'explication de la parabole de l'ivraie (Mt xiii, 36–43)", *RB*, 66 (1959), pp. 32–54. Cf. also Michaelis, *Gleichnisse*, pp. 49f; Strecker, *Weg*, p. 160, n. 2.

18. *Pro:* Vögtle, "Mt 28, 18–20", p. 289; Jeremias, "Deutung", p. 62; Manson, *Sayings*, p. 195. *Contra:* Trilling, *Israel*, pp. 124ff.

19. Contrary to de Goedt, op. cit., p. 40.

20. Cf. Jeremias, "Deutung", p. 62.

21. Kilpatrick, *Origins*, p. 97.

22. "Enderwartung", pp. 40f (ET, "End-Expectation", pp. 44f). Cf. also J. Weiss, *Die Predigt Jesu vom Reiche Gottes* (3. Aufl.; Göttingen, Vandenhoeck & Ruprecht, 1964), pp. 40f; Schmid, *Matthäus*, pp. 225.

23. *Der Menschensohn in der synoptischen Ueberlieferung* (2. Aufl.; Gütersloh, Gerd Mohn, 1963), pp. 64–8 (ET by D. M. Barton, *The Son of Man in the Synoptic Tradition* [London, S.C.M. Press, 1965], pp. 69–73). Cf. also Barth, "Gesetzesverständnis", pp. 55, 125, n. 6 (ET, "Law", pp. 59, 134, n. 2).

24. Tödt, op. cit., pp. 66f, 87 (ET, pp. 72, 93).

25. "Mt 28, 18–20", p. 288.

26. This term occurs 8 or 9 times in the first Gospel, and it means variously the "universe" as the sum total of all created things ([13.35]; 24.21; 25.34), the "earth" as the dwelling place of mankind and the locality where history takes place (4.8; 16.26 = Mk 8.36; 26.13 = Mk 14.9), or simply "mankind" in general, the "human race" (5.14; 18.7; 26.13). Cf. H. Sasse, *ThW*, III, pp. 882–91.

27. *Matthaei*, p. 71.

28. *Israel*, pp. 124ff. Cf. also Baumbach, *Verständnis des Bösen*, pp. 59f.

29. Trilling, *Israel*, pp. 125f.

30. Ibid., p. 126.

31. Ibid., pp. 124ff, 153.

32. Trilling's intention in halving the pericope, however, is valid, for he desires to distinguish between the "present" age of the Church in which the Gospel is proclaimed to all nations and the "future" coming of Jesus as Judge. Yet on this account one need not disrupt the unit (see below, pp. 98f).

33. Cf. 26.13, where the "world" denotes both the "earth" and "mankind": the "inhabited world".

34. Vögtle, "Mt 28, 18–20", p. 291. We of course refer to the "globe" as Matthew understood it.

35. See above, pp. 18f.

36. Cf. Strecker, *Weg*, p. 166, n. 7; Trilling, *Israel*, pp. 151–4. C. H. Dodd ("Matthew and Paul", *New Testament Studies* [Manchester, University Press, 1953], pp. 54–7) attempts to distinguish between the "Kingdom of Christ" and the "Kingdom of God" by restricting the former to the age between the Resurrection and the Parousia. Michaelis (*Matthäus*, II, p. 242) commits the opposite error and identifies the Kingdom of the Son of Man exclusively with the final Kingdom that God will establish at the End of the Age.

37. Tödt, op. cit., p. 67 (ET, p. 73).

38. Cf. Vögtle, "Mt 28, 18–20", p. 290; Manson, *Sayings*, p. 194.

39. Vögtle, "Mt 28, 18–20", pp. 290f; cf. also Lohmeyer, *Matthäus*, pp. 223f.

40. Vögtle, "Mt 28, 18–20", pp. 290f.

41. This is the concept we find in substance in the programmatic passages 1.23; 18.20; 28.16–20. Cf. also Bornkamm, "Enderwartung", pp. 38f.

(ET, "End-Expectation", pp. 42f); Barth, "Gesetzesverständnis", p. 125 (ET, "Law", p. 134), and the articles dealing with the role of Jesus Kyrios in the theology of Matthew cited on p. 142 under note 19.

42. Cf. 16.28; 26.64, and Vögtle's discussion of this problem, "Mt 28, 18–20", pp. 286f.

43. Cf. Enoch 53.3ff; 56.1ff; 100.4.

44. See above, pp. 68f. One should note, however, that while angels have their set place in apocalyptic literature, they never comprise specifically the retinue of the Son of Man (cf. J. W. Doeve, *Jewish Hermeneutics in the Synoptic Gospels and Acts* [Assen, Van Gorcum, 1953], pp. 136f). The latter is an innovation found in the Gospels (ibid., pp. 137, 149ff).

45. Genitive of origin and relationship.

46. The reader should observe that although the term "seed" ($\sigma\pi\epsilon\rho\mu\alpha$) denotes "persons" in harmony with Matthew's use of it in the parable of the Tares (13.24) and in his allusion to it in the Interpretation of the Parable of the Sower (13.19, 20, 22, 23), the concept of the seed as the "Word" (cf. the parable of the Sower) is still implicit, since it is the Word that has called the Church into being and sustains it.

47. Cf. Volz, *Eschatologie*, p. 352.

48. Contrary to D. Hill, "$\Delta\iota\kappa\alpha\iota\iota$ as a Quasi-Technical Term", *NTS*, 11 (1964/65), pp. 299f. Cf. also the much debated passage 10.40ff.

49. Cf. 7.21, 24; 12.50; 13.23; 10.14; 21.31;

50. Cf. 5.44–48; 7.12; 19.16–19; 22.34–40; 25.35–40.

51. See above, pp. 56f.

52. Ibid., pp. 69f.

53. W. Foerster, *ThW*, VII, p. 158.

54. Ibid., II, p. 78.

55. That Matthew intended Jesus to be revealed as the Messiah in the Temptation Story may be seen not only from the immediate context both backwards (3.13–17) and forwards (4.12–17), but also from the reference to the "Spirit" in 4.1 (cf. 3.16) and from the fact that "Son of God" is a messianic predication in the first Gospel (cf. Hummel, *Auseinandersetzung*, pp. 115f).

56. Cf. G. H. P. Thompson, "Called–Proved–Obedient: A Study in the Baptism and Temptation Narratives of Matthew and Luke", *JThS*, 11 (1960), pp. 1–10.

57. E. Fascher, *Jesus und der Satan* (Halle, Max Niemeyer Verlag, 1949), p. 31.

58. Genitive of origin and relationship. The word "evil" is masculine (cf. Jeremias, "Deutung", p. 61).

59. *Skandalon* (Gütersloh, C. Bertelsmann, 1930), pp. 146–9; cf. also Jülicher, *Gleichnisreden*, II, pp. 553f. *Contra*: Bugge, *Parabeln*, p. 142; Dodd, *Parables*, p. 147; C. W. F. Smith, "Mixed State", p. 152; and the translators of the RSV and the NEB.

60. See above, p. 59.

61. Cf. O. Cullmann, *Petrus: Jünger–Apostel–Märtyrer* (2. Aufl.; Zürich, Zwingli Verlag, 1960), pp. 200f, 205 (ET by F. V. Filson, *Peter: Disciple–Apostle–Martyr* [London, S.C.M. Press, 1953], pp. 174, 178).

62. O. Michel, *ThW*, IV, pp. 653ff. Cf. also Barth, "Gesetzesverständnis",

pp. 113–17 (ET, "Law", pp. 121–5); J. Gnilka, "Die Kirche des Matthäus und die Gemeinde von Qumran", *BZ*, 7 (1963), pp. 52f.

63. Note that 18.7a is a Matthaean supplement attached to a Q logion (18.7b = Lk 17.1b).

64. Contrary to Baumbach, *Verständnis des Bösen*, p. 114.

65. Cf. 5.44–48; 7.12; 19.16–22; 22.34–40.

66. E. Käsemann, "Die Anfänge christlicher Theologie", *Exegetische Versuche und Besinnungen* (Göttingen, Vandenhoeck & Ruprecht, 1964), II, p. 84.

67. Barth's discussion of the false prophets who are active within Matthew's Church is still perhaps the most balanced one ("Gesetzesverständnis", pp. 60–70, 149–54 [ET, "Law", pp. 64–75, 159–64]). Baumbach (*Verständnis des Bösen*, pp. 53–121) presents a comprehensive but questionable treatment of them, because he groups them with the Pharisees and views both as an intra-congregational faction (cf. esp. pp. 81–5). In other respects, J. Rohde (*Die redaktionsgeschichtliche Methode* [Hamburg, Furche Verlag, 1966], p. 53) joins Strecker (*Weg*, p. 137, n. 4) and Trilling (*Israel*, p. 211) in discounting Barth's thesis. The gist of their argument is that Matthew's warnings against the "false prophets" and "lawlessness" are merely one aspect of the conventional teaching activity of his Church, which explains why Barth does not succeed in providing a detailed characterization of these prophets. In defence of Barth's thesis, we are of the opinion that the sections 7.15–23 and 24.10ff, which are thoroughly Matthaean, reflect, not future or intangible, but actual conditions prevailing in Matthew's Church. Moreover, that Matthew even inserts 24.11 into his Gospel is noteworthy; this verse is not, strictly speaking, integral to the context, for Matthew reiterates the same thought only a few verses later, at 24.24. Might not this concern of Matthew to interject an additional reference to the false prophets indicate that he does indeed have to do with such a party? Again, that Matthew predicates "lawlessness" not only to the false prophets but also to the leaders of the Jews (23.28) does not suggest that lawlessness is so general a concept that Matthew does not attribute it to specific persons, but rather that in his eyes both of these groups were in fact guilty of offence against the will of God (cf. Matthew's varied application of the term σκάνδαλον). On the whole, if the thesis that Matthew's Church has to contend with a party of false prophets lacks extensive documentation, it nevertheless provides us with a better explanation of the data than the view set against it (cf. also Hummel [*Auseinandersetzung*, pp. 64–71], G. Bornkamm ["Der Auferstandene und der Irdische: Mt 28, 16–20", *Zeit und Geschichte*, edited by E. Dinkler (Tübingen, J. C. B. Mohr, 1964), pp. 179ff], and Davies, [*Sermon on the Mount*, pp. 199ff]).

68. The expression "End of the Ages" (plural) is found once in the letter to the Hebrews (9.26). Cf. also 1 Cor. 10.11.

69. Cf. Manson, *Sayings*, p. 194; Dalman, *Worte*, pp. 126f.

70. Cf. 24.3, 27, 30, 39.

71. Cf. 13.39–43, 49.

72. Cf. F. Lang, *ThW*, VI, p. 945. Of the evangelists, only Matthew makes use of such a rich variety of images in this respect. Frequent synonyms of the fiery furnace are the "unquenchable fire" (3.12 = Lk 3.17), the "Gehenna of fire" (5.22; 18.9), the "eternal fire" (18.8; 25.41), or, in the case of word-pictures (tree, darnel), the mere word "fire" itself (3.10 = Lk 3.9; 7.19; 13.40).

73. Billerbeck, IV, 2, p. 1032.

74. Ibid.

75. Cf. 3.10; 5.22; 7.19; 13.40ff; 18.8f; 25.31–46. Cf. also Billerbeck, IV, 2, p. 1052.

76. Enoch 108.3–6; cf. also Secrets of Enoch 40.12, Test. of Joseph 3.6.

77. Billerbeck, IV, 2, p. 1040; cf. also Rev. 16.10f, Ps 112.10.

78. K. H. Rengstorf, ThW, III, pp. 722, 724f.

79. The words "the righteous will shine", as we pointed out above, harbour a reference to Dan. 12.3 (cf. Judg. 5.31). At the same time, they are reminiscent of later texts such as 4 Ezra 7.97 and the Books of Adam and Eve 29.9, where we read, respectively, that the righteous are "destined to shine as the sun" and that "the just [righteous] shall shine like the sun in the sight of God" (cf. also 1 QM 1.8f).

80. Cf. S. Aalen, Die Begriffe 'Licht' und 'Finsternis' im Alten Testament, im Spätjudentum und im Rabbinismus (Oslo, I Kommisjon Hos Jacob Dybwad, 1951), p. 197.

81. 4 Ezra 7.97; Books of Adam and Eve 29.9; Secrets of Enoch 66.7.

82. 4 Ezra 7.97; Dan. 12.3; Enoch 39.7b; 104.2f; 2 Baruch 51.10.

83. 2 Baruch 51.5, 10.

84. Cf. Aalen, op. cit., pp. 198f, 319f.

85. Volz, Eschatologie, pp. 366f (my translation). Cf. also Aalen, op. cit., pp. 191, 196–9.

86. Cf. Vögtle, "Mt 28, 18–20", p. 292; Tödt, op. cit., pp. 65, 67 (ET, pp. 71f); de Goedt, op. cit., pp. 43f.

87. Cf. Vögtle, "Mt 28, 18–20", p. 292.

88. Cf. Barth, "Gesetzesverständnis", pp. 54–8 (ET, "Law", pp. 58–62); Strecker, Weg, pp. 158, 242.

89. O. Glombitza, "Der Perlenkaufmann", NTS, 7 (1960/61), pp. 156ff, 160; J. C. Fenton, "Expounding the Parables: IV. The Parables of the Treasure and the Pearl (Mt 13.44–46)", ExpT, 77 (1966), pp. 179f; Bultmann, Tradition, p. 187 (ET, p. 173); Jeremias, Gleichnisse, pp. 89f (ET, Parables, pp. 90f). Contra: C. W. F. Smith, Parables, p. 97; Michaelis, Gleichnisse, p. 61.

In the Gospel of Thomas, the parables of the Treasure (Logion 109) and of the Pearl (Logion 76) are not found as double parables. Yet it is questionable whether much significance should be attributed to this. For one may argue either that the disposition of these two parables in Thomas indicates that they were unattached in the earliest stages of the Gospel tradition (cf. H. Montefiore, Thomas and the Evangelists [London, S.C.M. Press, 1962], p. 66), or that these parables became disjoined in the course of the development of the Gospel tradition only after the time of Matthew (cf. W. Schrage, Das Verhältnis des Thomas-Evangeliums zur synoptischen Tradition und zu den koptischen Evangelienübersetzungen [Berlin, Verlag Alfred Töpelmann, 1964], p. 157). Until the literary and form-critical relationships between the Gospel of Thomas and the synoptic Gospels can be defined more exactly, the matter of whether or not the parables of the Hidden Treasure and of the Pearl were originally double parables remains unanswered.

A corollary to this problem is C.-H. Hunzinger's contention that Thomas's version of the parable of the Pearl is older and more authentic than Matthew's because it is more realistic in the sense of being true-to-life ("Unbekannte Gleichnisse Jesu aus dem Thomas-Evangelium", *Judentum, Urchristentum, Kirche* [Festschrift Joachim Jeremias], edited by W. Eltester [Berlin, Verlag Alfred Töpelmann, 1960], pp. 211, 219f). But exaggeration is not a foreign element in the parables of Jesus, and Hunzinger's thesis has not gained wide acceptance (cf. e.g. R. Schippers, "The Mashal-character of the Parable of the Pearl", *StEv*, II, pp. 236–41; Schrage, op. cit., p. 156).

90. The verbs in v. 44c do not contradict this statement, since the present tense is that of the historical present (cf. M'Neile, *Matthew*, p. 203).

91. Cf. Arndt—Gingrich, p. 611.

92. Cf., e.g. Bugge, *Parabeln*, p. 192; C. W. F. Smith, *Parables*, pp. 93f; Oesterley, *Parables*, pp. 81f; Linnemann, *Gleichnisse*, p. 104 (ET, *Parables*, pp. 98f). As far as the general principles of parable interpretation are concerned, this position can be defended. The question, however, is whether the interpreter need adopt it merely for the sake of expediency, i.e. in order to dispense at the outset with an aspect of this parable which is admittedly difficult to explain.

93. Cf. Oesterley, *Parables*, pp. 80f; Michaelis, *Gleichnisse*, pp. 62f; Jeremias, *Gleichnisse*, pp. 197f (ET, *Parables*, p. 199).

94. J. D. M. Derrett, "Law in the New Testament: The Treasure in the Field (Mt 13, 44)", *ZNW*, 54 (1963), p. 35. In refutation of Derrett's article, B. Noack ("En konstrueret lignelse", *DTT*, 26 [1963], pp. 238–43) challenges not only Derrett's reconstruction of this parable, but reiterates the argument we have just treated and agreed with at least in principle (cf. n. 92 above) according to which the whole issue of the morality of the man's act is not to be regarded as of central importance to the understanding of the parable. But while we grant this, it does not detract from the fact that Derrett succeeds in convincing us that his explanation of this problematic feature of the parable is plausible and helpful.

95. Derrett, loc. cit.

96. Ibid., p. 36.

97. Ibid., pp. 36f.

98. Ibid., pp. 37–41.

99. Ibid., p. 38.

100. Ibid.

101. Ibid., p. 41. Contrary e.g. to Dodd, *Parables*, p. 86, n. 1; Jeremias, *Gleichnisse*, p. 197 (ET, *Parables*, pp. 198f); Michaelis, *Matthäus*, II, p. 247.

102. Derrett, op. cit., pp. 41f.

103. Jeremias, *Gleichnisse*, p. 198 (ET, *Parables*, p. 199).

104. Concerning the place of the precious stone in Palestinian culture, cf. W. Frerichs, "Edelsteine", *BHH*, I, pp. 362–5.

105. F. Hauck, *ThW*, IV, p. 476.

106. B. T. D. Smith, *Parables*, p. 146.

107. When it is translated literally, the Greek text reads " 'one' very valuable pearl" (13.46). Jeremias (*Gleichnisse*, p. 198 [ET, *Parables*, pp. 199f]) argues that the Greek reproduces an Aramaic construction, so that the definite "one" should be rendered as an indefinite "a": " 'a' very valuable pearl". This Semitism is indicative not only of Jesus but also of Matthew (cf. e.g. 8.19; 21.19; 22.35).

108. Dodd, *Parables*, p. 86.

109. Jülicher, *Gleichnisreden*, II, pp. 581, 585; Bugge, *Parabeln*, pp. 193f, 198; Oesterley, *Parables*, pp. 82ff; E. Jüngel, *Paulus und Jesus* (Tübingen, J. C. B. Mohr, 1962), p. 143.

110. Schlatter, *Matthäus*, pp. 446f; B. T. D. Smith, *Parables*, pp. 146; Michaelis, *Gleichnisse*, pp. 65f; E. Percy, *Die Botschaft Jesu* (Lund, C. W. K. Gleerup, 1953), pp. 39f.

111. Linnemann, *Gleichnisse*, pp. 108ff. J. V. M. Sturdy, in his English translation of Linnemann's book, paraphrases "*der ganze Einsatz*" with the expression "risking all" (*Parables*, p. 101).

112. Jeremias, *Gleichnisse*, p. 199 (ET, *Parables*, pp. 200f). Cf. also Percy, op. cit. p. 215; Schmid, *Matthäus*, p. 227.

113. Dalman, *Worte*, p. 99; Schniewind, *Matthäus*, p. 173; T. H. Robinson, *Matthew*, p. 123; Lohmeyer, *Matthäus*, p. 226; E. Sjöberg, *Der verborgene Menschensohn in den Evangelien* (Lund, C. W. K. Gleerup, 1955), p. 195; Gnilka, *Verstockung*, p. 115; Glombitza, op. cit., p. 159; Jüngel, op. cit., p. 144.

114. On this point, cf. the remarks of Michaelis, *Gleichnisse*, pp. 65f.

115. Linnemann (*Gleichnisse*, pp. 105f [ET, *Parables*, p. 100]) and Jüngel (op. cit., p. 143) follow E. Fuchs in taking issue with the idea of "sacrifice" (*Opfer*). But, as far as the mere use of the term is concerned, whether it is appropriate or not would depend exclusively upon the manner in which the interpreter defines and employs it. Linnemann would seem to want to ban the word altogether.

116. Cf. Linnemann, *Gleichnisse*, pp. 105f (ET, *Parables*, pp. 99f). While it is true, as Jüngel points out (op. cit., p. 145), that Linnemann errs when she completely ignores the value of the discovered goods as a point of stress in these parables, it is equally true that Jüngel (ibid.) goes too far in the opposite direction when he refuses to recognize that the behaviour of the labourer and the merchant in these parables is also a major point of stress, in fact, the decisive one.

117. So e.g. Jülicher, *Gleichnisreden*, II, p. 559; Dodd, *Parables*, p. 150; Schmid, *Matthäus*, p. 228; Dahl, "Parables", p. 150; E. Jüngel, op. cit., p. 145; Jeremias, *Gleichnisse*, p. 89 (ET, *Parables*, p. 90); C. W. F. Smith, "Mixed State", pp. 154f; Baumbach, *Verständnis des Bösen*, p. 64.

118. See above, pp. 65f.

119. Ibid., pp. 72f.

120. Contrary to Strecker, *Weg*, pp. 218f.

121. Dodd, *Parables*, p. 140.

122. C. W. F. Smith, "Mixed State", p. 155.

123. So Jeremias, *Gleichnisse*, p. 223 (ET, *Parables*, p. 225); Schmid, *Matthäus*, p. 228.

124. Cf. B. T. D. Smith, *Parables*, p. 201; Baumbach, *Verständnis des Bösen*, p. 65.

125. A. E. Ross, "Nets", *DCG*, II, p. 242.

126. Cf. Dunkel, "Die Fischerei am See Genesareth und das Neue Testament", *Bib*, 5 (1924), p. 383; B. T. D. Smith, *Parables*, pp. 200f.

127. Cf. P. Reymond, *L'eau, sa vie, et sa signification dans l'Ancien Testament* (Leiden, E. J. Brill, 1958).

128. Cf. E. Hilgert, *The Ship and Related Symbols in the New Testament* (Assen, Van Gorcum, 1962), pp. 46–9; C. Edlund, "Fisch", *BHH*, I, p. 483.

129. Cf. E. R. Goodenough (*Jewish Symbols in the Greco-Roman Period* [New York, Pantheon Books, 1956], V, 1, p. 33) who states: "That the Israelites, especially those faithful to the Law, are little fishes swimming in the Torah, where alone they can live, must have been a very old conception. It was proverbial in the time of Akiba early in the second century after Christ. . . ".

130. Cf. Edlund, "Fisch", pp. 482f. In this connection, Goodenough (op. cit., V, 1, p. 34) remarks: the "Jews had proverbially compared the pious man to a fish who can survive only in his native element, that of Jewish legalism, and . . . this comparison had come over into Christianity with other Christian heritages from Judaism . . . with the necessity of reinterpretation. . . ". And again (ibid., p. 53): ". . . one cannot read Christian symbolism too readily back into Judaism. But we have seen at least striking suggestions that the Christians from the very beginning took the symbol [of the fish] over because in Judaism the fish was at least associated with the Messiah, if it was not the Messiah himself, and was certainly the food of the Messianic Age, the life-giving hope of immortality. Christians, we know, were everywhere telling men that the Jewish Messiah, who was to bring men life and hope, had already come in the person of Jesus."

131. Cf. Hilgert, op. cit., chap. 8; J. Mánek, "Fishers of Men", *NovTest*, 2 (1957), pp. 139f.

132. See above, pp. 98f.

133. Ibid., pp. 81, 86f.

134. Cf. C. W. F. Smith, "Mixed State", p. 154.

135. Ibid., p. 155.

136. Cf. the Manual of Discipline, esp. 3.13—4.26. Cf. also J. P. Audet, "Affinités littéraires et doctrinales du 'Manuel de Discipline' ", *RB*, 59 (1952), pp. 219–38; S. V. McCasland, "The Way", *JBL*, 77 (1958), pp. 222–30.

137. Cf. C. Edlund, *Das Auge der Einfalt* (Lund, C. W. K. Gleerup, 1952), pp. 62–79.

138. See above, pp. 100f.

139. Cf. Baumbach, *Verständnis des Bösen*, pp. 56–93.

140. Cf. Edlund, *Das Auge der Einfalt*, pp. 79, 110–13.

141. See above, pp. 105f.

142. Ibid, pp. 107f.

143. Almost without exception, scholars adopt the position that because vv. 49a, 50, echo 13.40b, 42, and appear to be more suited to the agricultural idiom than to the world of fishing, they must have been taken by Matthew from the Interpretation of the Parable of the Tares and rather clumsily appended also to the parable of the Net (cf. e.g. B. T. D. Smith, *Parables*, p. 201; Jeremias, *Gleichnisse*, pp. 83f [ET, *Parables*, p. 85]; C. W. F. Smith, *Parables*, p. 102; idem, "Mixed State", p. 154; Strecker, *Weg*, pp. 160f). This is, of course, a possibility. Yet the basis upon which this contention rests is, in the last analysis, no broader than the assertion that it is incongruous to depict fish as being burned. But how well these verses guard the propriety of the parable's picture is not the real issue. The weeping and gnashing of teeth,

for example, can be applied neither to burned darnel nor to fish. The thing to note is that regardless of whether we have to do with darnel or fish, these are but figures behind which Matthew envisages persons, and it is these persons (bad and good, evil and righteous) with whom Matthew is concerned. Consequently, one must be cautious in maintaining that vv. 49f are inappropriate to this parable's story and therefore necessarily secondary to 13.40b, 42. If these verses in both instances are the product of Matthew's editorial activity, as Jeremias believes (loc. cit.), then the question of priority is no longer relevant.

144. On this point, cf. the pertinent remarks of Lohmeyer, *Matthäus*, p. 228; T. H. Robinson, *Matthew*, p. 124.

145. See above, p. 94.

146. Ibid., pp. 41f, 95f.

147. Cf. e.g. Jülicher, *Gleichnisreden*, II, p. 133; Manson, *Sayings*, p. 198; B. T. D. Smith, *Parables*, pp. 171f. Concerning J. W. Doeve's lengthy discussion of the term "therefore" (*Jewish Hermeneutics in the Synoptic Gospels and Acts* [Assen, Van Gorcum, 1953], pp. 99–104), his conclusions regarding both this connective and the parable of Treasures New and Old are only partially acceptable, for there is reason to dispute that the word "scribe" in v. 52 refers to a particular group of learned men within Matthew's Church, that the parable is to be related either to the whole of chapter 13 or merely to the parable of the Net, that Matthew found this parable already attached to the parable of the Net, and that 13.24–43 and 13.44–52 are two blocks of material Matthew has simply appropriated. For our views on these matters, cf. the body of the study and see above, pp. 12–15.

148. Klostermann, *Matthäus*, p. 125. Jülicher (*Gleichnisreden*, II, p. 133) regards "therefore" as the vestige of an earlier source from which Matthew has extracted v. 52. Because this source is not available to us, Jülicher asserts that the logical force of "therefore" can no longer be determined.

149. Cf. J. Hoh, "Der christliche γραμματεύς (Mt 13, 52)", *BZ*, 17 (1926), pp. 265–9; B. W. Bacon, *Studies in Matthew* (London, Constable, 1930), chap. 10; Kilpatrick, *Origins*, p. 111; Stendahl, *School*, pp. 30, 34, n. 4; Doeve, op. cit., p. 99; Hummel, *Auseinandersetzung*, pp. 17f, 26ff; Trilling, *Israel*, p. 146; Strecker, *Weg*, pp. 30, 37, 192.

150. Cf. Arndt—Gingrich, p. 486.

151. Cf. Jülicher, *Gleichnisreden*, II, pp. 130f; Hoh, op. cit., pp. 261ff; B. T. D. Smith, *Parables*, pp. 172f.

152. Contrary to Arndt–Gingrich, p. 486; F. Blass and A. Debrunner, *A Greek Grammar of the New Testament and Other Early Christian Literature*, translated from the German by R. W. Funk (Chicago, University of Chicago Press, 1961), p. 82, para. 148.

153. Hoh, op. cit., pp. 262f; B. T. D. Smith, *Parables*, p. 173; Trilling, *Israel*, pp. 145f.

154. Michaelis, *Matthäus*, II, p. 256; Hoh, op. cit., pp. 256, 263; Wilkens, "Redaktion", p. 323, n. 64.

155. B. T. D. Smith, *Parables*, p. 173; Trilling, *Israel*, pp. 145f.

156. See above, p. 68.

# SELECTED BIBLIOGRAPHY

(The English translation of the Bible quoted in this study, except where the author has supplied his own, is that of the RSV. Publication details of works listed in the Selected Bibliography are not repeated in the footnotes.)

Allen, W. C., *A Critical and Exegetical Commentary on the Gospel according to S. Matthew*. The International Critical Commentary. 3rd reprinted edition. Edinburgh, T. & T. Clark, 1922 (= *Matthew*).

Barth, G., "Das Gesetzesverständnis des Evangelisten Matthäus", *Ueberlieferung und Auslegung im Matthäusevangelium*. Vol. 1 of Wissenschaftliche Monographien zum Alten und Neuen Testament. Zweite Auflage (Neukirchen, Neukirchener Verlag, 1961), pp. 54-154 (= "Gesetzesverständnis"). ET by P. Scott. "Matthew's Understanding of the Law", *Tradition and Interpretation in Matthew* (New Testament Library. London, S.C.M. Press, 1963), pp. 58-164 (= "Law").

Bauer, W., *A Greek-English Lexicon of the New Testament and Other Early Christian Literature*: translated and adapted from the German by W. F. Arndt and F. W. Gingrich. London, Cambridge University Press; Chicago, University of Chicago Press, 1957.

Baumbach, G., *Das Verständnis des Bösen in den synoptischen Evangelien*. Vol. XIX of Theologische Arbeiten. Berlin, Evangelische Verlagsanstalt, 1963 (= *Verständnis des Bösen*).

Billerbeck, P., and H. Strack, *Kommentar zum Neuen Testament aus Talmud und Midrasch*. 6 vols. Dritte Auflage. München, C. H. Beck'sche Verlagsbuchhandlung, 1961.

Blair, E. P., *Jesus in the Gospel of Matthew*. New York, Abingdon Press, 1960 (= *Matthew*).

Bonnard, P., *L'évangile selon Saint Matthieu*. Vol. 1 of Commentaire du Nouveau Testament. Neuchatel, Delachaux & Niestlé, 1963 (= *Matthieu*).

Bornkamm, G., "Enderwartung und Kirche im Matthäusevangelium", *Ueberlieferung und Auslegung in Matthäusevangelium*. Vol. 1 of Wissenschaftliche Monographien zum Alten und Neuen Testament. Zweite Auflage (Neukirchen, Neukirchener Verlag, 1961), pp. 13-47 (= "Enderwartung"). ET by P. Scott. "End-Expectation and Church in Matthew", *Tradition and Interpretation in Matthew* (New Testament Library. London, S.C.M. Press, 1963), pp. 15-51 (= "End-Expectation").

Bugge, C. A., *Die Haupt-Parabeln Jesu*. Giessen, J. Ricker'sche Verlagsbuchhandlung, 1903 (= *Parabeln*).

Bultmann, R., *Die Geschichte der synoptischen Tradition*. Vierte Auflage. Göttingen, Vandenhoeck & Ruprecht, 1958 (= *Tradition*). ET by J. Marsh.

*The History of the Synoptic Tradition.* Oxford, Blackwell, 1963 (= *Tradition*).

Cadoux, A. T., *The Parables of Jesus: Their Art and Use.* London, James Clarke & Co., n.d. (=*Parables*).

Cross, F. L., et al., eds., *Studia Evangelica.* Texte und Untersuchungen zur Geschichte der altchristlichen Literatur. 3 vols. Berlin, Akademie Verlag, 1959–64.

Dahl, N. A., "The Parables of Growth", *StTh,* 5 (1952), pp. 132–66 (= "Parables").

Dalman, G., *Die Worte Jesu.* Zweite Auflage. Leipzig, J. C. Hinrichs'sche Buchhandlung, 1930 (= *Worte*).

Davies, W. D., *The Setting of the Sermon on the Mount.* Cambridge University Press, 1964 (= *Sermon on the Mount*).

Dodd, C. H., *The Parables of the Kingdom.* Rev. ed. London, Nisbet, 1961 (= *Parables*).

Fiebig, P., *Altjüdische Gleichnisse und die Gleichnisse Jesu.* Tübingen, J. C. B. Mohr, 1904 (=*Altjüdische Gleichnisse*).

—— *Die Gleichnisreden Jesu im Lichte der rabbinischen Gleichnisse des neutestamentlichen Zeitalters.* Tübingen, J. C. B. Mohr, 1912 (= *Gleichnisreden Jesu*).

Gnilka, J., *Die Verstockung Israels.* Vol. III of Studien zum Alten und Neuen Testament. München, Kösel Verlag, 1961 (= *Verstockung*).

Hahn, F., *Das Verständnis der Mission im Neuen Testament.* Vol. 13 of Wissenschaftliche Monographien zum Alten und Neuen Testament. Neukirchen, Neukirchener Verlag, 1963 (= *Mission*). ET by F. Clarke. *Mission in the New Testament.* Vol. 47 of Studies in Biblical Theology. London, S.C.M. Press, 1965 (= *Mission*).

Hare, D. R. A., *The Theme of Jewish Persecution of Christians in the Gospel according to St Matthew.* Vol. 6 of Society for New Testament Studies Monograph Series. Cambridge University Press, 1967 (=*Jewish Persecution*).

Hastings, J., ed., *A Dictionary of the Bible.* 5 vols. Edinburgh, T. & T. Clark, 1898–1904.

—— *A Dictionary of Christ and the Gospels.* 2 vols. Edinburgh, T. & T. Clark, 1906–8.

Hermaniuk, M., *La Parabole Évangélique.* Vol. 38, series 11 of Universitas Catholica Lovaniensis. Louvain, Bibliotheca Alfonsiana, 1947 (=*Parabole*).

Hummel, R., *Die Auseinandersetzung zwischen Kirche und Judentum im Matthäusevangelium.* Vol. 33 of Beiträge zur evangelischen Theologie. München, Chr. Kaiser Verlag, 1963 (=*Auseinandersetzung*).

Jeremias, J., "Die Deutung des Gleichnisses vom Unkraut unter dem Weizen (Mt xiii 36–43)", *Neotestamentica et Patristica* (Festschrift Oscar Cullmann). Vol. VI of Supplements to Novum Testamentum, ed. B. Reicke and W. C. van Unnik (Leiden, E. J. Brill, 1962), pp. 59–63 (= "Deutung").

—— *Die Gleichnisse Jesu*. Sechste Auflage. Göttingen, Vandenhoeck & Ruprecht, 1962 (= *Gleichnisse*). ET of 6th German edn by S. H. Hooke. *The Parables of Jesus*. New Testament Library. London, S.C.M. Press, 1963 (= *Parables*).

Jülicher, A., *Die Gleichnisreden Jesu*. 2 vols. Nachdruck der Ausgabe Tübingen 1910. Darmstadt, Wissenschaftliche Buchgesellschaft, 1963 (= *Gleichnisreden*).

Kilpatrick, G. D., *The Origins of the Gospel according to St Matthew*. Reprinted edn. Oxford, Clarendon Press, 1950 (= *Origins*).

Kittel, G., and G. Friedrich, eds., *Theologisches Wörterbuch zum Neuen Testament*. 7 vols. Stuttgart, W. Kohlhammer Verlag, 1933–64.

Klostermann, E., *Das Matthäusevangelium*. Vol. 4 of Handbuch zum Neuen Testament. Zweite Auflage. Tübingen, J. C. B. Mohr, 1927 (= *Matthäus*).

Lagrange, M. J., *Évangile selon Saint Matthieu*. 8e édition. Paris, J. Gabalda, 1948 (= *Matthieu*).

Linnemann, E., *Gleichnisse Jesu*. Göttingen, Vandenhoeck & Ruprecht, 1961 (= *Gleichnisse*). ET of 3rd German edn by John Sturdy. *Parables of Jesus*. London, S.P.C.K., 1966 (= *Parables*).

Lohmeyer, E., *Das Evangelium des Matthäus*. A special volume in Meyer's Kritisch-exegetischer Kommentar über das Neue Testament, ed. W. Schmauch. Zweite Auflage. Göttingen, Vandenhoeck & Ruprecht, 1958 (= *Matthäus*).

M'Neile, A. H., *The Gospel according to St Matthew*. Reprinted edn. London, Macmillan, 1961 (= *Matthew*).

Manson, T. W., *The Sayings of Jesus*. Reprinted edn. London, S.C.M. Press, 1961 (= *Sayings*).

—— *The Teaching of Jesus*. 2nd edn. Cambridge University Press, 1935 (= *Teaching*).

Marxsen, W., "Redaktionsgeschichtliche Erklärung der sogenannten Parabeltheorie des Markus", *ZThK*, 52 (1955), pp. 255–71 ("Parabeltheorie").

Michaelis, W., *Das Evangelium nach Matthäus*. 2 vols. Prophezei. Zürich, Zwingli Verlag, 1948–9 (= *Matthäus*).

—— *Die Gleichnisse Jesu*. Vol. 32 of Die urchristliche Botschaft. Dritte Auflage. Hamburg, Furche Verlag, 1956 (= *Gleichnisse*).

Nepper-Christensen, P., *Das Matthäusevangelium, ein judenchristliches Evangelium?* Vol. 1 of Acta Theologica Danica. Aarhus, Universitetsforlaget, 1958 (= *Matthäusevangelium*).

Oesterley, W. O. E., *The Gospel Parables in the Light of their Jewish Background*. London, S.P.C.K., 1936 (= *Parables*).

Plummer, A., *An Exegetical Commentary on the Gospel according to S. Matthew*. London, Elliot Stock, 1909 (= *Matthew*).

Reicke, B., and L. Rost, eds., *Biblisch-Historisches Handwörterbuch*. 3 vols. Göttingen, Vandenhoeck & Ruprecht, 1962–66.

Robinson, T. H., *The Gospel of Matthew*. The Moffatt New Testament Commentary. London, Hodder & Stoughton, 1928 (= *Matthew*).

Schlatter, A., *Der Evangelist Matthäus*. Fünfte Auflage. Stuttgart, Calwer Verlag, 1959 (= *Matthäus*).

Schmid, J., *Das Evangelium nach Matthäus*. Vol. 1 of Regensburger Neues Testament. Vierte Auflage. Regensburg, Verlag Friedrich Pustet, 1959 (= *Matthäus*).

Schniewind, J., *Das Evangelium nach Matthäus*. Vol. 2 of Das Neue Testament Deutsch. Zehnte Auflage. Göttingen, Vandenhoeck & Ruprecht, 1962 (= *Matthäus*).

Smith, B. T. D., *The Parables of the Synoptic Gospels*. Cambridge University Press, 1937 (= *Parables*).

Smith, C. W. F., *The Jesus of the Parables*. Philadelphia, Westminster Press, 1948 (= *Parables*).

—— "The Mixed State of the Church in Matthew's Gospel", *JBL*, 82 (1963), pp. 149–68 (= "Mixed State").

Stendahl, K., *The School of St Matthew*. Vol. XX of Acta Seminarii Neotestamentici Upsaliensis. Uppsala, Almqvist & Wiksells, 1954 (= *School*).

Strecker, G., *Der Weg der Gerechtigkeit: Untersuchung zur Theologie des Matthäus*. Vol. 82 of Forschungen zur Religion und Literatur des Alten und Neuen Testaments. Göttingen, Vandenhoeck & Ruprecht, 1962 (= *Weg*).

Trilling, W., *Das wahre Israel*. Vol. X of Studien zum Alten und Neuen Testament. Dritte Auflage. München, Kösel Verlag, 1964 (= *Israel*).

Vögtle, A., "Das christologische und ekklesiologische Anliegen von Mt. 28, 18–20", *StEv*. II (Vol. 87 of "Texte und Untersuchungen zur Geschichte der altchristlichen Literatur"), pp. 266–94 (= "Mt 28, 18–20").

Volz, P., *Die Eschatologie der jüdischen Gemeinde im neutestamentlichen Zeitalter*. Tübingen, J. C. B. Mohr, 1934 (= *Eschatologie*).

Walker, R., *Die Heilsgeschichte im ersten Evangelium*. Göttingen, Vandenhoeck & Ruprecht, 1967 (= *Heilsgeschichte*).

Wellhausen, J., *Das Evangelium Matthaei*. Berlin, Georg Reimer, 1904 (= *Matthaei*).

Wilkens, W., "Die Redaktion des Gleichniskapitels Mark. 4 durch Matth.", *ThZ*, 20 (1964), pp. 304–27 (= "Redaktion").

Windisch, H., "Die Sprüche vom Eingehen in das Reich Gottes", *ZNW*, 27 (1928), pp. 163–92 (= "Eingehen").

Zahn, T., *Das Evangelium des Matthäus*. Vol. 1 of Kommentar zum Neuen Testament. Vierte Auflage. Leipzig, A. Deichertsche Verlagsbuchhandlung, 1922 (= *Matthäus*).

# INDEX OF NAMES

# INDEX OF BIBLICAL REFERENCES

Figures in bold type refer to the detailed treatment of the parables or other pericopes in Matthew 13

## OLD TESTAMENT

## APOCRYPHA AND PSEUDEPIGRAPHA

## EARLY CHRISTIAN WRITINGS